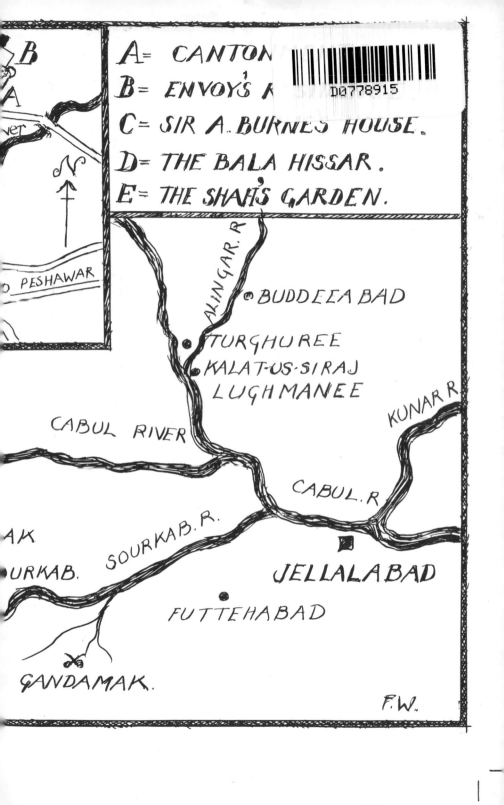

A= CANTON[...]
B= ENVOYS R[...]
C= SIR A. BURNES HOUSE.
D= THE BALA HISSAR.
E= THE SHAH'S GARDEN.

B

A

ver

N

O PESHAWAR

ALINGAR. R.

● BUDDEEABAD

● TURGHUREE
● KALAT-US-SIRAJ
LUGHMANEE

KUNAR R

CABUL RIVER

CABUL. R

AK

SOURKAB. R.

URKAB.

JELLALABAD

● FUTTEHABAD

GANDAMAK.

F.W.

D0778915

JOURNAL OF AN AFGHANISTAN PRISONER

The Bala Hissar, Cabul.

JOURNAL OF AN AFGHANISTAN PRISONER

Lieut Vincent Eyre
Bengal Artillery,
Late Deputy Commissary of Ordnance at Cabul

With an Introduction by James Lunt

Illustrated by Frank Wilson

ROUTLEDGE & KEGAN PAUL
London, Henley and Boston

Originally published in 1843 as
The Military Operations at Cabul,
which ended in the Retreat and Destruction
of the British Army, January 1842.
With a Journal of Imprisonment
in Affghanistan.
This edition
first published in 1976
by Routledge & Kegan Paul Ltd
39 Store Street,
London WC1E 7DD.
Broadway House.
Newtown Road.
Henley-on-Thames.
Oxon RG9 1EN and
9 Park Street,
Boston, Mass. 02108, USA
Printed in Great Britain by
Redwood Burn Limited
Trowbridge & Esher
Introduction © James Lunt 1976
No part of this book may be reproduced in
any form without permission from the
publisher, except for the quotation of brief
passages in criticism
ISBN 0 7100 8349 1

TO

MAJOR-GENERAL W. S. WHISH, C.B.

LATE COMMANDANT OF THE BENGAL ARTILLERY,

𝕿𝖍𝖎𝖘 𝖂𝖔𝖗𝖐 𝖎𝖘 𝖉𝖊𝖉𝖎𝖈𝖆𝖙𝖊𝖉,

AS A SLIGHT MARK OF ESTEEM FOR HIS PUBLIC AND
PRIVATE WORTH,

AND OF GRATITUDE FOR PAST KINDNESSES,

BY

HIS SINCERE FRIEND,

VINCENT EYRE.

NOTICE BY THE EDITOR.

THE original manuscript of this Journal was sent by Lieutenant Eyre in parts, as it was finished, and as opportunity offered, to a military friend in India. Even when the last part reached his hands, the eventual liberation of the Cabul prisoners was a matter of painful uncertainty ; and his judgment prompted him to transmit it entire, and without comment, to the Author's immediate relations in this country. There is a point connected with its publication *now*, which must not be thought to have been disregarded from any anxiety that this account should be the first : — it is, the question whether it should have been

A 3

withheld until the result of the inquiry now pending in India should be known. It is considered that sufficient delay has been already incurred to insure this end, and that all such investigations will have been closed before a copy of this book can find its way to India. The Journal is therefore at once printed as it came, in concurrence with the writer's own idea that it cannot fail to interest the British public.

E. EYRE.

Athenæum Club,
Dec. 29. 1842.

PREFACE BY THE AUTHOR.

THE following notes were penned to relieve the monotony of an Affghan prison, while yet the events which they record continued fresh in my memory. I now give them publicity in the belief that the information which they contain on the dreadful scenes lately enacted in Affghanistan, though clothed in a homely garb, will scarcely fail to be acceptable to many of my countrymen, both in India and England, who may be ignorant of the chief particulars. The time, from the 2d November, 1841, on which day the sudden popular outbreak at Cabul took place, to the 13th January, 1842, which witnessed the annihilation of the last small remnant of our unhappy force at Gundamuk, was one continued tragedy. The massacre of Sir Alexander Burnes and his associates, — the loss of our commissariat fort,—the defeat of our troops under Brigadier Shelton at Beymaroo, — the treacherous assassination of Sir William Macnaghten, our envoy and minister, — and lastly, the disastrous retreat and utter destruction * of a force consisting of 5000 fighting men and upwards of 12,000 camp-followers, — are events which will assuredly rouse the British Lion from his repose, and excite an indignant spirit of inquiry in every breast. Men will not be satisfied, in this case, with a bare statement of the facts,

* In the late accounts from Gen. Pollock's army at Cabul, it is stated that the number of *skeletons* found on the line of march was *very small* compared with the thousands which had been reported and believed to have perished. But too few have as yet *made their appearance* to require that the above statement should be qualified. The reader who continues to the end will have little hope that it can *ever* prove *very* incorrect. — EDITOR.

but they will doubtless require to be made acquainted with the causes which brought about such awful effects. We have lost six entire regiments of infantry, three companies of sappers, a troop of European horse artillery, half the mountain-train battery, nearly a whole regiment of regular cavalry, and four squadrons of irregular horse, besides a well-stocked magazine, which *alone*, taking into consideration the cost of transport up to Cabul, may be estimated at nearly a million sterling. From first to last, more than 100 British officers have fallen: their names will be found in the Appendix. I glance but slightly at the *political* events of this period, not having been one of the initiated; and I do not pretend to enter into *minute* particulars with regard to even our *military* transactions, more especially those not immediately connected with the sad catastrophe which it has been my ill-fortune to witness, and whereof I now endeavour to pourtray the leading features. In these notes I have been careful to state only what I know to be undeniable facts. I have set down nothing on mere hearsay evidence, nor any thing which cannot be attested by living witnesses, or by existing documentary evidence. In treating of matters which occurred under my personal observation, it has been difficult to avoid *altogether* the occasional expression of my own individual opinion: but I hope it will be found that I have made no observations bearing hard on men or measures, that are either uncalled for, or will not stand the test of future investigation. To Major Pottinger, C.B., the well-known hero of Herat, whose subsequent acts have amply sustained the fame which he there acquired, I am much indebted for a great deal of interesting matter relative to the events at Charekar. To Captain Colin Mackenzie of the Madras army, political assistant at Peshawur, my obligations are greater than I can express, for his most valuable aid in the preparation of these notes, as well as for his excellent account of the attack on Brigadier Anquetil's fort, and the sad detail of the Envoy's cruel murder, and the circumstances therewith connected. To Captain Lawrence, late military secretary to the Envoy, and to Captain Troup, late Brigade-Major to the Shah's force, I am likewise bound to offer my best acknowledgments for much important information.

The plan of cantonments and of the surrounding country, being drawn entirely from memory, requires indulgent criticism; but I trust it is sufficiently accurate to give the reader a tolerably correct idea of the nature of our position.

CONTENTS.

INTRODUCTORY CHAPTER.

CHAP. I.

a

CHAP. II.

CHAP. III.

CHAP. IV.

CHAP. V.

CHAP. VI.

CHAP. VII.

CHAP. VIII.

CHAP. IX.

GLOSSARY.

The following LIST OF WORDS used in this volume, with their meanings, may be useful to the English reader.*

Akukzye, or *Atchakzye*, the name of one of the great Affghan tribes.

Ameer, commander or chief; title assumed by Dost Mahomed Khan.

Atta, ground wheat.

Ayah, a nurse.

Bala Hissar, royal citadel, upper citadel.

Barukzye, name of one of the five great Dúráni or Dooranee tribes.

Bourge, tower.

Buniah, a trader, generally in grain.

Cafila, a convoy.

Char Chouk, public bazar. *Chaháa*, or *char*, means house, the bazar being introduced at right angles in the centre.

Chouk, bazar.

Chuprassie, a servant bearing a badge or brass plate.

Chuppao, a night surprise, or plundering attack.

Cossid, a messenger.

Debashee. Query whether this is an Indian or Kâbul term. Bashé means principal, as Káfila Bashé, the principal of the convoy, &c.

Dewan Kaneh, hall of audience.

Doohlie, palanquin for carrying sick.

* The *Editor*, having compiled this in haste from the information of Indian friends, begs that inaccuracies may be excused, and invites corrections, to be addressed to him at the publisher's.

Dooranee, name of five great tribes, the Popul-zai, Barak-zai, Núr-zai, Bármi-zai, and Abkhu-zai.

Ensofzyes, an Affghan tribe holding the territory north of Pesháwur.

Feringhee, European.

Ghazee, champion of religion.

Giljye, name of a great Affghan tribe.

Godown, storehouse.

Goorkha, a native of Népâl.

Havildar, a sergeant.

Hazirbash means " Be present."

Hurwah (uncertain).

Janbaz, Affghan horse.

Jeerghu, councell.

Jemandar, a native officer.

Juzail, long rifle.

Juzailchee, rifleman.

Kafir, infidel.

Khan, nobleman : the title in Kâbul is assumed by every one, even the lowest.

Kirkhee, a wicket, window.

Kujawur, a pannier carried on camels.

Kuzzilbash, descendant of the Persians, wearing a red cap.

Lascar, Indian term, an attendant on guns, magazines, &c.

Maund (of grain), 80 lb. weight.

Meerza, an appellation generally given to Mahomedan writers.

Meer Wyze (The) means a teacher; generally conferred on some one eminent for sanctity.

Mehmandar, a man of all work ; one who has charge of receiving guests, visitors, &c.

Moollah, priest.

Moonshee, interpreter or secretary.

Musjeed, a temple, place of worship.

Naib, deputy.

Nalkee, a sort of palanquin.

Nazir, steward.

Neencha, coat.

Nuwab, prince.

Pilāo, a dish of fowl with rice, &c.

Postheen, a sheepskin cloak.

Rajah, prince, an Indian term.

Ressala, a troop.

Sepoy, soldier, an Indian term; always *native* soldier.

Shah bagh, king's garden.

Shroff, a native banker.

Sirdar, a chief.

Subschoon, or *Shub-khoon* (the proper term), night surprise.

Sunga, stone breastwork.

Surwon, a man who takes care of camels.

Syud, a priest.

Wuzeer, vizier.

Yaboo, Affghan pony.

Zuna, dwelling; (*Kuneh*) private dwelling.

INTRODUCTION.

Not until the surrender of Singapore to the
Japanese almost exactly one hundred years later
were the British to suffer such a humiliating
defeat in Asia as that inflicted on them by the
Afghans in 1841-2. "From the beginning to end,"
wrote Sir John Fortescue of the campaign, "it
brought nothing but disgrace."

The ill-conceived decision to invade Afghanistan
in 1839, in order to restore the exiled Shah Shujah
to the throne and thereby to check imagined
Russian designs on Afghanistan, was the consequence of muddled thinking and quite staggering
complacency. And yet, at first, all went well with
British arms. The grandiloquently named "Army
of the Indus" crawled its way to Cabul via Sind,
Baluchistan and Ghazni. Having driven into exile
the reigning Amir, Dost Mahommed, the British
then installed in his place the unpopular Shah
Shujah and set about imposing his rule on his
unwilling subjects, most of whom cordially detested
him. This accomplished, the British made themselves as comfortable as the distance from their
bases in India permitted. An indefensible canton-

ment was constructed outside Cabul, families came up from India, cricket matches and race meetings were organised, and as a final act of folly the garrison was reduced to an unacceptable minimum.

By the beginning of 1841 Afghanistan was seething with discontent but the warnings of political officers living among the tribes fell on deaf ears. The British Envoy, Sir William Macnaghten, was convinced that all would turn out for the best, as was his principal adviser, Sir Alexander Burnes, who had originally advised against the campaign, but who now anticipated succeeding Macnaghten in the appointment of Envoy. To make matters worse a General arrived to command the Troops who had never before served in the East and who was crippled by gout. Poor Elphinstone, a physical and mental wreck, was not helped by the fact that his Second-in-Command, Brigadier Shelton, opposed him on nearly every issue. It would be hard to imagine a more certain recipe for disaster.

On 2 November 1841 the mob rose in Cabul and murdered Sir Alexander Burnes. Within a matter of days the whole of Afghanistan was in flames. All outlying British garrisons were attacked and the cantonment at Cabul besieged. From then on it was a story of divided counsels, appalling mismanagement, and even, on occasions, cowardice in face of the enemy. Macnaghten was murdered, Elphinstone dithered and drifted from one crisis to the next, while Shelton, although courageous in the field, was Cassandra-like in counsel. With all the remorselessness of a Greek tragedy mistake followed mistake until the entire army was cut to pieces while retreating through the snowclad passes on its way to India. Out of 4,500 fighting men who marched out of the Cabul cantonment on 6 January 1842, only one, Doctor Brydon, managed to reach the safety of the British lines in Jellalabad. Of the remainder, the majority were either killed or died of hunger and exposure in the bitter Afghan winter, and with them nearly 12,000 camp followers, men, women and children. A few were taken prisoner.

One of the prisoners was Lieutenant Vincent Eyre of the Bengal Artillery. He, his wife and child, fell into Afghan hands on 9 January 1842. This book is his description of the events leading up to his captivity, and thereafter of his experience as a prisoner of the Afghans until release on 17 September of the same year. By that date the armies of Generals Pollock and Nott had recaptured Cabul and Ghazni and in some small measure had restored the prestige of British arms – so far as that was possible.

Eyre's is a remarkable story, not least because the author writes so frankly and vividly of a disastrous episode in British history. He gives the impression that he is telling nothing but the truth, however unpalatable the truth must have been, but it is also a story of great courage, of men and women alike. Eyre was criticised at the time for publishing this account of his experiences before the inevitable court of enquiry had been able to decide upon the responsibility for the disaster in Cabul. However, it certainly did not hinder his subsequent career. He ended his service as General Sir Vincent Eyre, having been strongly recommended for the award of the Victoria Cross during the Indian Mutiny, and almost the last act in a long life of public service was his organisation of the Red Cross during the Franco-Prussian War. He must have been a remarkable man!

JAMES LUNT.

OPERATIONS

OF

THE BRITISH ARMY

AT

CABUL.

NOTES OF OPERATIONS,

ETC.

INTRODUCTORY CHAPTER.

INTERNAL STATE OF AFFGHANISTAN IN 1841. — DIS-
AFFECTION — ESPECIALLY IN KOHISTAN, AND MILITARY
OPERATIONS THERE. — MARCH OF GENERAL SALE FOR
JELLALABAD, WHO HAS TO FIGHT HIS WAY. — EARLIER
PREMONITORY SYMPTOMS OF DISTURBANCE.

WHEN Major-Gen. Elphinstone assumed the command of the troops in Affghanistan in April, 1841,
the country enjoyed a state of apparent tranquillity to which it had for many years been a
stranger. This remark applies more particularly
to those provinces which lie north-east of Ghuznee, comprehending Cabul proper, Kohistan,
Jellalabad, and the neighbouring districts. The
Giljye tribes, occupying a large portion of the
country between Ghuznee and Candahar, had
never been properly subdued, and the permanent
occupation of Khelat-i-Giljye by our troops had
so alarmed their jealous love of independence, as

B 2

to cause, during the months of July and August, a partial rising of the tribes, which, however, the valour of our Hindoostanee troops, under Colonel Wymer, at Huft-aseer, and of the 5th Bengal Cavalry under Col. Chambers at Mookoor, speedily suppressed. Some of the principal chiefs delivered themselves up as hostages, and quiet was restored. To the west of Candahar, a notorious freebooter, named Akter Khan, having collected about 7000 followers, horse and foot, was signally defeated near Girhisk, on the banks of the Heermund, in the month of July, by a detachment of the Shah's regular troops under Capt. Woodburn, consisting of only one infantry regiment, two H. A. guns, under Lieut. Cooper, besides two regiments of *Janbaz*, or Affghan horse: the latter, however, behaved ill, and can hardly be said to have shared in the glory of the unequal conflict. Capt. Griffin, with the Bengal 2d Native Infantry, was, a few days after, equally successful in an attack on the enemy in the same quarter. Akter Khan fled to the hills with a few followers, and the land again enjoyed repose. Kohistan, whose wild and turbulent chiefs had sturdily maintained their independence against the late ruler, Dost Mahommed Khan, seemed at last to have settled down into a state of quiet, though unwilling, subjection to Shah Shoojah. The Nijrow chiefs formed an almost solitary exception to this show of outward submission; and Sir William Macnaghten had strongly urged upon Lord Auckland, at an early period of the year, the expediency of sending a force into that country as soon as practicable.   Since our first occupation of Cabul, Nijrow had become a resort for all such restless and discontented characters as had rendered themselves obnoxious to the existing government. The fact of our having permitted them so long to brave us with impunity, had doubtless been regarded by the secret enemies of the new rule as a mark of conscious weakness, and may have encouraged them, in no slight degree, to hatch those treasonable designs against the state which were so suddenly developed in November, 1841, and which were for the time, unhappily, but too successful.*

Major Pottinger, having been appointed political agent in Kohistan, arrived from Calcutta in May, 1841, and was one of the first to prognosticate the coming storm.   He lost no time in representing to the Envoy the insufficiency of our military force in Kohistan, consisting at that time of merely two 6-pounder guns, and the Kohistanee regiment raised by Lieut. Maule of the Bengal Ar-

* The reader is particularly referred to a note at the end of the book.

tillery; which excellent young officer was, on the
first outbreak of the rebellion, cruelly butchered
by his own men, or, which is the same thing, with
their consent.   This regiment was stationed at
Charekar, a post of no strength, and ill adapted
for making a protracted defence, as was afterwards
proved.   The Major was, however, considered in
the light of an alarmist, and he only succeeded in
procuring a few Hazirbash horsemen and a 17-
pounder gun, with a small detachment of the
Shah's artillery, and a very scanty supply of ammunition.

About the end of September, Major Pottinger
came to Cabul for the purpose of impressing on
the Envoy that, unless strong measures of pre-
vention were speedily adopted, he considered a
rise in Kohistan as in the highest degree probable.
His apprehensions were considered by the Envoy
as not altogether unfounded, and he was em-
powered to retain as hostages the sons of the
leading chiefs, whose fidelity he suspected.   The
first interruption to the state of outward tranquillity, which I have described above, occurred
early in September.   Capt. Hay, in command of
some Hazirbashes, and Lieut. Maule, with his
Kohistanee regiment, (which had been relieved at
Charekar by the Goorkah, or 4th regiment, the
Shah's subsidized force officered from the line,

under Capt. Codrington,) and two 6-pounder guns, had been sent into the Zoormut valley to collect the annual revenue, with orders likewise to make an attempt to seize certain noted plunderers, among whom were some of the murderers of Col. Herring, who had long infested the road between Ghuznee and Cabul. The revenue was in the course of being quietly paid, when Capt. Hay was mischievously informed by Moollah Momin, collector of revenue in Zoormut (who shortly after distinguished himself as one of our bitterest foes), that the men, whom he wished to seize, were harboured in a certain neighbouring fort of no strength whatever, and that the inhabitants would doubtless give them up rather than risk a rupture with the government. Capt. Hay immediately proceeded thither, but found the place much stronger than he had been led to expect, and the people obstinately prepared to resist his demands. On approaching the fort, he was fired upon ; and finding the six-pounder shot, of which he gave a few rounds in return, made no impression on the mud walls, he had no alternative but to retreat.

The Envoy, on receiving Capt. Hay's report, immediately despatched a sufficient force to punish the rebels. It consisted of 200 of H. M. 44th Inf., 5th N. I., 6th regt. S. S. F., 4 guns of Abbot's battery, 2 iron nine-pounders mountain

train, 2 comp. Shah's Sappers, and 2 squadrons
of Anderson's horse. These were under the
command of Lieut.-Col. Oliver, and were accompanied by Capt. G. H. Macgregor, the political agent at Gundamuck, who happened to
be then at Cabul on business. The force commenced its march on the 27th September, and
reached the Zoormut valley without the slightest
interruption. On the approach of our troops the
rebels had fled to the hills in the greatest consternation, leaving their forts at our mercy. The
principal strongholds were destroyed with powder,
and the force prepared to return to Cabul.

Meanwhile the hydra of rebellion had reared
its head in another far more formidable quarter.
Early in October three Giljye chiefs of note suddenly quitted Cabul, after plundering a rich
Cafila at Tezeen, and took up a strong position
in the difficult defile of Khoord-Cabul, about ten
miles from the capital, thus blocking up the pass,
and cutting off our communication with Hindo-
stan. Intelligence had not very long previously
been received that Mahomed Akber Khan, second son of the ex-ruler Dost Mahomed Khan,
had arrived at Bameean from Khooloom for the
supposed purpose of carrying on intrigues against
the government. It is remarkable that he is
nearly connected by marriage with Mahomed

Shah Khan and Dost Mahomed Khan*, also Giljyes, who almost immediately joined the above-mentioned chiefs. Mahomed Akber had, since the deposition of his father, never ceased to foster feelings of intense hatred towards the English nation; and, though often urged by the fallen ruler to deliver himself up, had resolutely preferred the life of a houseless exile to one of mean dependence on the bounty of his enemies. It seems therefore in the highest degree probable that this hostile movement on the part of the Eastern Giljyes was the result of his influence over them, combined with other causes which will be hereafter mentioned. The march of Gen. Sale's brigade to their winter quarters at Jellala-bad, and ultimately to India, had only been deferred until the return of the force from Zoormut, but was now hastened in consequence of this unwelcome news. On the 9th October the 35th regt. N. I. under Col. Monteath, C.B., 100 of the Shah's Sappers under Capt. G. Broadfoot, a squadron of the 5th cavalry under Capt. Oldfield, and 2 guns of Capt. Abbott's battery under Lieut. Dawes, were sent on in advance to the entrance of the pass at Bootkhak, where, on the following night, it was attacked by a large num

* This chief must not be confounded with the ex-ruler o the same name.

ber of rebels, who, taking advantage of the high
ground and deep ravines in the neighbourhood of
the camp, maintained a sharp fire upon it for
several hours, by which 35 Sepoys were killed
and wounded.

On the morning of the 11th Gen. Sale marched
from Cabul with H. M. 13th Lt. Inf. to join the
camp at Bootkhak, and on the following morning
the whole proceeded to force the pass.   Intelligence had been received that the enemy, besides
occupying the heights of this truly formidable
defile, which in many places approach to within
fifty yards of each other, rising up almost per-
pendicularly to an elevation of 500 or 600 feet,
had erected a *sunga*, or stone breastwork, in the
narrowest part of the gorge, flanked by a strong
tower.   The advance guard, con-isting of the
Shah's Sappers, a company of H. M. 13th foot,
another of the 35th N. I., and 2 guns under
Lieut. Dawes, was met about midway through
the pass, which is nearly five miles long, by a
sharp and continued discharge of juzails from the
strong posts of the enemy.   This was returned by
our men with precision and effect, notwithstanding
the disadvantages of their situation ; flanking
parties gallantly struggled up the height to dislodge the enemy from thence, while the Sappers
rushed on to destroy the above-mentioned breast-

work: through this, however, the stream which flows down the middle of the defile had already forced a passage; and, as the enemy abandoned it, as well as the flanking tower, on the approach of our troops, Lieut. Dawes passed his guns through the interval at full speed, getting them under the shelter of a rock beyond the sustained and murderous fire of the enemy's juzailchees, it being impossible to elevate the guns sufficiently to bear upon them. The flankers did their duty nobly, and the fight had lasted for about half an hour, during which the conduct of the Shah's Sappers under Capt. Broadfoot was creditable in the highest degree, when the approach of the main column under Gen. Sale, who had been already shot through the leg, enabled Capt. Seaton of the 35th regiment, who commanded the advance guard, to push on. This he did, running the gauntlet to the end of the pass, by which time the enemy, fearful of being taken in rear, abandoned their position, and retired towards Kubbur-i-Jubbar, on the road to Tezeen. The 35th regiment, Shah's Sappers, Lieut. Dawes's guns, and a party of Hazirbash under Capt. Trevor, encamped at Khoord-Cabul, H. M.'s 13th Lt. Inf. returning to Bootkhak. During their return, parties who still lurked among the rocks fired upon the column, thereby doing some mischief.

In these positions the divided force remained encamped for several days, awaiting the return to Cabul of the troops from Zoormut. During this time several *shub-khoons*, or night attacks, were made on the two camps, that on the 35th regiment at Khoord-Cabul being peculiarly disastrous from the treachery of the Affghan horse, who admitted the enemy within their lines, by which our troops were exposed to a fire from the least suspected quarter : many of our gallant Sepoys and Lieut. Jenkins thus met their death.

On the 20th October, Gen. Sale moved with his force to Khoord-Cabul, having been previously joined by the 37th regiment under Major Griffiths, Capt. Abbot's guns, the mountain train under Capt. Backhouse, 100 of Anderson's irregular horse under Lieut. Mayne, and the remainder of the Shah's sappers and miners. About the 22d the whole force there assembled, with Capt. Macgregor, political agent, marched to Tezeen, encountering much determined opposition on the road.

By this time it was too evident that the whole of the Eastern Giljyes had risen in one common league against us. Their governor, or viceroy, Humza Khan, had in the interval gone forth under pretence of bringing back the chiefs to their allegiance ; on his return, however, which took place nearly at the time at which Gen. Sale marched from Khoord-Cabul, the treacherous nature of his proceedings had been discovered, and he was placed by the Shah in confinement : he was suspected, indeed, before.   Gen. Sale remained at Tezeen until the 26th October.

It must be remarked that, for some time previous to these overt acts of rebellion, the always strong and ill-repressed personal dislike of the Affghans towards Europeans had been manifested in a more than usually open manner in and about Cabul.   Officers had been insulted and attempts made to assassinate them.   Two Europeans had been murdered, as also several camp followers ; but these and other signs of the approaching storm had unfortunately been passed over as mere ebullitions of private angry feeling.   This incredulity and apathy is the more to be lamented, as it was pretty well known that on the occasion of the *shub-khoon*, or first night attack on the 35th N. I. at Bootkhak, a large portion of our assailants consisted of the armed retainers of the different men of consequence in Cabul itself, large parties of whom had been seen proceeding from the city to the scene of action on the evening of the attack, and afterwards returning. Although these men had to pass either through the heart or round the skirts of our camp at

Seeah Sung, it was not deemed expedient even to question them, far less to detain them.

On the 26th October, Gen. Sale started in the direction of Gundamuck, Capt. Macgregor, political agent, having, during the halt at Tezeen, half frightened half cajoled the refractory Giljye chiefs into what the sequel proved to have been a most hollow truce ; for the term *treaty* can scarcely be applied to any agreement made with men so proverbially treacherous, as the whole race of Affghans have proved themselves to be, from our first knowledge of their existence up to the present moment. Of the difficulties experienced by Gen. Sale during his march to Gundamuck, and of the necessity which induced him subsequently to push on to Jellalabad, the public are aware. On the day of his departure from Tezeen the 37th N. I., 3 companies of the Shah's sappers, under Capt. Walsh, and 3 guns of the mountain train, under Lieut. Green, retraced their steps towards Cabul, and encamped at Kubbur-i-Jubbar, to wait as an escort to the sick and convalescent. The sappers continued their march back to Cabul unopposed ; the rest remained here unmolested until the 1st November, when they broke ground for Khoord-Cabul. Here, in the afternoon of the 2d, Major Griffiths, who commanded the detachment, received a peremptory order from Gen. Elphinstone to force his way without loss of time to Cabul, where the insurrection had already broken out in all its violence.   While striking his camp he was attacked by the mountaineers, who now began to assemble on the neighbouring heights in great numbers ; and his march through the pass from Bootkhak to Cabul was one continued conflict, nothing saving him from heavy loss but the steadiness and gallantry of his troops, and the excellence of his own dispositions.   He arrived in cantonments before daybreak on the morning of the 3d November.

The two great leaders of the rebellion were Ameenoollah Khan, the chief of Logue, and Abdoollah Khan, Achukzye, a chief of great influence, and possessing a large portion of the Pisheen valley.

Ameenoollah Khan had hitherto been considered one of the staunchest friends of the existing government; and such was the confidence placed in him by the wuzeer, that he had selected him to take charge of Humza Khan, the lately superseded governor of the Giljyes, as a prisoner to Ghuznee.   This man now distinguished himself as one of our most inveterate enemies.   To illustrate the character of his coadjutor, Abdoollah Khan it will be sufficient to relate the following anecdote. In order to get rid of his elder brother, who stood between him and the inheritance, he caused him to be seized and buried up to the chin in the earth. A rope was then fastened round his neck, and to the end of it was haltered a wild horse: the animal was then driven round in a circle, until the unhappy victim's head was twisted from his shoulders. This same man is also mentioned in terms of just abhorrence by Capt. A. Conolly in his Travels.

But though the two above-named chiefs took a leading part in the rebellion, there can be little doubt that it had its origin in the deep offence given to the Giljyes by the ill-advised reduction of their annual stipends — a measure which had been forced upon Sir William Macnaghten by Lord Auckland.* This they considered, and with some show of justice, as a breach of faith on the part of our government: at all events, that was surely mistaken economy which raised into hostility men, whose determined spirit under a sense of wrong the following anecdote may illustrate. When oppressed by Nadir Shah, the Giljye tribes, rather than succumb to the tyrant's will, took refuge in the mountains amidst the snow, where with their families they fed for

---

* The editor invites particular attention to a note on this subject at the end.

months on roots alone: of these they sent a
handful to Nadir, with the message, that, so long
as such roots could be procured, they would continue to resist his tyranny.   Such were many
of the men now leagued together by one common
feeling of hatred against us.

A passage occurring in a posthumous memo-
randum by the Envoy, now in Lady Macnaghten's
possession, requires insertion here : —

" The immediate cause of the outbreak in the
capital was a seditious letter addressed by Abdoollah Khan to several chiefs of influence at
Cabul, stating that it was the design of the Envoy
to seize and send them all to London !   The
principal rebels met on the previous night, and,
relying on the inflammable feelings of the people
of Cabul, they pretended that the king had issued
an order to put all infidels to death; having previously forged an order from him for our destruction, by the common process of washing out the
contents of a genuine paper, with the exception
of the seal, and substituting their own wicked
inventions."

Such at least is the generally received version
of the story, though persons are not wanting who
would rashly pronounce the king guilty of the
design imputed to him.

But, however that may be, it is certain that

the events, which I have already narrated, ought to have been enough to arouse the authorities from their blind security. It ought, however, to be stated that, alarmed by certain symptoms of disaffection in different parts of the country, and conscious of the inadequacy of the means he then possessed to quell any determined and general insurrection, Sir William had, a few months previously, required the presence of several more regiments: he was however induced to cancel this wise precautionary measure. But, even had this additional force arrived, it is next to certain that the loss of British honour, subsquently sustained, could only have been deferred for a period. A fearfully severe lesson was necessary to remove the veil from the eyes of those, who, drawing their conclusions from their wishes, *would* consider Affghanistan as a settled country. It is but justice to Sir William Macnaghten to say that such recommendations from him as were incompatible with the retrenching system were not received at head-quarters in a way encouraging to him as a public officer.

CHAPTER I.

OUTBREAK OF THE REBELLION. — MURDER OF SIR
ALEXANDER BURNES. — WANT OF ENERGY. — ATTACKS
ON CAPT. LAWRENCE AND LIEUT. STURT. — CHARACTER
OF GEN. ELPHINSTONE. — UNMILITARY POSITION AND
CONSTRUCTION OF THE CANTONMENT AT CABUL.

November 2d, 1841. — AT an early hour this morning, the startling intelligence was brought from the city, that a popular outbreak had taken place; that the shops were all closed; and that a general attack had been made on the houses of all British officers residing in Cabul. About 8 A. M. a hurried note was received by the Envoy in cantonments from Sir Alexander Burnes *, stating that the minds of the people had been strongly excited by some mischievous reports, but expressing a hope that he should succeed in quelling the commotion. About 9 A. M., however, a rumour was circulated, which afterwards proved but too well founded, that Sir Alexander had been murdered, and Capt. Johnson's treasury

* The Envoy lived in the cantonment, and Sir A. Burnes in the city.

plundered. Flames were now seen to issue from that part of the city where they dwelt, and it was too apparent that the endeavour to appease the people by quiet means had failed, and that it would be necessary to have recourse to stronger measures. The report of firearms was incessant, and seemed to extend through the town from end to end.

Sir William Macnaghten now called upon Gen. Elphinstone to act. An order was accordingly sent to Brigadier Shelton, then encamped at Seeah Sung, about a mile and half distant from cantonments, to march forthwith to the *Bala Hissar, or royal citadel,* where his Majesty Shah Shooja resided, commanding a large portion of the city, with the following troops; viz. one company of H. M. 44th foot; a wing of the 54th regiment N. I., under Major Ewart; the 6th regiment Shah's infantry, under Capt. Hopkins; and 4 horse artillery guns, under Capt. Nicholl; and on arrival there to act according to his own judgment, after consulting with the King.

The remainder of the troops encamped at Seeah Sung were at the same time ordered into cantonments; viz. H. M. 44th foot under Lieut-Col. Mackerell; 2 horse artillery guns under Lieut. Waller; and Anderson's irregular horse. A messenger was likewise despatched to recall the 37th

N. I. from Khoord-Cabul without delay. The troops at this time in cantonments were as follows: viz. 5th regiment N. I., under Lieut.-Col. Oliver; a wing of 54th N. I.; 5 six-pounder field guns, with a detachment of the Shah's artillery, under Lieut. Warburton; the Envoy's body-guard; a troop of Skinner's horse, and another of local horse, under Lieut. Walker; three companies of the Shah's sappers, under Capt. Walsh; and about 20 men of the Company's sappers, attached to Capt. Paton, Assist.-Qr.-Mast.-Gen.

Widely spread and formidable as this insurrection proved to be afterwards, it was at first a mere insignificant ebullition of discontent on the part of a few desperate and restless men, which military energy and promptitude ought to have crushed in the bud. Its commencement was an attack by certainly not 300 men on the dwellings of Sir Alexander Burnes and Capt. Johnson, paymaster to the Shah's force; and so little did Sir Alexander himself apprehend serious consequences, that he not only refused, on its first breaking out, to comply with the earnest entreaties of the wuzeer to accompany him to the Bala Hissar, but actually forbade his guard to fire on the assailants, attempting to check what he supposed to be a mere riot, by haranguing the attacking party from the gallery of his house.

The result was fatal to himself; for, in spite of the devoted gallantry of the Sepoys, who composed his guard, and that of the paymaster's office and treasury on the opposite side of the street, who yielded their trust only with their latest breath, the latter were plundered, and his two companions, Lieut. William Broadfoot of the Bengal European regiment, and his brother Lieut. Burnes of the Bombay army, were massacred, in common with every man, woman, and child found on the premises, by these bloodthirsty miscreants. Lieut. Broadfoot killed five or six men with his own hand, before he was shot down.

No man, surely, in a highly responsible public situation — especially in such a one as that held by the late Sir Alexander Burnes — ought ever to indulge in a state of blind security, or to neglect salutary warnings, however small. It is indisputable that such warnings had been given to him; especially by a respectable Affghan named Taj-Mahomed, on the very previous night, who went in person to Sir A. Burnes to put him on his guard, but retired disgusted by the incredulity with which his assertions were received. It is not for me to comment on *his* public character. It is the property of the civilized portion of the world; but it is due to another, little known beyond the immediate sphere in which he moved, to say that,

had this outbreak been productive of no effects
beyond the death of *Lieut. William Broadfoot,* it
could not be sufficiently deplored : in him was lost
to the state not only one of its bravest and most
intelligent officers, but a man who for honesty of
purpose and soundness of judgment, I may boldly
aver, could not be surpassed.

The King, who was in the Bala Hissar, being
somewhat startled by the increasing number of
the rioters, although not at the time aware, so far
as we can judge, of the assassination of Sir A.
Burnes, despatched one of his sons with a number
of his immediate Affghan retainers, and that corps
of Hindoostanees commonly called Campbell's
regiment, with two guns, to restore order : no
support, however, was rendered to these by our
troops, whose leaders appeared so thunderstruck
by the intelligence of the outbreak, as to be incapable of adopting more than the most puerile
defensive measures.   Even Sir William Macnaghten seemed, from a note received at this time
from him by Captain Trevor, to apprehend little
danger, as he therein expressed his perfect confidence as to the speedy and complete success of
Campbell's Hindoostanees in putting an end to the
disturbance.   Such, however, was not the case ;
for the enemy, encouraged by our inaction, increased rapidly in spirit and numbers, and drove

back the king's guard with great slaughter, the guns being with difficulty saved.

It must be understood that Capt. Trevor lived at this time with his family in a strong *bourge*, or tower, situated by the river side, near the Kuzzil-bash quarter, which, on the west, is wholly distinct from the remainder of the city. Within musket shot, on the opposite side of the river, in the direction of the strong and populous village of Deh Affghan, is a fort of some size, then used as a godown, or storehouse, by the Shah's commissariat, part of it being occupied by Brigadier Anquetil, commanding the Shah's force. Close to this fort, divided by a narrow watercourse, was the house of Capt. Troup, Brigade Major of the Shah's force, perfectly defensible against musketry. Both Brigadier Anquetil and Capt. Troup had gone out on horseback early in the morning towards cantonments, and were unable to return ; but the above fort and house contained the usual guard of Sepoys ; and in a garden close at hand called the *Yaboo-Khaneh*, or lines of the baggage-cattle, was a small detachment of the Shah's sappers and miners, and a party of Captain Ferris's juzailchees. Capt. Trevor's tower was capable of being made good against a much stronger force than the rebels at this present time could have collected, had it been properly garrisoned.

As it was, the Hazirbash, or King's life-guards, were, under Capt. Trevor, congregated round their leader, to protect him and his family; which duty, it will be seen, they well performed under very trying circumstances. For what took place in this quarter I beg to refer to a communication made to me at my request by Capt. Colin Mackenzie, Assistant Political Agent at Peshawur, who then occupied the godown portion of the fort above mentioned, which will be found hereafter.*

I have already stated that Brigadier Shelton was early in the day directed to proceed with part of the Seeah Sung force to occupy the Bala Hissar, and, if requisite, to lead his troops against the insurgents. Capt. Lawrence, military secretary to the Envoy, was at the same time sent forward to prepare the King for that officer's reception. Taking with him four troopers of the body-guard, he was galloping along the main road, when, shortly after crossing the river, he was suddenly attacked by an Affghan, who, rushing from behind

---

* I am sorry to say that this document has not reached me with the rest of the manuscript. I have not struck out the reference, because there is hope that it still exists, and may be yet appended to this narrative. The loss of any thing else from Capt. Mackenzie's pen will be regretted by all who read his other communication, the account of the Envoy's murder. — EDITOR.

a wall, made a desperate cut at him with a large two-handed knife. He dexterously avoided the blow by spurring his horse on one side; but, passing onwards, he was fired upon by about fifty men, who, having seen his approach, ran out from the Lahore gate of the city to intercept him. He reached the Bala Hissar safe, where he found the King apparently in a state of great agitation, he having witnessed the assault from the window of his palace. His Majesty expressed an eager desire to conform to the Envoy's wishes in all respects in this emergency.

Capt. Lawrence was still conferring with the King, when Lieut. Sturt, our executive engineer, rushed into the palace, stabbed in three places about the face and neck. He had been sent by Brigadier Shelton to make arrangements for the accommodation of the troops, and had reached the gate of the *Dewan Khaneh*, or hall of audience, when the attempt at his life was made by some one who had concealed himself there for that purpose, and who immediately effected his escape. The wounds were fortunately not dangerous, and Lieut. Sturt was conveyed back to cantonments in the king's own palanquin, under a strong escort. Soon after this, Brig. Shelton's force arrived; but the day was suffered to pass without any thing being done demonstrative of

British energy and power. The murder of our countrymen, and the spoliation of public and private property, were perpetrated with impunity within a mile of our cantonment, and under the very walls of the Bala Hissar.

Such an exhibition on our part taught the enemy their strength — confirmed against us those who, however disposed to join in the rebellion, had hitherto kept aloof from prudential motives, and ultimately encouraged the nation to unite as one man for our destruction.

It was, in fact, the crisis of all others calculated to test the qualities of a military commander. Whilst, however, it is impossible for an unprejudiced person to approve the military dispositions of this eventful period, it is equally our duty to discriminate. The most *responsible* party is not always the most culpable. It would be the height of injustice to a most amiable and gallant officer not to notice the long course of painful and wearing illness, which had materially affected the nerves, and probably even the intellect, of Gen. Elphinstone; cruelly incapacitating him, so far as he was personally concerned, from acting in this sudden emergency with the promptitude and vigour necessary for our preservation. Major-Gen. Elphinstone had some time before represented to Lord Auckland the shattered state of

his health, stating plainly and honestly that it
had unfitted him to continue in command, and
requesting permission to resign.   Lord Auckland
at first pressed him to remain, but ultimately
acceded to his wishes; and the General was on
the point of returning to India, thence to embark
for England, when the rebellion unhappily broke
out.* No one, who knew Gen. Elphinstone, could
fail to esteem his many excellent qualities both
in public and private life.   To all under his command, not excepting the youngest subaltern, he
was ever accessible, and in the highest degree
courteous and considerate : nor did he ever exhibit, either in word or practice, the slightest
partiality for officers of his own service over those
of the Company. His professional knowledge was
extensive; and, before disease had too much
impaired his frame for active exertion, he had
zealously applied himself to improve and stimu-
late every branch of the service. He had, indeed,
but one unhappy fault as a general — the result,
probably, of age and infirmity — and this was a
want of confidence in his own judgment, leading
him to prefer every body's opinion to his own,
until, amidst the conflicting views of a multitude
of counsellors, he was at a loss which course to
take.   Hence much of that indecision, procrastination, and want of method, which paralyzed all

* See a note at the end of the book.

our efforts, gradually demoralised the troops, and ultimately, not being redeemed by the qualities of his second in command, proved the ruin of us all. I might add that, during the siege, no one exposed his person more fearlessly or frequently to the enemy's fire than Gen. Elphinstone : but his gallantry was never doubted. Unhappily, Sir William Macnaghten at first made light of the insurrection, and, by his representations as to the general feeling of the people towards us, not only deluded himself, but misled the General in council. The unwelcome truth was soon forced upon us, that in the whole Affghan nation we could not reckon on a single friend.

But though no active measures of aggression were taken, all necessary preparations were made to secure the cantonment against attack. It fell to my own lot to place every available gun in position round the works. Besides the guns already mentioned, we had in the magazine 6 nine-pounder iron guns, 3 twenty-four pounder howitzers, 1 twelve-pounder ditto, and 3 $5\frac{1}{2}$-inch mortars ; but the detail of artillerymen fell very short of what was required to man all these efficiently, consisting of only 80 Punjabees belonging to the Shah, under Lieut. Warburton, very insufficiently instructed, and of doubtful fidelity.

To render our position intelligible, it is necessary to describe the cantonment, or fortified lines so called. It is uncertain whether, for the faults which I am about to describe, any blame justly attaches to Lieut. Sturt, the engineer, a talented and sensible officer, but who was often obliged to yield his better judgment to the spirit of false economy which characterised our Affghan policy. The credit, however, of having selected a site for the cantonments, or controlled the execution of its works, is not a distinction now likely to be *claimed* exclusively by *any one*. But it must always remain a wonder that any Government, or any officer or set of officers, who had either science or experience in the field, should, in a *half*-conquered country, fix their forces (already inadequate to the services to which they might be called) in so extraordinary and injudicious a military position. Every engineer officer who had been consulted, since the first occupation of Cabul by our troops, had pointed to the Bala Hissar as the only suitable place for a garrison which was to keep in subjection the city and the surrounding country ; but, above all, it was surely the only proper site for the *magazine*, on which the army's efficiency depended. In defiance, however, of rule and precedent, the position eventually fixed upon for our magazine and cantonment was a piece of low swampy ground, commanded on all sides by hills

or forts. It consisted of a low rampart and a
narrow ditch in the form of a parallelogram,
thrown up along the line of the Kohistan road,
1000 yards long and 600 broad, with round flanking bastions at each corner, every one of which
was commanded by some fort or hill. To one
end of this work was attached a space nearly half
as large again, and surrounded by a simple wall.
This was called the " Mission Compound :" half
of it was appropriated for the residence of the
Envoy, the other half being crowded with build-
ings, erected without any attempt at regularity,
for the accommodation of the officers and assist-
ants of the mission, and the Envoy's body-guard
This large space required in time of siege to be
defended, and thus materially weakened the garrison ; while its very existence rendered the whole
face of the cantonment, to which it was annexed,
nugatory for purposes of defence. Besides these
disadvantages, the lines were a great deal too
extended, so that the ramparts could not be properly manned without harassing the garrison.
On the eastern side, about a quarter of a mile off,
flowed the Cabul river in a direction parallel with
the Kohistan road. Between the river and cantonments, about 150 yards from the latter, was a wide
canal. Gen. Elphinstone, on his arrival in April,
1841, perceived at a glance the utter unfitness of

the cantonment for purposes of protracted defence, and when a new fort was about to be built for the magazine on the south side, he liberally offered to purchase for the government, out of his own funds, a large portion of the land in the vicinity, with the view of removing some very objectionable inclosures and gardens, which offered shelter to our enemy within two hundred yards of our ramparts; but neither was his offer accepted, nor were his representations on the subject attended with any good result. He lost no time, however, in throwing a bridge over the river, in a direct line between the cantonments and the Seeah Sung camp, and in rendering the bridge over the canal passable for guns; which judicious measure shortened the distance for artillery and infantry by at least two miles, sparing, too, the necessity which existed previously of moving to and fro by the main road, which was commanded by three or four forts, as well as from the city walls. Moreover, the Cabul River being liable to sudden rises, and almost always unfordable during the rainy season (March and April), it will easily be understood that the erection of this bridge was a work of much importance. But the most unaccountable oversight of all, and that which may be said to have contributed most largely to our subsequent disasters, was that of having *the commissariat stores detached from cantonments,* in an old fort which, in an outbreak, would be almost indefensible. Capt. Skinner, the chief commissariat officer, at the time when this arrangement was made, earnestly solicited from the authorities a place *within* the cantonment for his stores, but received for answer that " no such place could be given him, as they were far too busy in erecting barracks for the men to think of commissariat stores." The Envoy himself pressed this point very urgently, but without avail. At the south-west angle of cantonments was the bazar village, surrounded by a low wall, and so crowded with mud huts as to form a perfect maze. Nearly opposite, with only the high road between, was the small fort of Mahomed Shereef, which perfectly commanded our south-west bastion. Attached to this fort was the Shah Bagh, or King's garden, surrounded by a high wall, and comprising a space of about half a square mile. About two hundred yards higher up the road towards the city, was the commissariat fort, the gate of which stood very nearly opposite the entrance of the Shah Bagh. There were various other forts at different points of our works, which will be mentioned in the course of events. On the east, at the distance of about a mile, was a range of low hills dividing us from the Seeah Sung camp ; and on the west, about the same distance off, was another somewhat higher range, at the north-east flank of which, by the road-side, was the village of *Beymaroo*, commanding a great part of the Mission Compound. In fact, we were so hemmed in on all sides, that, when the rebellion became general, the troops could not move out a dozen paces from either gate, without being exposed to the fire of some neighbouring hostile fort, garrisoned too by marksmen who seldom missed their aim. The country around us was likewise full of impediments to the movements of artillery and cavalry, being in many places flooded, and every where closely intersected by deep water-cuts.

I cannot help adding, in conclusion, that almost all the calamities that befel our ill-starred force may be traced more or less to the defects of our position ; and that our cantonment at Cabul, whether we look to its situation or its construction, must ever be spoken of as a disgrace to our military skill and judgment.

CHAP. II.

THE 37TH REGIMENT ATTACKED ON ITS RETURN FROM
KHOORD-CABUL. — MURDER OF LIEUTS. MAULE AND
WHEELER. — LOSS OF THE COMMISSARIAT FORT. — THE
GENERAL'S INDECISION. — MAJOR THAIN AND CAPT.
PATON. — SUCCESSFUL ATTACK ON THE FORT OF MA-
HOMED SHEREEF. — ENGAGEMENTS WITH AFFGHAN
HORSE AND FOOT. — THE ENEMY'S PLAN TO REDUCE
THE BRITISH BY STARVATION. — BRIGADIER SHELTON
SENT FOR FROM BALA HISSAR.

November 3d. — AT 3 A. M. the alarm was sounded
at the eastern gate of cantonments, in consequence
of a brisk file-firing in the direction of Seeah
Sung, which turned out to proceed from the
37th regiment N. I. on its return from Khoord-
Cabul, having been closely followed up the whole
way by a body of about 3000 Giljyes. The
regiment managed, nevertheless, to save all its
baggage excepting a few tents, which were left
on the ground for want of carriage, and to bring
in all the wounded safe.

A more orderly march was never made under
such trying circumstances, and it reflects the
highest credit on Major Griffiths and all concerned. This regiment was a valuable acqui-
c 6

sition to our garrison, being deservedly esteemed one of the best in the service. Three guns of the mountain train under Lieut. Green accompanied them, and were of the greatest use in defending the rear on the line of march. In consequence of their arrival, a reinforcement was sent into the Bala Hissar, consisting of the left wing 54th N. I., with Lieut. Green's guns, 1 iron nine-pounder, 1 twenty-four-pounder howitzer, 2 $5\frac{1}{2}$-inch mortars, and a supply of magazine stores. They all reached it in safety, though a few shots were fired at the rear-guard from some orchards near the city. Brigadier Shelton was ordered to maintain a sharp fire upon the city from the howitzers and guns, and to endeavour to fire the houses by means of shells and carcasses from the two mortars; should he also find it practicable to send a force into the city, he was to do so.

Early in the afternoon, a detachment under Major Swayne, consisting of two companies 5th N. I., one of H. M. 44th, and 2 H. A. guns under Lieut. Waller, proceeded out of the western gate towards the city, to effect, if possible, a junction at the Lahore gate with a part of Brigadier Shelton's force from the Bala Hissar. They drove back and defeated a party of the enemy who occupied the road near the Shah Bagh, but had to encounter a sharp fire from the Kohistan gate of the city, and from the walls of various enclosures, behind which a number of marksmen had concealed themselves, as also from the fort of Mahmood Khan commanding the road along which they had to pass.   Lieut. Waller and several Sepoys were wounded.   Major Swayne, observing the whole line of road towards the Lahore gate strongly occupied by some Affghan horse and juzailchees, and fearing that he would be unable to effect the object in view with so small a force unsupported by cavalry, retired into cantonments.   Shortly after this, a large body of the rebels having issued from the fort of Mahmood Khan, 900 yards south-east of cantonments, extended themselves in a line along the bank of the river, displaying a flag ; an iron nine-pounder was brought to bear on them from our south-east bastion, and a round or two of shrapnell caused them to seek shelter behind some neighbouring banks, whence, after some desultory firing on both sides, they retired.

Whatever hopes may have been entertained, up to this period, of a speedy termination to the insurrection, they began now to wax fainter every hour, and an order was despatched to the officer commanding at Candahar to lose no time in sending to our assistance the 16th and 43d regiments N. I. (which were under orders for India), together with a troop of horse artillery, and half a regiment of cavalry; an order was likewise sent off to recall Gen. Sale with his brigade from Gundamuck. Capt. John Conolly, political assistant to the Envoy, went into the Bala Hissar early this morning, to remain with the King, and to render every assistance in his power to Brigadier Shelton.

On this day Lieut. Richard Maule, commanding the Kohistanee regiment, which on its return from Zoormut had been stationed at Kahdarra in Kohistan, about twenty miles north-west of Cabul, with the object of keeping down disaffection in that quarter, being deserted by his men, was, together with local Lieut. Wheeler, his adjutant, barbarously murdered by a band of rebels. They defended themselves resolutely for several minutes; but at length fell under the fire of some juzails. Lieut. Maule had been previously informed of his danger by a friendly native, but chose rather to run the risk of being sacrificed than desert the post assigned him. Thus fell a noble-hearted soldier and a devout Christian.

November 4th.—The enemy having taken strong possession of the *Shah Bagh,* or King's Garden, and thrown a garrison into the fort of Mahomed Shereef, nearly opposite the bazar, effectually prevented any communication between the cantonment and commissariat fort, the gate of which latter was commanded by the gate of the Shah Bagh on the other side of the road.

Ensign Warren of the 5th N. I. at this time occupied the commissariat fort with 100 men, and having reported that he was very hard pressed by the enemy, and in danger of being completely cut off, the General, either forgetful or unaware at the moment of the important fact that upon the possession of this fort we were entirely dependent for provisions, and anxious only to save the lives of men whom he believed to be in imminent peril, hastily gave directions that a party under the command of Capt. Swayne of H. M.'s 44th Regt. should proceed immediately to bring off Ensign Warren and his garrison to cantonments, abandoning the fort to the enemy. A few minutes previously an attempt to relieve him had been made by Ensign Gordon, with a company of the 37th N. I. and eleven camels laden with ammunition ; but the party were driven back, and Ensign Gordon killed. Capt. Swayne now accordingly proceeded towards the spot with two companies of H. M.'s 44th ; scarcely had they issued from cantonments ere a sharp and destructive fire was poured upon them from Mahomed Shereef's fort, which, as they proceeded, was taken up by the marksmen in the Shah Bagh, under whose deadly aim both officers and men suffered severely; Capts. Swayne and Robinson of the 44th being killed, and Lieuts. Hallahan, Evans, and Fortye wounded, in this disastrous business.   It now seemed to the officer, on whom the command had devolved, impracticable to bring off Ensign Warren's party, without risking the annihilation of his own, which had already sustained so rapid and severe a loss in officers; he therefore returned forthwith to cantonments.   In the course of the evening, another attempt was made by a party of the 5th Lt. Cavalry; but they encountered so severe a fire from the neighbouring enclosures as to oblige them to return without effecting their desired object, with the loss of 8 troopers killed and 14 badly wounded.   Capt. Boyd, the Assist.-Com.-Gen., having meanwhile been made acquainted with the General's intention to give up the fort, hastened to lay before him the disastrous consequences that would ensue from so doing.   He stated that the place contained, besides large supplies of wheat and atta, all his stores of rum, medicine, clothing, &c., the value of which might be estimated at four lacs of rupees; that to abandon such valuable property would not only expose the force to the immediate want of the necessaries of life, but would infallibly inspire the enemy with tenfold courage. He added that we had not above two days' supply of provisions in cantonments, and that neither himself nor Capt. Johnson of the Shah's commissariat had any prospect of procuring them elsewhere under existing circumstances. In consequence of this strong representation on the part of Capt. Boyd, the General sent immediate orders to Ensign Warren to hold out the fort to the last extremity. (Ensign Warren, it must be remarked, denied having received this note.) Early in the night a letter was received from him to the effect that he believed the enemy were busily engaged in mining one of the towers, and that such was the alarm among the Sepoys that several of them had actually made their escape over the wall to cantonments; that the enemy were making preparations to burn down the gate; and that, considering the temper of his men, he did not expect to be able to hold out many hours longer, unless reinforced without delay. In reply to this he was informed that he would be reinforced by 2 A. M.

At about 9 o'clock P. M. there was an assembly of staff and other officers at the General's house, when the Envoy came in and expressed his serious conviction that, unless Mahomed Shereef's fort were taken that very night, we should lose the commissariat fort, or at all events be unable to bring out of it provisions for the troops. The disaster of the morning rendered the General extremely unwilling to expose his officers and men to any similar peril; but, on the other hand, it was urged that the darkness of the night would nullify the enemy's fire, who would also most likely be taken unawares, as it was not the custom of the Affghans to maintain a very strict watch at night. A man in Capt. Johnson's employ was accordingly sent out to reconnoitre the place; he returned in a few minutes with the intelligence that about twenty men were seated outside the fort near the gate, smoking and talking; and from what he overheard of their conversation, he judged the garrison to be very small, and unable to resist a sudden onset. The debate was now resumed, but another hour passed and the General could not make up his mind. A second spy was despatched, whose report tended to corroborate what the first had said. I was then sent to Lieut. Sturt, the engineer, who was nearly recovered from his wounds, for his opinion. He at first expressed himself in favour of an immediate attack, but, on hearing that some of the enemy were on the watch at the gate, he judged it prudent to defer the assault till an early hour in the morning : this decided the General, though not before several hours had slipped away in fruitless discussion.

Orders were at last given for a detachment to be in readiness at 4 A. M. at the Kohistan gate ; and Capt. Bellew, Deputy Assist.-Quar.-Mast.-Gen., volunteered to blow open the gate ; another party of H. M.'s 44th were at the same time to issue by a cut in the south face of the rampart, and march simultaneously towards the commissariat fort, to reinforce the garrison. Morning had, however, well dawned ere the men could be got under arms; and they were on the point of marching off, when it was reported that Ensign Warren had just arrived in cantonments with his garrison, having evacuated the fort. It seems that the enemy had actually set fire to the gate; and Ensign Warren, seeing no prospect of a reinforcement, and expecting the enemy every moment to rush in, led out his men by a hole which he had prepared in the wall. Being called upon in a public letter from the Assist.-Adj.-Gen. to state his reasons for abandoning his post, he replied that he was ready to do so before a court of inquiry, which he requested might be assembled to investigate his conduct ; it was not, however, deemed expedient to comply with his request.

It is beyond a doubt that our feeble and in-effectual defence of this fort, and the valuable booty it yielded, was the first *fatal* blow to our supremacy at Cabul, and at once determined those chiefs — and more particularly the Kuzzil-bashes — who had hitherto remained neutral, to join in the general combination to drive us from the country.

Capt. Trevor, having held out his house against the rebels until all hope of relief was at an end, was safely escorted into cantonments this morn-ing, with his wife and seven children, by his Ha-zirbash horsemen, who behaved faithfully, but now, out of regard for their families, dispersed to their houses. Capt. Mackenzie likewise, after defending his fort until his ammunition was ex-pended, fought his way into cantonments late last night, having received a slight wound on the road. His men had behaved with the utmost bravery, and made several successful sallies.   See his own account.*

November 5th.—It no sooner became generally known that the commissariat fort, upon which we were dependent for supplies, had been abandoned, than one universal feeling of indignation per-vaded the garrison; nor can I describe the im-

* I have already stated with regret that this interesting paper is missing. — EDITOR.

patience of the troops, but especially the native portion, to be led out for its recapture—a feeling that was by no means diminished by their seeing the Affghans crossing and re-crossing the road between the commissariat fort and the gate of the *Shah Bagh*, laden with the provisions upon which had depended our ability to make a protracted defence. Observing this disposition among the troops, and feeling the importance of checking the triumph of the enemy in its infancy, I strenuously urged the General to send out a party to capture Mahomed Shereef's fort by blowing open the gate, and volunteered myself to keep the road clear from any sudden advance of cavalry with two H. A. guns, under cover of whose fire the storming party could advance along the road, protected from the fire of the fort by a low wall, which lined the road the whole way. The General agreed; a storming party under Major Swayne, 5th H. I., was ordered; the powder bags were got ready; and at about 12 mid-day we issued from the western gate : the guns led the way, and were brought into action under the partial cover of some trees, within one hundred yards of the fort. For the space of twenty minutes the artillery continued to work the guns under an excessively sharp fire from the walls of the fort; but Major Swayne, instead of rushing forward with

his men, as had been agreed, had in the mean
time remained stationary under cover of the wall
by the road side. The General, who was watch-
ing our proceedings from the gateway, observing
that the gun ammunition was running short, and
that the troops had failed to take advantage of the
best opportunity for advancing, recalled us into
cantonments : thus the enemy enjoyed their triumph undiminished; and great was the rage of
the Sepoys of the 37th N. I., who had evinced
the utmost eagerness to be led out, at this disappointment of their hopes. It must be acknowledged that the General was singularly unfortunate
in many of the coadjutors about him, who, with
all the zeal and courage which distinguish British
officers, were sadly lacking in that military judgment and quicksightedness which are essential to
success in a critical moment. Let me here, however, pay a just tribute to the memory of two of
his staff officers, now, alas ! no more. Few men
have ever combined all the excellent qualities
which constitute the good soldier and the good
man more remarkably than did *Major Thain* of
H. M.'s 21st Fusileers, A. D. C. to Gen. Elphinstone ; while of *Capt. Paton*, Deputy Quarter-
master-general, it may be safely affirmed, that
in solid practical sense and genuine singleness of
heart he was never surpassed. Would that all,

to whom the General was in the habit of deferring, had been equally wise to counsel and prompt to execute with the two above-named gallant men !

November 6th.—It was now determined to take the fort of Mahomed Shereef by regular breach and assault. At an early hour, 3 iron nine-pounder guns were brought to bear upon its north-east bastion, and 2 howitzers upon the con-tiguous curtain. I took charge of the former, and Lieut. Warburton of the latter. In the space of about two hours a practicable breach was ef-fected, during which time a hot fire was poured upon the artillerymen from the enemy's sharp-shooters, stationed in a couple of high towers which completely commanded the battery, whereby, as the embrasures crumbled away from the con-stant concussion, it became at length a difficult task to work the guns. A storming party, com-posed of 3 companies, viz. 1 comp. H. M. 44th, under Ensign Raban, 1 comp. 5th N. I. under Lieut. Deas, 1 comp. 37th under Lieut. Steer, the whole commanded by Major Griffiths, speedily carried the place. Poor Raban was shot through the heart, when conspicuously waving a flag on the summit of the breach.

As this fort adjoined the Shah Bagh, it was deemed advisable to dislodge the enemy from the

latter, if possible. Learning that there was a large
opening in the wall in the north side of the garden,
I took a six-pounder gun thither, and fired several
rounds of grape and shrapnell upon parties of the
enemy assembled within under the trees, which
speedily drove them out ; and had a detachment
of infantry taken advantage of the opportunity
thus afforded to throw themselves into the building at the principal entrance by the road side,
the place might have been easily carried per-
manently, and immediate repossession could have
been then taken of the commissariat fort opposite,
which had not yet been emptied of half its contents.   While this was going on, a reconnoitring
party under Major Thain, A. D. C., consisting of
1 H. A. gun, 1 troop 5th cavalry, and 2 comps. of
infantry, scoured the plain to the west of cantonments ; and having driven the enemy from several
enclosures, were returning homeward, when large
numbers of Affghan horse and foot were observed
to proceed from the direction of the city towards
the south-west extremity of a hill, which runs in
a diagonal direction from north-east to south-west
across the plain, to the west of cantonments.   A
resallah of Anderson's horse had been stationed
on the summit of this hill all the morning as a
picket, whence they had just been recalled, when
a large body of the enemy's horse reached the

base, and proceeded to crown the summit. Major
Thain's party, observing this, came to a halt;
and a few minutes afterwards a reinforcement
opportunely arrived, consisting of 1 resallah of
irregular horse under Capt. Anderson, 1 troop
of ditto under Lieut. Walker, and 2 troops 5th
cavalry under Capts. Collyer and Bott. I now considered it my duty to join the H. A. gun, which
had no officer with it, and I accordingly left the six-
pounder gun under the protection of Capt. Mackenzie, who, with a few of his juzailchees, had
now joined me, having been engaged in skirmish-
ing across the plain towards the west end of the
Shah Bagh, where, finding an opening, he had
crept in with his men, and cleared that part of
the garden, but, not being supported, had been
obliged to retire with a loss of 15 killed out of 95.

I now advanced with the H. A. gun, supported
by a troop of the 5th cavalry, to the foot of the
hill, and opened fire upon the enemy, while the
rest of the cavalry, headed by Anderson's horse,
rode briskly up the slope to force them off. The
officers gallantly headed their men, and encountered about an equal number of the enemy, who
advanced to meet them. A hand to hand encounter
now took place, which ended in the Affghan horse
retreating to the plain, leaving the hill in our
possession. In this affair Capt. Anderson per-

D

sonally engaged, and slew the brother-in-law of
Abdoollah Khan. Meanwhile the enemy began
to muster strong on the plain to the west of the
Shah Bagh, whence they appeared to be gradually
extending themselves towards the cantonments,
as if to intercept our return; it was therefore
deemed prudent to recall the cavalry from the
height, and show front in the plain, where they
could act with more effect. A reinforcement of
two companies of infantry and one H. A. gun was
sent out, and the whole force was drawn up in
order of battle, anticipating an attack, with one
gun on either flank. In this position a distant
fire was kept up by the enemy's juzailchees, which
was answered principally by discharges of shrapnell and round shot from the guns; the heights,
too, were again crowned by the Affghan horse,
but no disposition was manifested by them to encounter us in open fight, and, as the night gradually
closed in, they slowly retired to the city. On
this occasion about 100 of the enemy fell on the
hill, while the loss on our side was 8 troopers
killed, and 14 wounded.

It will be remembered that I left a six-pounder
gun at the opening in the wall of the Shah Bagh.
After my departure, large numbers of the enemy's
infantry had filled the west end of the Shah Bagh,
and, stealing up among the trees, and close to the

high wall, towards the gun, kept up so hot and precise a fire as to render its removal absolutely necessary. Capt. Mackenzie had been joined by a party of H. M.'s 44th; with whom, and with a few of his own men, he endeavoured to cover the operation, which was extremely difficult, it being necessary to drag the gun by hand over bad ground. Several of the Shah's gunners were killed, and many of the covering party knocked over, the gun being barely saved. I may here add, that from this time forward the juzailchees, under the able direction of Capt. Mackenzie, who volunteered to lead them, were forward to distinguish themselves on all occasions, and continued to the very last a most useful part of our force.

November 8th. — An attempt was made by the enemy to mine one of the towers of the fort we captured on the 6th, which could not have happened had we taken possession of the gate of the Shah Bagh at the same time. Our chief cause of anxiety now was the empty state of our granary. Even with high bribes and liberal payment, the Envoy could only procure a scanty supply, insufficient for daily consumption, from the village of Beymaroo, about half a mile down the Kohistan road, to the north. The object of the enemy undoubtedly was to starve us out; to effect which the chiefs exerted their whole influence to prevent

our being supplied from any of the neighbouring
forts.   Their game was a sure one ;   and, so long
as they held firmly together, it could not fail to be
sooner or later successful.   During the short interval of quiet, which ensued after our capture of
the fort, the rebels managed to rig out a couple
of guns which they procured from the workyard
of Lieut. Warburton (in charge of the Shah's
guns), situated, unfortunately, in the city.   These
they placed in a position near Mahmood Khan's
fort, opposite the south-east bastion of cantonments.   All this time a cannonade was daily kept
up on the town by Capt. Nicholl of the Horse
Artillery in the Bala Hissar; but, though considerable damage was thereby done, and many of
the enemy killed, it required a much more powerful battery than he possessed to ruin a place of
such extent.   On the morning of the 2d, when
the rebellion commenced, the two guns, which
were sent with Campbell's Hindoostanees into the
city, had been left outside the gate of the Bala
Hissar in the confusion and hurry of retreat,
where they had ever since remained.   So jealous
a watch was kept over these by the enemy from
the houses of the Shah Bazar, that it was found
impossible to get them back into the fort ; and it
was necessary for our troops to maintain an
equally strict watch to prevent their being removed

by the enemy, who made several desperate efforts to obtain them. An attempt of this kind took place to-day, when the rebels were driven back into the city with considerable loss.

November 9th. — The General's weak state of health rendering the presence of a coadjutor absolutely necessary, to relieve him from the command of the garrison, Brigadier Shelton, the second in command, was, at the earnest request of the Envoy, summoned in from the Bala Hissar, in the hope that, by heartily co-operating with the Envoy and General, he would strengthen their hands and rouse the sinking confidence of the troops. He entered cantonments this morning, bringing with him 1 H. A. gun, 1 mountain train ditto, 1 company H. M. 44th, the Shah's 6th infantry, and a small supply of atta.

CHAP. III.

DESPONDENCY IN CANTONMENT. — DIFFERENCE OF OPINION BETWEEN BRIGADIER SHELTON AND SIR WILLIAM MACNAGHTEN. — ANNOYANCE FROM THE FIRE OF THE ENEMY OUT OF SEVERAL FORTS. — STORMING OF THE RIKA-BASHEE FORT, UNDER BRIGADIER SHELTON. — PERILOUS SITUATION AND BRAVERY OF LIEUT. BIRD. — FURTHER ENGAGEMENTS WITH THE ENEMY. — SUPERIORITY OF THE AFFGHANS IN THE USE OF FIRE-ARMS.

November 10*th*.—HENCEFORWARD Brigadier Shelton bore a conspicuous part in the drama upon the issue of which so much depended. He had, however, from the very first, seemed to despair of the force being able to hold out the winter at Cabul, and strenuously advocated an immediate retreat to Jellalabad.

This sort of despondency proved, unhappily, very infectious. It soon spread its baneful influence among the officers, and was by them communicated to the soldiery. The number of *croakers* in garrison became perfectly frightful, lugubrious looks and dismal prophecies being encountered every where. The severe losses sustained by H. M.'s 44th under Capt. Swayne, on the 4th instant, had very much discouraged the men of that regiment; and it is a lamentable fact that some of those European soldiers, who were naturally expected to exhibit to their native brethren in arms an example of endurance and fortitude, were among the first to lose confidence and give vent to feelings of discontent at the duties imposed on them. The evil seed, once sprung up, became more and more difficult to eradicate, showing daily more and more how completely demoralising to the British soldier is the very idea of a retreat.

Sir William Macnaghten and his suite were altogether opposed to Brigadier Shelton in this matter, it being in his (the Envoy's) estimation a duty we owed the Government to retain our post, at whatsoever risk. This difference of opinion, on a question of such vital importance, was attended with unhappy results, inasmuch as it deprived the General, in his hour of need, of the strength which unanimity imparts, and produced an uncommunicative and disheartening reserve in an emergency which demanded the freest interchange of counsel and ideas.

But I am digressing. — About 9 A.M. on the 10th the enemy crowned the heights to the west in great force, and almost simultaneously a large body of horse and foot, supposed to be Giljyes, who had just arrived, made their appearance on the Seeah Sung hills to the east, and, after firing a feu de joie, set up a loud shout, which was answered in a similar way by those on the opposite side of us. This was supposed to be a preconcerted signal for a joint attack on the cantonments. No movement was however made on the western side to molest us, but on the eastern quarter parties of the enemy, moving down into the plain, took possession of all the forts in that direction. One of these, called the Rika-bashee fort, was situated directly opposite the Mission Compound, at the north-east angle of cantonments, within musket-shot of our works, into which the enemy soon began to pour a very annoying fire; a party of sharp-shooters at the same time, concealing themselves among the ruins of a house immediately opposite the north-east bastion, took deadly aim at the European artillerymen who were working the guns, one poor fellow being shot through the temple in the act of sponging. From 2 howitzers and a 5½-inch mortar, a discharge of shells into the fort was kept up for two hours.

At this time not above two days' supply of provisions remained in garrison, and it was very clear that, unless the enemy were quickly driven out from their new possession, we should soon be completely hemmed in on all sides. At the Envoy's urgent desire, he taking the entire responsibility on himself, the General ordered a force to hold themselves in readiness under Brigadier Shelton to storm the Rika-bashee fort. About 12 A. M. the following troops assembled at the eastern gate : — 2 H. A. guns, 1 mountain train gun, Walker's horse, H. M.'s 44th foot under Col. Mackerell, 37th N. I. under Major Griffiths, 6th regiment of Shah's force under Capt. Hopkins. The whole issued from cantonments, a storming party consisting of two companies from each regiment taking the lead, preceded by Capt. Bellew, who hurried forward to blow open the gate. Missing the gate, however, he blew open a wicket of such small dimensions as to render it impossible for more than two or three men to enter abreast, and these in a stooping posture. This, it will be seen, was one cause of discomfiture in the first instance; for the hearts of the men failed them when they saw their foremost comrades struck down, endeavouring to force an entrance under such disadvantageous circumstances, without being able to help them. The signal, however, was given for the storming party, headed by Col. Mackerell. On nearing the wicket, the detachment encountered an excessively sharp fire from the walls, and the small passage, through which they endeavoured to rush in, merely served to ex-

pose the bravest to almost certain death from the
hot fire of the defenders.   Col. Mackerell, however, and Lieut. Bird of Shah's 6th infantry,
accompanied by a handful of Europeans and a
few Sepoys, forced their way in; Capt. West-
macott of the 37th being shot down outside, and
Capt. M'Crae sabred in the entrance.   The garrison, supposing that these few gallant men were
backed by the whole attacking party, fled in
consternation out of the gate, which was on the
opposite side of the fort, and which ought to have
been the point assailed.   Unfortunately, at this
instant a number of the Affghan cavalry charged
round the corner of the fort next the wicket: the
cry of " Cavalry!" was raised, a cry which too often,
during our operations, paralyzed the arms of those,
whose muskets and bayonets we have been accustomed to consider as more than a match for a desultory charge of irregular horsemen; the Europeans gave way simultaneously with the Sepoys—
a bugler of the 6th infantry, through mistake,
sounded the retreat—and it became for the time a
scene of *sauve qui peut*.   In vain did the officers,
especially Major Scott of H. M.'s 44th, knowing the
fearful predicament of his commanding officer, ex-
hort and beseech their men to charge forward—not
a soul would follow them, save a private of the 44th
named Steward, who was afterwards promoted for

his solitary gallantry.   Let me here do Brigadier
Shelton justice : his acknowledged courage redeemed the day; for, exposing his own person to
a hot fire, he stood firm amidst the crowd of fugitives, and by his exhortations and example at
last rallied them ; advancing again to the attack,
again our men faltered, notwithstanding that the
fire of the great guns from the cantonments, and
that of Capt. Mackenzie's juzailchees from the
N. E. angle of the Mission Compound, together
with a demonstration on the part of our cavalry,
had greatly abated the ardour of the Affghan
horse.   A third time did the Brigadier bring on
his men to the assault, which now proved successful.   We became masters of the fort.   But what,
in the mean time, had been passing inside the fort,
where, it will be remembered, several of our brave
brethren had been shut up, as it were, in the
lions' den ?

On the first retreat of our men, Lieut. Bird,
with Col. Mackerell and several Europeans, had
hastily shut the gate by which the garrison had
for the most part evacuated the place, securing
the chain with a bayonet : the repulse outside,
however, encouraged the enemy to return in great
numbers, and, it being impossible to remain near
the gate on account of the hot fire poured in
through the crevices, our few heroes speedily had

the mortification to see their foes not only re-entering the wicket, but, having drawn the bayonet, rush in with loud shouts through the now re-opened gate. Poor Mackerell, having fallen, was literally hacked to pieces, although still alive at the termination of the contest. Lieut. Bird, with two Sepoys, retreated into a stable, the door of which they closed; all the rest of the men, endeavouring to escape through the wicket, were met and slaughtered. Bird's place of concealment at first, in the confusion, escaped the observation of the temporarily triumphant Affghans; at last it was discovered, and an attack commenced at the door. This, being barricaded with logs of wood, and whatever else the tenants of the stable could find, resisted their efforts, while Bird and his now solitary companion, a Sepoy of the 37th N. I. (the other having been struck down), maintained as hot a fire as they could, each shot taking deadly effect from the proximity of the party engaged. The fall of their companions deterred the mass of the assailants from a simultaneous rush, which must have succeeded; and thus that truly chivalrous, high-minded, and amiable young gentleman, whose subsequent fate must be ranked among the mysterious dispensations of Providence which we cannot for the present fathom, stood at bay with his equally brave comrade for upwards of a

quarter of an hour, when, having only five car-
tridges left, in spite of having rifled the pouch of
the dead man, they were rescued as related above.
Our troops literally found the pair " grim and
lonely there," upwards of thirty of the enemy
having fallen by their unassisted prowess.

Our loss on this occasion was not less than 200
killed and wounded. Four neighbouring forts
were immediately evacuated by the enemy, and
occupied by our troops: they were found to contain about 1400 maunds of grain; in removing
which no time was lost, but as it was not found
practicable to bring off more than half before
night-fall, Capt. Boyd, the Assist.-Com.-Gen.,
requested Brig. Shelton that a guard might be
thrown into a small fort, where it must be left
for the night; this was, however, refused, and on
the following morning, as might have been expected, the grain was all gone: permanent possession was, however, taken of the Rika-bashee
and Zulfekar forts, the towers of the remainder
being blown up on the following day.

Numbers of Giljie horse and foot still maintaining their position on the Seeah Sung heights,
Brig. Shelton moved his force towards that
quarter. On reaching the base of the hill, fire
was opened from the two H. A. guns, which,
with the firm front presented by our troops,

caused the enemy shortly to retire towards the city, and ere we turned homeward not a man remained in sight.

November 13th. The enemy appeared in great force on the western heights, where, having posted two guns, they fired into cantonments with considerable precision. At the earnest entreaty of the Envoy, it was determined that a party, under Brigadier Shelton, should sally forth to attack them, and, if possible, capture their guns. The force ordered for this service was not ready until 3 P.M. It consisted of the following troops: —2 squadrons 5th Light Cavalry, under Col. Chambers; 1 squadron Shah's 2d Irregular Horse, under Lieut. Le Geyt; 1 troop of Skinner's Horse, under Lieut. Walker; the Body Guard; 6 companies her Majesty's 44th, under Major Scott; 6 companies 37th, under Major Swayne; 4 companies Shah's 6th Infantry, under Capt. Hopkins; and 1 H. A. gun and 1 Mountain Train do. under myself, escorted by a company of 6th Shah's under Capt. Marshall. After quitting cantonments, the troops took the direction of a gorge between the two hills bounding the plain, distant about a mile (the enemy's horse crowning that to the left), and advanced in separate columns at so brisk a pace, that it seemed a race which should arrive first at the scene of action. The infantry had actually reached the foot of the hill, and were on the point of ascending to the charge, ere the H. A. gun, which had been detained in the rear by sticking fast in a canal, could be got ready for action ; nor had more than one round of grape been fired, ere the advance, led on by the gallant Major Thain, had closed upon the foe, who resolutely stood their ground on the summit of the ridge, and unflinchingly received the discharge of our musketry, which, strange to say, even at the short range of ten or twelve yards, did little or no execution! From this cause the enemy, growing bolder every moment, advanced close up to the bayonets of our infantry, upon whom they pressed so perseveringly, as to succeed in driving them backwards to the foot of the hill, wounding Major Thain on the left shoulder, and sabring several of the men. Several rounds of grape and shrapnell were now poured in, and threw them into some confusion, whereupon a timely charge of our cavalry, Anderson's horse taking the lead, drove them again up the hill, when our infantry once more advancing carried the height, the enemy retreating along the ridge, closely followed by our troops, and abandoning their guns to us. The H. A. gun now took up a position in the middle of the gorge, whence it played with effect on a large body of horse as-

sembled on the plain west of the hill, who forthwith retreated to a distance.

Our troops had now got into ground where it
was impracticable for Horse-Artillery to follow.
I accordingly pushed forward with one artillery-
man and a supply of drag-ropes and spikes, to
look out for the deserted guns of the enemy;
one of these, a 4-pounder, was easily removed
along the ridge by a party of the Shah's 8th
Infantry; but the other, a 6-pounder, was awk-
wardly situated in a ravine half way down the
side of the hill, our troops, with the Mountain-
Train 3-pounder, being drawn up along the ridge
just above it. The evening was now fast closing
in, and a large body of Affghan infantry occupied
some enclosures on the plain below, whence they
kept up so hot a fire upon the gun, as to render
its removal by no means an easy task; but the
Envoy having sent us a message of entreaty that
no exertions might be spared to complete the
triumph of the day by bringing off *both* the
enemy's guns, Major Scott, of her Majesty's
44th, repeatedly called on his men to descend with
him to drag the 6-pounder away; but, strange to
say, his frequent appeals to their soldierly feelings
were made in vain : with a few gallant exceptions
they remained immovable, nor could the Sepoys
be induced to lead the way where their European

brethren so obstinately hung back. Meanwhile
it became nearly dark, and the further detention
of the troops being attended with risk, as the
enemy, though driven from the hill, still maintained a threatening attitude below, I descended
with the Horse Artillery gunner, and, having
driven in a spike, returned to assist in making
sure of the captured 4-pounder. This, from the
steepness of the hill, and the numerous water-
cuts which every where intersected the plain,
proved a somewhat troublesome business. Lieut.
Macartney, however, with a company of the
Shah's 6th Infantry, urged on his men with zeal,
and we at last had the satisfaction to deposit our
prize safe within the cantonment gates. Meanwhile the enemy, favoured by the darkness, pressed
hard upon our returning troops, and by dint of
incessant firing and shouting rendered their homeward march somewhat disorderly, effecting, however, but little damage.

It was no small disadvantage under which we
laboured, that no temporary success of our troops
over those of the enemy could be followed up,
nor even possession be retained of the ground
gained by us at the point of the bayonet, owing
to the necessity of withdrawing our men into their
quarters at night. On reaching the cantonment,
we found the garrison in a state of considerable

alarm, and a continual blaze of musketry illumi-
nating the whole line of rampart. This had arisen
from a demonstration of attack having been made
by the enemy on the south-west bastion, which
had been immediately checked by a few rounds
of grape from the guns, and by a well-directed
fire from the juzailchees under Capt. Mackenzie;
but it was long ere quiet could be restored, the
men continuing to discharge their pieces at they
knew not what.

Our infantry soldiers, both European and
Native, might have taken a salutary lesson from
the Affghans in the use of their fire-arms; the
latter invariably taking steady deliberate aim, and
seldom throwing away a single shot; whereas our
men seemed to fire entirely at random, without
any aim at all; hence the impunity with which
the Affghan horsemen braved the discharge of
our musketry in this day's action within twelve
yards, not one shot, to all appearance, taking
effect.   In this affair Capt. Paton, Assist.-Quart.-
Mast.-Gen., had the misfortune to receive a
wound in the left arm, which rendered amputation
necessary, and the valuable services of one of our
most efficient staff officers were thus lost.   This
was the last success our arms were destined to
experience.   Henceforward it becomes my weary
task to relate a catalogue of errors, disasters, and

difficulties, which, following close upon each other, disgusted our officers, disheartened our soldiers, and finally sunk us all into irretrievable ruin, as though Heaven itself, by a combination of evil circumstances for its own inscrutable purposes, had planned our downfall. But here it is fit I should relate the scenes that had all this while been enacting at our solitary outpost in Kohistan.

CHAP. IV.

ON the 15th November, Major Pottinger, C. B.
and Lieut. Haughton, Adjt. of the Shah's 4th,
or Goorkha regiment, came in from Charekar,
both severely wounded, the former in the leg, and
the latter having had his right hand amputated,
besides several cuts in the neck and left arm.
Their escape was wonderful.

The following is an outline of what had taken
place in Kohistan, from the commencement of the
insurrection up to the present date.

It appears, from Major Pottinger's account of
the transactions of that period, that it was not
without reason he had so urgently applied to Sir
William Macnaghten for reinforcements. Towards the end of October, premonitory signs of

the coming tempest had become so unequivocally threatening as to confirm Major Pottinger in his worst suspicions, and in his conviction that order could not possibly be restored without a departure on the part of government from the long-suffering system which had been obstinately pursued with respect to Nijrow in particular; but his conviction alone could do little to stem the torrent of coming events.

About this time Meer Musjeedee, a contumacious rebel against the Shah's authority, who had been expelled from Kohistan during General Sale's campaign in that country in 1840, and who had taken refuge in Nijrow after the fashion of many other men of similar stamp, obstinately refusing to make his submission to the Shah even upon the most favourable terms, openly put himself at the head of a powerful and well-organised party, with the avowed intention of expelling the Feringees and overturning the existing government. He was speedily joined by the most influential of the Nijrow chiefs. A few of these made their appearance before Lughmanee, where Major Pottinger resided, and proffered their services towards the maintenance of the public tranquillity. It will be seen that their object was the blackest treachery.

I shall here relate Major Pottinger's story, almost in his own words, as given to me.

In the course of the forenoon of the 3d of November, Major Pottinger had an interview with a number of the more influential chiefs in his house or fort, and, about noon, went into the garden to receive those of inferior rank, accompanied by his visiters: here they were joined by Lieut. Charles Rattray, Major Pottinger's Assistant. In discussing the question of the rewards to which their services might entitle them, the head men declared that, although *they* were willing to agree to Major Pottinger's propositions, they could not answer for their clansmen, and the above-mentioned petty chiefs, who were awaiting the expected conference at some little distance. Mr. Rattray, accordingly, in company with several of the principal, joined the latter, and, shortly after, proceeded with them to an adjoining field, where numbers of their armed retainers were assembled, for the purpose of ascertaining their sentiments on the subject of the conference. While thus engaged, this most promising and brave young officer apparently became aware of intended foul play, and turned to leave the field, when he was immediately shot down. At this time Major Pottinger was still sitting in his garden, in company with several of the above-

mentioned chiefs, and had just received intelligence of the purposed treachery from Mahomed
Kasim Khan, a debashee of Hazirbash, a small
detachment of which composed a part of his escort:
he had with difficulty comprehended the man's
meaning, which was conveyed by hints, when the
sound of firing was heard :— the chiefs that were
with him rose and fled, and he escaped into the
fort by the postern gate; which having secured,
he, from the terre-plein of the rampart, saw poor
Mr. Rattray lying badly wounded in the field at
the distance of some 300 yards, and the late pretended negotiators making off in all directions
with the plunder of the camp of the Hazirbash
detachment. Of these plunderers a party passing
close to Mr. Rattray, and observing that life was
not extinct, one of them put his gun close to his
head, and blew his brains out,—several others
discharging their pieces into different parts of his
body.

Major Pottinger's guard, being by this time on
the alert, opened a fire, which speedily cleared the
open space; but the enemy, seeking shelter in the
numerous watercourses, and under the low walls
surrounding the fort, harassed them incessantly
until the appearance of Lieut. Haughton, adjutant
of the Goorkha regiment, who, advancing from
Charekar, where the corps was cantoned, distant

about three miles, speedily drove the assailants
from their cover.   Capt. Codrington, who commanded the regiment, chanced to be in Lughmanee
at this very time; and, on Mr. Haughton's approach, he led out a sortie and joined him: the
skirmish was sharp, and the enemy suffered severely, Capt. Codrington remaining in possession
of an adjacent canal, the bank of which was immediately cut, to supply the tank of the fort with
water in case of accidents.

The evening had now closed in, and the enemy
had retired, taking up a position which seemed to
threaten the Charekar road.   Capt. Codrington
accordingly left Lughmanee in haste, strengthen-
ing Major Pottinger's party to about 100 men,
these having to garrison four small forts.   He
promised, however, to relieve them the next
morning, and to send a further supply of ammunition, of which there only remained 1500 rounds.
Capt. Codrington reached Charekar unmolested;
and the enemy, returning to their former point of
attack, carried off their dead with impunity, the
garrison being too weak to make a sally.   On the
morning of the 4th, Capt. Codrington despatched
four companies with a six-pounder gun, according
to promise.   Their march caused numbers of the
enemy now assembled on all sides to retreat; but
one large body remained in position on the skirts

of the mountain range to their right, and threatened their flank. Mr. Haughton, who commanded, detached Ensign Salisbury with a company to disperse them, which, in spite of the disparity of numbers, was effected in good style. Unhappily the Goorkhas, being young soldiers, and flushed with success, pressed forward in pursuit with too much eagerness, regardless of the recalling bugle, when at last Mr. Salisbury with difficulty halted them, and endeavoured to retrace his steps. The enemy, observing the error they had committed in separating themselves too far from their main body, rallied and followed them in their retreat so closely, as to oblige Mr. Salisbury to halt his little band frequently, and face about. Mr. Haughton, consequently, in order to extricate the compromised company, halted his convoy, and despatched the greatest part of his men in the direction of the skirmish. All this encouraged the other parties of the enemy who had retired to return, against whom, in numbers not less than 4000 men, Mr. Haughton maintained his ground until rejoined by his subaltern, when, seeing the hopelessness of making good his way to Lugh-manee, he retreated, and regained in safety the fortified barracks at Charekar. Many of the men fell in this expedition, which would have proved infinitely more disastrous, from the number of the

E

enemy's cavalry, who latterly seemed to gain confidence at every stage, but for the extraordinary
gallantry and conduct of Mr. Haughton, who,
with a handful of men and a gun, protected the
rear of our over-matched troops. Mr. Salisbury
was mortally wounded, and the trail of the gun
gave way just as the party reached Charekar.

This disappointment led Major Pottinger to
believe that no second attempt would be made
to relieve them; and as he had no ammunition
beyond the supply in the men's pouches, he determined to retreat on Charekar after dark: the
better to hide his intention, he ordered grain to
be brought into the fort. Meantime the Charekar
cantonment was attacked on all sides, and in the
afternoon large bodies of the enemy were detached thence, and, joining others from that part
of the valley, recommenced their investment of
Lughmanee. That part of the Major's garrison
which occupied the small fort to the east of the
principal one, defended by himself, although their
orders were not to vacate their posts until after
dark, being panic-stricken, did so at once, gaining
the stronger position, but leaving behind several
wounded comrades and their havildar, who remained
staunch to his duty: these, however, were brought
off. Major Pottinger then strengthened the garrison of a cluster of adjacent huts, which, being

surrounded by a sort of rude fortification, formed
a tolerably good out-work; but the want of European officers to control the men was soon la-
mentably apparent, and in a short time the
Goorkhas, headed by their native officer, abandoned the hamlet, followed as a matter of course
by the few Affghan soldiers attached to Capt. Codrington's person, who had remained faithful until
then.   This last misfortune gave the enemy cover
up to the very gate of the main stronghold, and
before dark they had succeeded in getting possession of a gun-shed built against its outer wall,
whence they commenced mining.

As soon as night had fairly closed in, Major
Pottinger drew together the Goorkha garrison outside the postern gate, under pretence of making a
sortie, and thus separated them from the Affghans
and their followers, who remained inside; he then
marched for Charekar, the garrison of the remaining fort joining him as he drew on; he passed by
the investing posts in perfect silence, taking his
route along the skirts of the mountains to avoid the
main road, and arrived in safety at Charekar.   In
Lughmanee he abandoned the hostages whom he
had taken from the Kohistan chiefs, two boxes of
treasure containing 2000 rupees, about sixty stand
of juzails, all his office records, Mr. Rattray's,
Dr. Grant's, and his own personal property, and a

number of horses belonging to himself and the
above-mentioned two officers, and to some horsemen who had not deserted — for the greater part
of his mounted escort had fled in the beginning
of the affray.   The Heratees, and seven or eight
Peshawarees, were the only Affghans who adhered to him: the Cabulees, had deserted to a
man, immediately on the murder of Mr. Rattray;
they had been much disgusted the preceding
month, as well as their comrades who proved un-
faithful too, by the sudden reduction of a portion
of his escort, which naturally led them to apprehend that their livelihood from the British service
was of a precarious nature.

On the morning of 5th Nov. large bodies of the
enemy closed in round the Charekar barracks,
and about 7 o'clock they attacked the outposts
with a spirit engendered by the success of the
preceding evening.   Capt. Codrington requested
Major Pottinger to take charge of what artillery
he had, and to move a squadron in support of the
skirmishers, which he did.   The skirmishers were
driven in, and, while retreating, Major Pottinger
was wounded in the leg by a musket-shot.   Encouraged by this, and by the unfinished state of
the works round the barracks, in the entrance of
which there was no gate, the enemy advanced
with great determination to the attack, and dis-

lodged the Goorkhas from some mud huts outside, which were still occupied by a part of the
regiment. In this affair Capt. Codrington, an
officer of whose merits it is difficult to speak too
highly, fell mortally wounded. The main post
was, however, successfully defended, and the
enemy driven back with considerable loss; upon
which Mr. Haughton (who had now succeeded
to the command, the only remaining officer being
Mr. Rose, a mere youth,) made a sortie and drove
the enemy out of the gardens occupied by them
in the morning, maintaining his ground against
their most desperate efforts until after dark.
Relief was then sent to the garrison (consisting
of about 50 men) of Khaja Meer's fort, which it
had been found expedient to occupy previously,
because it commanded the interior of the barracks
on the southern side.

From this time the unfortunate horses and
cattle of the garrison were obliged to endure the
extremity of thirst, there being *no* water for *them*,
and the supply for even the fighting men scanty
in the extreme, obtained only from a few pools in
the ditch of the rampart, which had been formed
by a seasonable fall of rain. During the 6th the
enemy renewed their attack in augmented numbers, the whole population of the country ap-

parently swarming to the scene of action. Notwithstanding two successful sorties, all the outposts
were driven in by dark, and thenceforth the garrison was confined to the barrack itself.

On the 7th the enemy got possession of Khoja
Meer's fort: the regimental moonshee had been
gained over, and through him the native officer
was induced to surrender. From the towers of
that fort, on the 8th, the enemy offered terms, on
the condition that all the infidels should embrace
Mahomedanism. Major Pottinger replied, that
they had come to aid a Mahomedan sovereign in
the recovery of his rights; that they consequently
were within the pale of Islam, and exempt from
coercion on the score of religion. The enemy
rejoined, that the King himself had ordered them
to attack the Kaffirs, and wished to know if
Major Pottinger would yield on receiving an
order. He refused to do so, except on the produc-
tion of a written document. All this time the
garrison was sorely galled from the post of vantage
in possession of the enemy.

On the 9th, the enemy were enabled by the
carelessness of the guard to blow up a part of the
south-west tower of the barracks; but, before they
could profit by the breach and the panic of the
men, Mr. Haughton rallied the fugitives, and,

leading them back, secured the top of the parapet wall with a barricade of boards and sand-bags.

On the 10th, the officers drew their last pool of water, and served out *half a wineglass* to each fighting man.

On the 11th, all could not share even in that miserable proportion, and their sufferings from thirst were dreadful. During the night a sortie was made, and some of the followers brought in a little water from a distant place, the sight of which only served to aggravate the distress of the majority ; still, however, the fortitude of these brave and hardy soldiers remained unshaken, although apathy, the result of intense suffering, especially among Hindoos, began to benumb their faculties.

On the 12th, after dark, Mr. Haughton ordered out a party to cover the water-carriers in an attempt to obtain a supply ; but the over-harassed Sepoys, unable to restrain themselves, dashed out of the ranks on approaching the coveted element, instead of standing to their arms to repel the enemy, and, consequently, the expedition failed in its object. Another sortie, consisting of two companies under Ensign Rose, was then ordered out, one of which, having separated from the other, dispersed in search of water ; that under Mr. Rose

himself fell on a post of the besiegers, every man
of which they bayoneted; but, being unaccountably
struck with a panic, the men fled back to the
barracks, leaving Mr. Rose almost alone, who was
then obliged to return, having accomplished his
object but partially.   These circumstances were
communicated by Mr. Haughton to Major Pottinger (whose wound had disabled him from
active bodily co-operation in these last events),
together with the startling intelligence, that the
corps was almost wholly disorganised from the
large amount of killed and wounded, the hardships it had undergone, the utter inefficiency of
the native officers, who had no sort of control
over the soldiers, the exhaustion of the men from
constant duty, and the total want of water and
provisions.

Relief from Cabul, for which Major Pottinger
had written repeatedly, seemed now hopeless,
and an attempt at protracted defence of the post
appeared likely to ensure the destruction of its
brave defenders.   Major Pottinger considered
that the only remaining chance of saving any
portion of the regiment was a retreat to Cabul;
and, although that was abundantly perilous, he
entertained a hope that a few of the most active
men who were not encumbered with wives and
children might escape.   Then was felt most bit-

terly, the impolicy of the encouragement which had been held out to all the recruits to bring their families with them, on what, even at the time of their being raised, was looked on by the most able officers as likely to prove a campaign of several years. Mr. Haughton coincided in the Major's views, and it was agreed, to ensure secrecy, that the men should not be informed of their intentions until paraded for the march.

This wretched state of things continued until the afternoon of the 13th, when Mr. Haughton discovered amongst the Punjabee artillerymen two who had deserted a few days previously, and who apparently had returned for the purpose of seducing their comrades. He immediately seized them; but, while he was in the act of their apprehension, the jemadar of the artillery, himself a Punjabee Mussulman, snatched a sword from a bystander, and cut down that officer, repeating his blows as he lay on the ground. Before the astonished Goorkhas could draw their knives or handle their muskets, this miscreant, followed by all the artillerymen and the greater number of the Mahomedans in the barracks, rushed out of the gate and escaped. The tumult and confusion occasioned by this impressed Major Pottinger with the idea that the enemy had driven the men from the walls ; under this impression, he caused himself to be carried to the main gate, but on his arrival he found that Dr. Grant had secured that point, and rallied the men. The native officers immediately gathered round him, with many of the Sepoys, to assert their fidelity ; but demoralization had evidently progressed fearfully, as may be judged from the fact that the garrison had plundered the treasure and the quarters of the deceased Capt. Codrington the instant the Major had left them, and that in the face of the enemy's fire they had pulled down the officers' boxes, which had been piled up as traverses to protect the doorway, broken them open, and pillaged them. Dr. Grant then amputated Mr. Haughton's right hand, and hastily dressed the severe wounds which he had received in his left arm and on his neck. In the evening the doctor spiked all the guns with his own hands, and the garrison then left the barracks by the postern gate. The advance was led by Major Pottinger (Mr. Haughton, who accompanied him, being unable to do more than sit passively on his horse), Dr. Grant brought out the main body, and Ensign Rose, with the Quart.-Mast.-Serjt., commanded the rear.

Notwithstanding the previous sufferings of these unfortunate men, it may be said that here com-

menced their real disasters.   In vain did Major
Pottinger attempt to lead his men to seize a
building generally occupied by the enemy after
night-fall, by the possession of which the exit of
the main body from the barracks might be covered.
In fact, it was with much difficulty that he eventually succeeded in halting them at about half a
mile from the barracks until the main body and
rear should close up.   The men were naturally
occupied entirely with their families, and such
property as it had been impossible to prevent
their bringing away;   and discipline, the only
source of hope under such circumstances, was at
an end.

After the junction of the main body and rear,
Dr. Grant suddenly disappeared, and was not
afterwards seen.

The regiment then proceeded along the road
to Sinjit Durrah, where Major Pottinger knew
that water could be procured.   On reaching the
first stream, the last remnant of control over this
disorderly mob was lost;   much delay took place,
and, in moving on, the advance became suddenly
separated from the main body.   After an anxious
search Major Pottinger effected a rejunction.

At Sinjit Durrah they quitted the road to avoid
alarming the villages and any outposts that might
be stationed there;   and much time was lost in

regaining the track from the other side : at Istalif the same manœuvre was practised. Major Pottinger now found very few inclined to push on ; exhaustion from the pain of his wound precluded the possibility of his being of any further use as a leader; and he determined to push on with Mr. Haughton towards Cabul, although with faint hope that the strength of either would prove adequate to the exertion. Having no guide, they got into many difficulties; and day was breaking by the time they reached the range of mountains half way between Charekar and Cabul. Men and horses were by this time incapable of further endurance : the latter, it must be remembered, had been ten days without water previously to starting, and five days without food; they were still upwards of twenty miles from any place of safety ; their sufferings from their wounds, fatigue, hunger, and thirst, made life a burden, and at this time despair had almost obtained a victory — but God sustained them. By Mr. Haughton's advice they sought shelter in a very deep but dry ravine, close to a small village, hoping that their proximity to danger might prove a source of safety ; as it was probable that the inhabitants, who by this time must have been on the alert, would scarcely think of looking for their prey close to their own doors. The companions of Major Pottinger and Mr.

Haughton were a sepoy of the regiment, a moon-shee, and the regimental *buniah*. In the forenoon they were alarmed by a firing on the mountains above them; the cause of this, as it appeared afterwards, was that a few of the fugitive Goorkhas had ascended the hills for safety (which, indeed, it was Major Pottinger's wish to do, until he yielded to the arguments of his companion), whither they were pursued and massacred by the country people. The rest of the day passed in tranquillity; and again, under the friendly shroud of darkness, having previously calculated their exact position, did this sorely-bestead little party resume their dangerous route. It was providential that Major Pottinger had, from his habits as a traveller through unknown and difficult regions, accustomed himself to ascertain and remember the bearings of the most conspicuous landmarks of the countries he traversed; it was therefore comparatively easy for him to lead the way over the steep and rugged peaks, by which alone they might hope to find a safe path, — for the main road, and even the more accessible tracks across the tops of the mountains, were closely beset, and watch-fires gleamed in all directions. Indeed Gholam-Moyun-ood-deer, a distinguished partizan in the service of the rebels, had been despatched from Cabul, with a number of his most active

followers, purposely to intercept and seize the
Major, of whose flight intelligence had been early
received, and actually was at that time patrolling
those very heights over which the fugitives passed.
But the protecting hand of Providence was displayed not only in leading them unharmed
through the midst of their enemies, but in supplying them with mental fortitude and bodily
strength. Weak and exhausted, their hardy and
usually sure-footed Toorkman horses could scarcely
strain up the almost impracticable side of the
mountain, or preserve their equilibrium in the
sharp sudden descents which they encountered,
for path there was none. On one occasion Mr.
Haughton, whose desperate wounds I have already
described, fell off, and, being unable to rise, declared his determination of awaiting his fate where
he lay. The Major refused to desert him, and both
slept for about one hour, when, nature being a
little restored, they pushed on until they descended
into the plain of Alifat, which they crossed,
avoiding the fort of that name, and, struggling up
the remaining ridge that separated them from the
plain of Cabul, they entered it by the southern
end of the Cabul lake. Intending now to cross
the cultivation, and to reach cantonments by the
back of the Shah's garden, Major Pottinger
missed his road close to Kila-i-bolund, and found

himself within the enemy's sentries; but being unwilling to alarm them by retracing his steps, after discovering his mistake, he led the way towards Deh Affghan. Here they were challenged by various outposts, to whom they answered after the fashion of Affghan horsemen; but they were compelled, in order to avoid suspicion, actually to enter the city of Cabul, their only hope now being in the slumberous security of the inhabitants at that hour (it being now about 3 A. M.), and in the protection of their Affghan dress and equipments. The Goorkha sepoy, who, strange to say, had kept up with them *on foot*, had *his* outward man concealed by a large *postheen*, or sheepskin cloak. They pursued their way through the lanes and bazar of the city, without any interruption, except the occasional gruff challenge of a sleepy watchman, until they gained the skirts of the city. There they were like to have been stopped by a picket which lay between them and the cantonment. The disposition to a relaxation of vigilance as the morning approaches, which marks the Affghan soldier, again befriended them; they had nearly passed the post before they were pursued. Desperation enabled them to urge their wearied horses into a pace which barely gave them the advantage over their enemies, who were on foot; and they escaped with a volley from the now aroused picket, the little Goorkha freshening his way in the most surprising manner, considering his previous journey. A few hundred yards further brought them within the ramparts of our cantonment, where they were received by their brethren in arms as men risen from the dead.

CHAP. V.

REMOVAL FROM CANTONMENT TO BALA HISSAR DISCUSSED.——
THE IDEA ABANDONED. —— GENERAL SALE'S RETURN IM-
PRACTICABLE. —— MAHMOOD KHAN'S FORT——ANNOYANCE
FROM IT —— BUT LEFT IN ENEMY'S POSSESSION.——LETTER
FROM THE ENVOY TO THE GENERAL. —— UNPROFITABLE
OPERATIONS AT THE VILLAGE OF BEYMAROO. —— ARRI-
VAL OF MAHOMED AKBER KHAN AT CABUL.

November 16*th*. —— THE impression made on the
enemy by the action of the 13th was so far salutary, that they did not venture to annoy us again
for several days. Advantage was taken of this
respite to throw magazine supplies from time to
time into the Bala Hissar, a duty which was ably
performed by Lieut. Walker, with a resalah of
irregular horse under cover of night. But even
in this short interval of comparative rest, such
was the wretched construction of the cantonment,
that the mere ordinary routine of garrison duty,
and the necessity of closely manning our long
line of rampart both by day and night, was a
severe trial to the health and patience of the
troops; especially now that the winter began to

show symptoms of unusual severity. There seemed, indeed, every probability of an early fall of snow, to which all looked forward with dread, as the harbinger of fresh difficulties and of augmented suffering.

These considerations, and the manifest superiority of the Bala Hissar as a military position, led to the early discussion of the expediency of abandoning the cantonment and consolidating our forces in the above-mentioned stronghold. The Envoy himself was, from the first, greatly in favour of this move, until overruled by the many objections urged against it by the military authorities; to which, as will be seen by a letter from him presently quoted, he learned by degrees to attach some weight himself; but to the very last it was a measure that had many advocates, and I venture to state my own firm belief that, had we at this time moved into the Bala Hissar, Cabul would have been still in our possession. The chief objections urged were, 1st, the difficulty of conveying our sick and wounded; 2dly, the want of firewood; 3dly, the want of forage for the cavalry; 4thly, the triumph that our abandonment of cantonments would afford the enemy; 5thly, the risk of defeat on the way thither. On the other hand it was advanced, 1st, that, though to carry the sick would be *difficult*, it still was not *impossible;* for so short a distance two, or even three, men could be conveyed on each doolie; some might manage to walk, and the rest could be mounted on the yaboos and camels, on top of their loads; 2dly, although wood was scarce in the Bala Hissar, there was enough for purposes of cooking, and for the want of fires the troops would be amply compensated by the comparative ease and comfort they would enjoy in other respects; 3dly, the horses must, in the case of there being no forage, have been shot; but the want of cavalry would have been little felt in such a situation; 4thly, as we should have destroyed all that was valuable before leaving, the supposed triumph of the enemy would have been very short-lived, and would soon have given way to a feeling of disappointment at the valueless nature of their acquisition, and of dismay at the strength and security of our new position; 5thly, the distance did not exceed two miles, and one half of that distance was protected by the guns of the Bala Hissar. If we had occupied the Seeah Sung hills with a strong party, placing guns there to sweep the plain on the cantonment side, the enemy could have done little to impede our march, without risking a battle with our whole force in a fair field, to which they were generally averse, but which would, perhaps, have been the *best* mode for *us* of deciding the struggle.

To remove so large a force, clogged with so
many thousands of camp followers, without loss
of some kind, was, of course, next to impossible;
but ought such considerations to have interfered
with a step which would have been attended in
the long run with such great military and political
advantages? Our troops, once collected in the
Bala Hissar, could have been spared for offensive
operations against the city and the neighbouring
forts, by which means plenty of food and forage
would in all probability have been readily procured, while the commanding nature of the position would have caused the enemy to despair of
driving us out, and a large party would probably
have been ere long formed in our favour. Such
were the chief arguments employed on either side;
but Brigadier Shelton having firmly set his face
against the movement from the first moment of
its proposition, all serious idea of it was gradually
abandoned, though it continued to the very last
a subject of common discussion.

November 18*th.*—Accounts were this day received
from Jellalabad, that Gen. Sale, having sallied
from the town, had repulsed the enemy with considerable loss. At the beginning of the insurrection, Gen. Sale's brigade was at Gundamuk; and
I have already mentioned, that an order recalling
it to Cabul was immediately despatched by the

Envoy.   Gen. Sale, on receipt of it, summoned a
council of war, by whom it was unanimously agreed
to be impracticable to obey the order.   The circumstances of his march to Jellalabad are already
well known to the public.   The hope of his return
had tended much to support our spirits; our disappointment was therefore great to learn that all
expectation of aid from that quarter was at an
end.   Our eyes were now turned towards the
Candahar force as our last resource, though an
advance from that quarter seemed scarcely practicable so late in the year.

Much discussion took place this evening regarding the expediency of taking Mahmood Khan's
fort.   There were many reasons to urge in favour
of making the attempt.   It was one of the chief
resorts of the rebels during the day, and they had
established a battery of two guns under the walls,
from which they constantly fired upon our foraging parties, and upon the south-east bastion of
cantonments.   It was about 900 yards distant
from our rampart, which was too far for breaching
with the 9-pounders; but a dry canal, which ran
towards it in a zigzag direction, afforded facilities
for a regular approach within 300 yards, of which
advantage might have been taken to enable the
artillery to make a breach.   Secondly, this fort
commanded the road all the way up to the Bala

Hissar, and the possession of it would at once have secured to us an easy communication with that place, and with the city. Thirdly, the Envoy declared his opinion that the moral effect derived from its possession would be more likely to create a diversion in our favour than any other blow we could strike, as the Affghans had always attached great importance to its occupation. These considerations had decided the General in favour of making the attempt this very night, by blowing open the gate, and a storming party was actually warned for the duty, when Lieut. Sturt, the engineer officer, raising some sudden objection, the plan was given up, and never afterwards resumed by the military. It was, however, the cause of no small astonishment to the officers in the Bala Hissar, who, from their commanding situation, could observe all that took place on both sides, that Mahmood Khan's fort should have been suffered to remain in the hands of the enemy, though at night it was often garrisoned by a mere handful of men. This fort, nevertheless, gave abundant occupation to the artillery, who, when nothing else was going on, were frequently employed in disturbing the enemy in that quarter with one of the iron 9-pounders, and an occasional shelling from the mortar.

November 19*th.*— A letter was this day received

by the General from the Envoy to the following effect : — " That, all hope of assistance from Jellalabad being over, it behoved us to take our future proceedings into consideration. He himself conceived it our imperative duty to hold on as long as possible in our present position, and he thought we might even struggle through the whole winter by making the Mahomedans and Christians live chiefly upon flesh, supposing our supplies of grain to fail ; by which means, as the essentials of wood and water were abundant, he considered our position might be rendered impregnable. A retreat towards Jellalabad would teem not only with disaster, but dishonour, and ought not to be contemplated until the very last extremity. In eight or ten days we should be better able to judge whether such extremity should be resorted to. In that case, we should have to sacrifice not only the valuable property of Government, but his majesty Shah Shoojah, to support whose authority we were employed by Government ; and even were we to make good our retreat to Jellalabad, we should have no shelter for our troops, and our camp followers would all be sacrificed. He had frequently thought of negotiating, but there was no party of sufficient power and influence to protect us. Another alternative would be to throw ourselves into the Bala Hissar ; but he feared that would be also a disastrous retreat, to effect which much property must be necessarily sacrificed. Our heavy guns might be turned against us, and food and fuel might be scarce, for a further supply of which we might be dependent on sorties into the city, in which, if beaten, we must of course be ruined. On the whole, he was decidedly of opinion that we should hold out; it was still possible that reinforcements might arrive from Candahar, or something might turn up in our favour; there were hopes, too, that, on the setting in of winter, the enemy would disperse. He had been long disposed to recommend a blow being struck to retrieve our fortunes, such as taking Mahmood Khan's fort; but he had since reason to believe this would not answer. In eight or ten days, he concluded, it would remain for the military authorities to determine whether there was any chance of improving our position, and to decide whether it would be more prudent to attempt a retreat to Jellalabad, or to the Bala Hissar. If provision sufficient for the winter could be procured, on no account would he leave the cantonment."

November 22d.—The village of Beymaroo (or " *husbandless*," from a beautiful virgin who was buried there) was situated about half a mile to the north of cantonments, on the Kohistan road,

at the north-east extremity of a hill which
bounded the plain to the west.   As it was built
on a slope, and within musket-shot, the upper
houses commanded a large portion of the Mission
Compound.   From this village we for a long
time drew supplies, the Envoy largely bribing the
proprietor, to which, however, the enemy in some
measure put a stop by taking possession of it
every day.   This morning, large bodies of Affghan
horse and foot, having again issued from the city,
proceeded to crown the summit of the above-
mentioned hill.   It was determined, at the recommendation of the Envoy, to send a party of
our troops to forestall the enemy in the occupation
of the village; and Major Swayne, 5th N. I., was
appointed to that duty, with a detachment composed as follows: — a Wing 5th N. I., 2 Re-
sallas Irregular Horse, 1 Resalla 5th Light
Cavalry, and one Mountain-train gun.   The
party had already reached the village, when it
was deemed proper to send after it a Horse Artillery gun, which I was requested by the General
to accompany.   Major Swayne, however, it would
seem by his own account, found the village
already occupied by a body of Kohistanees, and
the entrance blocked up in such a manner that
he considered it out of his power to force a

F

passage. On arriving at the place with the H. A.
gun, I found him in an orchard on the road-side,
the trees of which partially protected the men
from a very sharp fire, poured in amongst them
from the houses. There being no shelter for the
gun here, nor any mode of employing it to advantage, it was ordered to cross some fields to the
right, and take up a position where it could best
fire upon the village, and upon the heights above
it, which were now crowded with the enemy's
infantry. In order to protect the horses, I drew
up the gun near the fort of Zoolfa Khan, under
the walls of which they had shelter; but for the
gun itself no other position could be found than
in the open field, where it was exposed to the full
fire of the enemy posted in the village and behind
the neighbouring walls. The Mountain-train
gun was also with me, and both did some execution among the people on the summit of the hill,
though to little purpose.

Major Swayne, whose orders were to storm the
village, would neither go forward nor retire; but,
concealing his men under the cover of some low
wall, he all day long maintained an useless fire
on the houses of Beymaroo, without the slightest
satisfactory result. The cavalry were drawn up
in rear of the gun on the open plain, as a conspicuous mark for the Kohistanees, and where,

as there was nothing for them to do, they accordingly did nothing. Thus we remained for five or six hours, during which time the artillery stood exposed to the deliberate aim of the numerous marksmen who occupied the village and its immediate vicinity, whose bullets continually sang in our ears, often striking the gun, and grazing the ground on which we stood. Only two gunners, however, out of six were wounded, but the cavalry in our rear had many casualties both among men and horses.

Late in the evening, a party of Affghan horse, moving round from behind Beymaroo, proceeded towards a fort in our rear, whence a cross fire was opened upon us. Brigadier Shelton now joined, bringing with him a reinforcement from the 5th N. I., under Col. Oliver. Major Swayne, with two companies, was then sent to reconnoitre the fort whence the fire proceeded, and the H. A. gun was at the same time moved round, so as to bear upon the Affghan cavalry, who hovered among the trees in the same quarter. While engaged in this operation, I received a bullet through the left hand, which for the present terminated my active services. Shortly after this the troops were recalled into cantonments.

It is worthy of note, that Mahomed Akber

Khan, second son of the late Ameer Dost Mahomed Khan, arrived in Cabul this night from Bameean. This man was destined to exercise an evil influence over our future fortunes. The crisis of our struggle was already nigh at hand.

CHAP. VI.

A SECOND EXPEDITION TO BEYMAROO. — INCREASING NUM-
BERS AND VIGILANCE OF THE ENEMY. — OUR FORCE
DRIVEN BACK WITH SEVERE LOSS. — OBSERVATIONS.

November 23d. — THIS day decided the fate of
the Cabul force. At a council held at the
General's house on the night of the 22d it was
determined, on the special recommendation of the
Envoy, that, in consequence of the inconvenience
sustained by the enemy so frequently taking possession of Beymaroo, and interrupting our foraging
parties, a force, under Brigadier Shelton, should on
the following morning take the village by assault,
and maintain the hill above it against whatever
number of the enemy might appear. Accordingly,
at 2 A. M. the under-mentioned troops* moved out
of cantonments in perfect silence by the Kohistan

* 1 H. A. gun, under Sergt. Mulhal.
   5 Cos. H. M. 44th, under Capt. Leighton.
   6 Cos. 5th N. I., under Lieut.-Col. Oliver.
   6 Cos. 37th N. I., under Major Kershaw, H. M. 13th.
   Sappers, 100 men, under Lieut. Laing.
   1 Squadron 5th Lt. Cav., under Capt. Bott.
   1 Ditto Irregular Horse, under Lieut. Walker.
   100 men, Anderson's Horse.

F 3

gate, and skirting the musjed immediately opposite, which was held by a company of Her Majesty's
44th, took the direction of the gorge at the further extremity of the Beymaroo hill, which they
ascended, dragging the gun to the top with great
difficulty, from the rugged and steep nature of the
side, which labour was greatly facilitated by the
exertions of 200 commissariat surwoons, who had
volunteered for the occasion. The whole force
then moved to the knoll at the N. E. extremity
of the hill, which overhung the village of Beymaroo. The gun was placed in position commanding
an enclosure in the village, which, from its fires,
was judged to be the principal bivouac of the
enemy, and a sharp fire of grape commenced,
which evidently created great confusion, but it
was presently answered by a discharge of juzails;
the enemy forsaking the open space, and covering
themselves in the houses and towers: to this we
replied in the intervals of the cannonade by discharges of musketry. It was suggested by Capt.
Bellew and others to Brigadier Shelton to storm
the village, while the evident panic of the enemy
lasted, under cover of the darkness, there being
no moon: to this the Brigadier did not accede.

When the day broke, parties of the enemy were
descried hurrying from the village, and taking
across the plain towards the distant fort, their fire

having previously slackened from the failure of their ammunition. At this time, certainly, not above 40 men remained in the village. A storming party, consisting of 2 companies 37th N. I. and some Europeans, under Majors Swayne and Kershaw, were ordered to carry the village; but Major Swayne, taking a wrong direction, missed the principal entrance, which was open, and arrived at a small *kirkhee*, or wicket, which was barricaded, and which he had no means of forcing, so that he was obliged to cover himself and his men as well as he could from the sure aim of the enemy's marksmen, by whose fire his party suffered considerably, himself being shot through the neck.

After remaining thus for about half an hour, he was recalled by the Brigadier, who observed large bodies of armed men pouring out from the city towards the scene of conflict. Meanwhile Lieut. Walker had been directed to lead his irregular horse down into the plain on the west side of the hill, to cut off such fugitives from the village as he might be able to intercept, and to cover himself from the fire of infantry under the walls of an old fort not far from the base of the hill. Brigadier Shelton, leaving three companies of the 37th N. I. in the knoll above Beymaroo as a reserve, under

Major Kershaw, moved back with the troops and guns to the part of the hill which overlooked the gorge.

Shortly after this it was suggested to raise a *sunga*, or stone breastwork, for the protection of the troops wholly exposed to the distant fire of the enemy's juzails; but this proposition was not acted on. Immense numbers of the enemy, issuing from the city, had now crowned the summits of the hill opposite the gorge,—in all, probably 10,000 men. The plain on the west of the two hills was swept by swarms of their cavalry, who evidently designed to cut off the small party of Irregular Horse under Lieut. Walker; while the failure of our attempt to storm the village had rendered it easy for the enemy to throw strong reinforcements into it, and to supply the ammunition of which they had been in great want.

About 7 A. M., the fire from the enemy's hill was so galling, that the few skirmishers sent to the brow of our hill could with difficulty retain their posts. As an instance of the backwardness which now began to develop itself among our men, it must be mentioned, that Lieut.-Col. Oliver endeavoured to induce a party of his own regiment to follow him to the brow of the hill, to keep down the sharp fire of a number of the enemy, who had ensconced themselves in a small

ravine commanding the foremost square ; not a
man would follow him, — and it was only after
that brave officer had gone forward himself into
the thickest of the fire, saying, " Although my
men desert me, I myself will do my duty," that
about a dozen were shamed into performing
theirs. The remainder of the troops (the infantry formed into two squares, and the cavalry
being drawn up *en masse* immediately in their
rear) suffered severely without being able to re-
taliate, from the comparatively short range of the
musket. Our single gun maintained as hot a fire
on the masses of the enemy as possible, doing
great execution ; but the want of a second gun
to take up the fire was sensibly felt, inasmuch as,
after a short time, the vent became too hot for the
artillerymen to serve. This state of things continued until between 9 and 10 o'clock, when a
large party of the enemy's cavalry threatened our
right flank, and, to prevent his destruction, Lieut.
Walker was recalled. This demonstration, however, was repulsed by a well-directed discharge of
shrapnell from the H. A. gun, by one of which a
chief of consequence, supposed to be Abdoollah
Khan, Achukzye, was mortally wounded.

By the recall of Lieut. Walker the enemy were
enabled to surround our position at all points, except that facing the cantonments ; our gun am-

munition was almost expended, and the men were faint with fatigue and thirst (no water being procurable), while the number of killed and wounded was swelled every instant.

About this time (between 10 and 11 A. M.), large bodies of the enemy's infantry advanced across the plain from the Shah Bagh to the end of the hill, to cut off the supplies of ammunition coming from cantonments, as also the *dhoolies* on which we endeavoured to send off a few of the wounded. These, however, were checked by a party of our troops in the musjed, opposite the Kohistan gate, and by about fifty juzailchees under the temporary command of Capt. Trevor, (Capt. Mackenzie, their leader, having been requested by Brigadier Shelton to act as one of the staff for the day,) who lined some low walls and watercourses, as well as by frequent discharges of round shot and shrapnell from the cantonment guns under Lieut. Warburton.

Previously to this, numbers of the most daring Ghazees had descended into the gorge, and, taking advantage of some hillocks on the ascent towards our position, had crept gradually up, maintaining a deadly fire on our skirmishers, who were, unfortunately, wholly exposed; they became at length disheartened, and gave way. At this moment the Brigadier offered a reward of

100 rupees to any man who should take a flag of
the enemy, which had been planted behind a
tumulus about thirty yards in front of the square,
and he fruitlessly endeavoured to induce the men
to charge bayonets; several of the officers at the
same time advanced to the front, and actually
pelted the enemy with stones.* All attempts,
however, to encourage our men were in vain.
The attacking party were now emboldened to
make a rush upon our gun; our cavalry were
ordered to charge, but again in vain, for the
men would not follow their officers.† The panic
spread, and our troops gave way, except the
second square, which had been formed about 200
yards in the rear, and three companies under
Major Kershaw at the other extremity of the
hill; behind this second square the officers with
great difficulty rallied the fugitives, leaving the

---

* The names of this little band of heroes deserve to be
recorded: they were Capt. Macintosh and Lieut. Laing, who
were almost instantly killed, and Capts. Mackenzie, Troup,
and Leighton; the latter fell in the retreat of the army from
Cabul, the other two happily still survive to fight their
country's battles: of such men the Indian army may well be
proud.

† Capts. Bott and Collyer, 5th Light Cavalry; Lieut.
Walker, Irregular Horse; Russular Ishmael Khan, Jemadar
Synd, Mahomed Synd, and Mirza Musseer Bey, of Ander-
son's Horse.

gun in the hands of the enemy, who lost no time in walking off with the limber and horses.

By this time the news of Abdoolah Khan's wound had spread among the ranks of the enemy, causing great confusion, which extended to the Ghazees now in possession of the gun. This, and the tolerably firm attitude resumed by our troops, induced them to content themselves with the limber and horses, and retire. Their retreat gave fresh courage to our disheartened soldiers, who again took possession of the gun, and advanced to the brow of the hill, where were found the bodies of Capt. Macintosh and Lieut. Laing, as well as those of the soldiers slain in the onset, including two H. A. men, who, with a devotedness worthy of British soldiers, had perished while vainly endeavouring to defend their charge. Some fresh gun-ammunition having now arrived from cantonments, carried by Lascars, a fire was again opened on the ranks of the enemy; but we were unable to push the advantage gained by the momentary disorder alluded to above, because, in fact, the cavalry would not act. In the observations on this action, made hereafter, there will be found some palliation for the backwardness of the cavalry on this occasion, in spite of the gallant bearing of their leaders; the infantry were too few, and too much worn out and disheartened, to be able to make a forward movement. The consequence was, that not only did the whole force of the enemy come on with renewed vigour and spirits, maintaining at the same time the fatal juzail fire which had already so grievously thinned our ranks, but fresh numbers poured out of the city, and from the surrounding villages, until the hill occupied by them scarcely afforded room for them to stand.

This unequal conflict having lasted until past noon, during which period reinforcements and an additional gun had been in vain solicited from the cantonments, Brigadier Shelton sent Capt. Mackenzie to request Major Kershaw to move up his reserve (which could scarcely so be called, having been the whole day hard pressed by large bodies of the enemy in the village, and by parties occupying ruins and broken ground on the skirts of his position). The Major, fearing that, if he abandoned the knoll on which he had been stationed, our retreat to the cantonments (then becoming more and more imperatively necessary) might be cut off, made answer, that " he begged to suggest, that the Brigadier should fall back upon him." Before this message could be delivered, the front ranks of the advanced square, at the Brigadier's extremity of the hill, had been literally mowed down ; — most of the artillerymen, who performed their duty in a manner which is beyond praise, shared the same fate. The manœuvre practised by the Ghazees previously was repeated by still greater numbers. The evident unsteadiness of our troops, and the imminent danger to which the gun was a second time exposed, induced the Brigadier, after repeated suggestions from Serg. Mulhall, who commanded the battery, to order the gun to be limbered up — a second limber having arrived from cantonments — and to retire towards Major Kershaw's position. Scarcely had this movement been commenced, when a rush from the Ghazees completely broke the square; — all order was at an end: — the entreaties and commands of the officers, endeavouring to rally the men, were not even listened to, and an utter rout ensued down the hill in the direction of cantonments, the enemy closely following, whose cavalry, in particular, made a fearful slaughter among the unresisting fugitives. Major Kershaw's party, perceiving this disaster, endeavoured to escape; but strong parties, issuing from the village, cut off their retreat, and thus great numbers of our Sepoys perished: the grenadier company, especially, was all but annihilated. The mingled tide of flight and pursuit seemed, to those who manned the walls of cantonment, to be about to enter the gate together; and, by some fatality, the ammunition of the great guns in battery within the cantonments was almost expended. A heavy fire, however, was opened from the Shah's 5th Infantry in the Mission Compound: a fresh troop of the 5th Cavalry, under Lieut. Hardyman, charged across the plain towards the enemy, joined by Lieut. Walker, who had rallied fifteen or twenty of his own men; during which gallant effort this most promising and brave young officer received a mortal wound. These operations, assisted by a sharp discharge from the juzailchees under Capt. Trevor, contributed to check the pursuit; and it was observed at the time, and afterwards ascertained to be correct, that a chief (Osman Khan) voluntarily halted his followers, who were among the foremost, and led them off; which may be reckoned, indeed, the chief reason why *all* of our people, who on that day went forth to battle, were not destroyed. Our loss *was* tremendous; the principal part of the wounded having been left in the field, including Lieut.-Col. Oliver, where they were miserably cut to pieces. Our gun and second limber, which, while endeavouring to gallop down the hill, had overturned on rough ground, we had the mortification to behold triumphantly carried off by the enemy.

About half an hour previous to the flight of our troops, a note had been written to the Assist.-

Adjt.-Gen. by Capt. Troup, earnestly requesting
that the Mountain-train gun, which had by that
time been repaired, might be sent out with the
least possible delay ; and the first idea that suggested itself to that officer after our defeat was,
that by quickly bringing this gun to bear upon
the H. A. gun, then in the hands of the enemy,
the latter might still be saved. He therefore
galloped with speed to cantonments, where finding
the Mountain-train gun just ready to start, he
was on the point of leading it out of the gate,
when his progress was interrupted by the Assist.-
Adjt.-Gen., on the plea that it would now be of
no use. This is the more to be lamented, as, from
the spot occupied by Capt. Trevor's juzailchees,
who, protected by a low wall, still kept up a sharp
and effectual fire on the enemy, the range to the
side of the hill whence the Affghans were endeavouring to carry off the captured gun, about
which they clustered in thousands, was so short,
that grape, even from a small caliber, must have
prevented the execution of their intentions. Had
the company of fresh infantry, which was drawn
up outside the gate under command of Lieut.
Alexander, moved forward in company with the
mountain gun to the support of the above gallant
handful of juzailchees, excellent service might

have been rendered. But it seemed as if we were under the ban of Heaven.

OBSERVATIONS.

In this miserable and disastrous affair no less than six great errors must present themselves, even to the most unpractised military eye, each of which contributed in no slight degree to the defeat of our troops, opposed as they were by overwhelming numbers.

1st. The first and perhaps most fatal mistake of all was the taking out a *single* gun. The General Order by the Marquess of Hastings, expressly forbidding less than two guns to take the field, under any circumstances or on any pretence whatever, when another is available, must be well known at least to every officer who has served in India. This positive prohibition was the offspring of dearly-bought experience; and the action of Beymaroo affords another convincing example of the risk to which a single gun is exposed, when unsupported by the fire of a second. It was certainly the Brigadier's intention to take the mountain gun also; but this had unfortunately been disabled on the previous day, and it had been twice specially reported, both to the Brigadier and to the General

the foregoing night, by Capt. Troup, that it could
not be got ready before 12 A. M. on the following
day.

2dly. The second error is scarcely less evident
than the first. — Had immediate advantage been
taken of the panic which our unexpected cannonade created among the possessors of the village,—whose slack fire afforded sufficient evidence
of the actual fact that they were not only con-
temptible in numbers, but short of ammunition,
—had, I say, a storming party been led to the
attack under cover of the darkness, which would
have nullified the advantage they possessed in
being under cover, the place must inevitably have
fallen into our hands, and thus would the principal
object of the sally have been gained, and a good
line of retreat secured for our troops in case of
necessity.

3dly. The third error was so manifest as to be
quite unaccountable. A party of 100 sappers
had accompanied the force for the express purpose
of raising a *sunga*. The fittest place for such a
work would have been half-way along the ridge
occupied by us, where our troops would then have
been wholly protected from the fire of the juzails
from the opposite hill, while the enemy could not
have advanced to the attack without exposing
themselves to the full effects of our musketry and

grape. It would, in fact, have infused into our troops a sense of security from any sudden charge of the enemy's horse, and at the same time have enabled our own cavalry to issue forth with the assurance of having in their rear a place of defence, on which to fall back, if hard pressed by the enemy. It has been seen that no such defence was raised.

4thly. All have heard of the British SQUARES at *Waterloo*, which defied the repeated desperate onsets of Napoleon's choicest *cavalry*. At *Beymaroo* we formed squares to resist the *distant fire of infantry*, thus presenting a solid mass against the aim of perhaps the best marksmen in the world, the said squares being securely perched on the summit of a steep and narrow ridge, up which no cavalry *could* charge with effect. A Peninsular General would consider this to be a novel fashion ; yet Brigadier Shelton had the benefit of Peninsular experience in his younger days, and, it must be owned, was never surpassed in dauntless bravery.

5thly. Our cavalry, instead of being found upon the plain, where they might have been useful in protecting our line of communications with the cantonments, and would have been able to advance readily to any point where their services might have been required, were hemmed in between two

infantry squares, and exposed for several hours to
a destructive fire from the enemy's juzails, on
ground where, even under the most favourable
circumstances, they could not have acted with
effect.   This false and unsatisfactory position of
course discouraged the troopers; and, when the
infantry finally gave way, the two arms of the
service became mixed up in a way that greatly
increased the general confusion, and rendered it
impossible for the infantry to rally, even had they
been so disposed.   The truth is, that the cavalry
were not allowed fair play, and such a position
must have disgusted and dispirited *any* troops.

6thly. Shortly after our regaining possession of
the gun, one of the Brigadier's staff, Capt. Mackenzie, feeling convinced that, from the temper
of the troops, and from the impossibility of recti-
fying the false position in which the force was
placed, not only was success beyond hope, but
that defeat in its most disastrous shape was fast
approaching, proposed to the Brigadier to endeavour to effect a retreat, while it was yet in his
power to do so with comparative impunity.   His
reply was, " Oh, no! we will hold the hill some
time longer."   At that time, even if the slaughter
of the soldiery, the loss of officers, the evident
panic in our ranks, and the worse than false
nature of our position, had not been sufficient to

open all eyes as to the impossibility even of partial success, (for the real object of the expedition, viz. the possession of the village of Beymaroo, had been, as it were, abandoned from the very first,) the weakness and exhaustion of both men and horses, who were not only worn out by bodily fatigue, but suffering grievously from extreme thirst and the debility attendant on long fasting, ought to have banished all idea of further delaying a movement, in which alone lay the slightest chance of preserving to their country lives, by the eventual sacrifice of which not even the only solace to the soldier in the hour of misfortune, the consciousness of unimpaired honour, was likely to be gained.

CHAP. VII.

OUR PASSIVENESS. — CONFERENCES AND NEGOTIATIONS
WITH THE INSURGENT CHIEFS. — LOSS OF MAHOMED
SHEREEF'S FORT. — TERMS AGREED ON.

November 24th. — OUR troops had now lost all
confidence ; and even such of the officers as had
hitherto indulged the hope of a favourable turn
in our affairs began at last reluctantly to entertain gloomy forebodings as to our future fate.
Our force resembled a ship in danger of wrecking
among rocks and shoals, for want of an able pilot
to guide it safely through them. Even now, at
the eleventh hour, had the helm of affairs been
grasped by a hand competent to the important
task, we might perhaps have steered clear of destruction ; but, in the absence of any such deliverer,
it was but too evident that Heaven alone could
save us by some unforeseen interposition. The
spirit of the men was gone ; the influence of the
officers over them declined daily ; and that boasted
discipline, which alone renders a handful of our
troops superior to an irregular multitude, began
fast to disappear from among us. The enemy, on
the other hand, waxed bolder every day and every

hour, nor was it long ere we got accustomed to be bearded with impunity from under the very ramparts of our garrison.

I have already mentioned the new bridge thrown over the river by Gen. Elphinstone: this the enemy, advancing up the bed of the river under cover of the bank, to-day began to demolish. I must do Brigadier Shelton the justice to say that he, seeing the vast importance of the bridge in case of a retreat (an alternative of which he never lost sight), had strongly urged the erection of a field-work for its protection; in fact, there was a small unfinished fort near at hand, which one night's work of the sappers would have rendered fit for the purpose, and a small detachment thrown into it would have perfectly commanded the bridge. But madness was equally apparent in all that was done or left undone: even this simple precaution was neglected, and the result will be seen in the sequel.

Capt. Conolly now wrote in from the Bala Hissar, strongly advising an immediate retreat thither, on which movement several of the chief military and all the political officers considered our only hope of holding out through the winter to depend. But the old objections were still urged against the measure by Brigadier Shelton and others; and the General, in a letter this day addressed to the Envoy, expressed his opinion that " the movement, if not altogether impossible, would be attended with great difficulty, encumbered as we should be with numerous sick and wounded. The enemy would doubtless oppose us with their whole force, and the greater part of the troops would be required to cover the operation, thus leaving the cantonments imperfectly defended; that the men were harassed, dispirited, and greatly reduced in numbers; and failure would be attended with certain destruction to the whole force. To remove the ammunition and stores would be the work of several days, during which the enemy would hover around, and offer every obstacle to our operations. Our wounded were increased, whilst our means of conveying them were diminished. Would the Bala Hissar hold the force with all the followers ? Water was already said to be selling there at a high price.* We had barely twenty days' supply of provisions in the cantonments; and, even supposing we could find means to carry it with us, there was no prospect of obtaining more in the Bala Hissar. A retreat thence would be worse than from our present position, after having abandoned our cattle; and the sick and wounded must be left

* This report was entirely untrue.

behind us." In these opinions Brigadier Shelton entirely concurred. An appalling list of objections, it must be confessed, but insufficient to shake my belief that a removal of the force into the Bala Hissar was not only practicable but necessary for our safety and honour; while the risks attending it, though formidable, were only such as we ought, as soldiers, to have unhesitatingly incurred. Shah Shoojah had moreover declared himself impatient to receive us; and, even had the dreaded ruin overwhelmed us in the attempt, would it not have been a more manly and honourable course, than the inglorious treaty we shortly afterwards entered into with a treacherous band of rebels, by which we deserted the sovereign whom it was our duty to protect to the last drop of our blood? Had we boldly sallied forth, preferring death to dishonour, would not the fate of our poor fellows have been an hundredfold happier than that they subsequently experienced in their miserable retreat, inasmuch as they would have died in the consciousness of having bravely done their duty? Never were troops exposed to greater hardships and dangers; yet, sad to say, never did soldiers shed their blood with less beneficial result than during the investment of the British lines at Cabul. While, therefore, justice is done to the memory of the dead,

G

and those, who encountered a thousand perils in the brave and skilful performance of their duty, must be held up to that honour which is their due — while the tear of pity may well be shed at their untimely fate — the blame and discredit also must be *theirs*, who rendered nugatory all the oblations of blood that were offered, all the advantages that were gained, and finally involved a still formidable force in ruin and disgrace. But to return to my narrative.

A letter to the address of the Envoy was this day received from Osman Khan *, Barukzye, a near relative of the new King, and generally supposed to have a favourable bearing towards us, wherein he took credit to himself for having " checked the ardour of his followers in their pursuit of our flying troops on the preceding day, when, by following up their success, the loss of our cantonments and the destruction of our force was inevitable; but that it was not the wish of the chiefs to proceed to such dreadful extremities, their sole desire being that we should quietly evacuate the country, leaving them to govern it according to their own rules, and with a king of their own choosing." On the receipt of this friendly communication, the Envoy requested the

* This chief had sheltered Capt. Drummond in his own house since the first day of the outbreak.

General to state his opinion regarding the possibility, in a military point of view, of retaining our position in the cantonments; as, in case of a negative reply, he might be able to enter into negotiations with the existing rulers of the country.

The General replied to the effect that "we had now been in a state of siege for three weeks; our provisions were nearly expended, and our forage entirely consumed, without the prospect of procuring a fresh supply; that our troops were much reduced by casualties, and the large number of sick and wounded increased almost daily; and that, considering the difficulty of defending the extensive and ill-situated cantonment, the near approach of winter, the fact of our communications being cut off, and that we had no prospect of reinforcement, with the whole country in arms against us, he did not think it possible to retain our present position in the country, and therefore thought the Envoy ought to avail himself of the offer to negotiate, which had been made him."

November 27th. — Nothing else of consequence took place until this morning, when two deputies from the assembled chiefs, having made their appearance at the bridge, were ushered into cantonments by Capts. Lawrence and Trevor, the

Envoy having agreed to confer with them, on condition that nothing should be proposed which it would be derogatory in him to consider. The interview took place in the officers' guard-room at the eastern gate; the exact particulars did not transpire, but the demands made by the chiefs were such as it was impossible to comply with, and the deputies took leave of the Envoy with the exclamation that "we should meet again in battle!" "We shall at all events meet," replied Sir William, "at the day of judgment." At night the Envoy received a letter from the chiefs, proposing terms of so disgraceful and insulting a nature as seemed at once to preclude all hope of terminating our difficulties by treaty. The tenor of them was as follows: "That we should deliver up Shah Shoojah and his whole family; lay down our arms; and make an unconditional surrender; when they might perhaps be induced to spare our lives, and allow us to leave the country on condition of never returning." The Envoy's reply was such as well became the representative of his country's honour. "He was astonished," he said, "at their departing from that good faith for which he had given them credit, by violating the conditions on which he had been led to entertain proposals for a pacific arrangement; that the terms they proposed were too dishonourable to be entertained for a moment; and that, if they persisted in them, he must again appeal to arms, leaving the result to the God of battles."

December 1st. — No active renewal of hostilities took place until to-day, when a desperate effort was made by the enemy to gain possession of the Bala Hissar, which they endeavoured to effect by a night attack, in the first instance, on the *Bourge-i-lakh,* an isolated tower forming an outwork to the fortress, and from its elevated position commanding almost the entire works. This point was, however, strongly reinforced without delay by Major Ewart, commanding the garrison, and notwithstanding the determined spirit exhibited by the enemy, who made repeated charges up the hill, they were repulsed with considerable slaughter.

December 4th. — At an early hour the enemy moved out in force from the city, and, having crowned the Beymaroo hills, posted two guns in the gorge, from which they maintained a tolerably brisk fire for several hours into the cantonments, effecting fortunately but little mischief; in the evening they, as usual, retired to their respective haunts. During the night a rush was suddenly made by a party of Affghans to the gate of Mahomed Shereeff's fort, garrisoned by our troops, which they attempted, in imitation of our own method at the taking of Ghuznee, to blow open with powder bags, but without success.

December 5th.— This day the enemy completed the destruction of our bridge over the river, which they commenced on the 24th ult., no precaution having been taken to prevent the evil. Day after day we quietly looked on without an effort to save it, orders being in vain *solicited* by various officers for preventive measures to be adopted. In consequence of the enemy having commenced mining one of the towers of Mahomed Shereeff's fort, the garrison was reinforced, and Lieut. Sturt succeeded during the night in destroying the mine. This, however, could only be effected at the expense of opening a passage under the walls, which it became necessary to barricade; and although this measure of precaution was efficiently executed, such was the nervous state of the party composing the garrison, that no reliance could be placed on their stability in case of an attack.

December 6th. — The garrison of Mahomed Shereeff's fort was relieved at an early hour by one company of H. M.'s 44th, under Lieut. Grey, and one company 37th N. I. under Lieut. Hawtrey, an amply sufficient force for the defence of the place against any sudden onset; but, unhappily, the fears of the old garrison were communicated to the new,

and, owing to the representations of Lieut. Hawtrey, the defences were minutely examined by
Lieut. Sturt, the garrison engineer, and by him
pronounced to be complete. Scarcely, however, had
that officer returned to cantonments, ere information was conveyed to the General that the detachment, having been seized with a panic, had
taken flight over the walls, and abandoned the
fort to the enemy.   It would appear that a small
party of juzailchees, having crept up to the un-
dermined tower under cover of the trees in the
Shah Bagh, had fired upon the garrison through
the barricaded breach which I have above described, unfortunately wounding Lieut. Grey,
upon whose departure for medical aid the Europeans, deprived of their officer, lost what little
confidence they had before possessed, and, collecting their bedding under the walls, betrayed
symptoms of an intention to retreat. The enemy
meanwhile, emboldened by the slackened fire of
the defenders, approached momentarily nearer to
the walls, and, making a sudden rush to the barricade, completed the panic of the garrison, who
now made their escape over the walls in the
greatest consternation, deaf to the indignant re-
monstrances of their gallant commander, who in
vain entreated them not to disgrace themselves
and him by such cowardly proceedings. Even

the Sepoys, who at first remained staunch, contaminated by the bad example set them by their European brethren, refused to rally; and Lieut. Hawtrey, finding himself deserted by all, was obliged reluctantly to follow, being the last to leave the fort. It is, however, worthy of mention, that two Sepoys of the 37th N. I. were left dead in the fort, and two others were wounded, while not a man of the 44th was touched, excepting one whose hand suffered from the accidental explosion of a grenade.

The enemy, though at first few in numbers, were not slow to avail themselves of the advantage afforded them by this miserable conduct of our troops, and their banner was soon planted in triumph on the walls, amidst the exulting shouts of hundreds. Much recrimination took place between the Europeans and the Sepoys engaged in this affair, each declaring the other had been the first to run; and a court of inquiry was assembled to investigate the matter, the result of which, though never entirely divulged, was generally supposed to be favourable to the Sepoys, it being a known fact, that the Europeans had brought off nearly all their bedding safe, whilst the Sepoys had left everything behind. At all events, a circumstance soon occurred, which abundantly testified the impression made on those in command. At this time the bazar village was garrisoned by a party of H. M.'s 44th, who, on observing the flight of the soldiers from Mahomed Shereeff's fort, were actually on the point of abandoning their own post, when they were observed and stopped by some officers, of whom one was Lieut. White, the adjutant of the regiment; but so little dependence could now be placed on their stability, that a guard from the 37th N. I. was stationed at the entrance of the bazar, with strict orders to prevent the exit of any Europeans on duty in the place.

December 7th. — The European garrison was this day withdrawn from the bazar, and a company of the 37th N. I. substituted in their room! This, being the weakest point of our defences, had hitherto been protected entirely by parties of H. M.'s 44th, which post of honour they were now considered unworthy to retain.

I may here be excused for offering a few brief remarks.

In the course of this narrative, I have been compelled by stern truth to note down facts nearly affecting the honour and interests of a British regiment. It may, or rather I fear it must, inevitably happen that my unreserved statements of the Cabul occurrences will prove unacceptable to many, whose private or public feel-

ings are interested in glossing over or suppressing
the numerous errors committed and censures
deservedly incurred.   But my heart tells me that
no paltry motives of rivalry or malice influence
my pen ; rather a sincere and honest desire to
benefit the public service, by pointing out the
rocks on which our reputation was wrecked, the
means by which our honour was sullied and our
Indian empire endangered, as a warning to future
actors in similar scenes.   In a word, I believe that
more good is likely to ensue from the publication
of the whole unmitigated truth, than from a mere
garbled statement of it.   A kingdom has been
lost — an army slain ; — and surely, if I can show
that, had we been but true to ourselves, and had
vigorous measures been adopted, the result might
have been widely different, I shall have written
an instructive lesson to rulers and subjects, to
generals and armies, and shall not have incurred
in vain the disapprobation of the self-interested
or the proud.   It is notorious that the 44th foot
had been for a long time previous to these occurrences in a state of woful deterioration.   I firmly
believe that in this, and in every other respect, they
stood alone as a regiment of that noble army whose
glorious deeds in all quarters of the globe have
formed, with those of the British navy, the foundation of our national pride, and have supplied for

ages to come a theme of wonder and admiration. The regiment in question fell a prey to a vital disease, which the Horse Guards alone could have remedied, and which is now beyond the reach of proper investigation. May a redeeming glory and renown rise from its ashes!

The alarming discovery having been made that our supply of provisions had been materially overrated, and that not even a sufficiency for one day remained in store, Capt. Hay was despatched with a convoy of military stores into the Bala Hissar, with orders to bring back the animals laden with grain. He started several hours before daybreak, but on reaching the Seeah Sung hill, a few straggling shots being fired upon his rear, the men riding the laden *yaboos* (Affghan ponies) were panic-stricken, and, hastily casting the loads to the ground, galloped for safety to the front. Much private property was lost at the same time, for, notwithstanding all the opposition that had been made to the proposal of a retreat to the Bala Hissar, the General in some degree deferred to the opinions of those who favoured the movement, by adopting the half-measure of sending in magazine supplies from time to time by driblets. This led many to suppose that the whole force would sooner or later retreat thither, and accordingly advantage was taken of

every opportunity to send in a few private necessaries in advance.   On this occasion the attempt
failed in the manner I have above related; but
Capt. Hay nevertheless accomplished the primary
object of his journey, by bringing back as much
provisions as could be collected on so short a
notice.

December 8th. — The Envoy, having addressed
a public letter to the General, requested him to
state " whether or not it was his opinion that
any further attempt to hold out against the
enemy would merely have the effect of sacrificing
both His Majesty Shah Shoojah and ourselves; and
whether, supposing this to be so, the only alternative left was not to negotiate for our safe retreat out of the country, on the most favourable
terms possible ?"   The General, in reply, stated
his conviction that " the present situation of the
troops was such, from the want of provisions and
the impracticability of procuring more, that no
time ought to be lost in entering into negotiations for a safe retreat from the country : That,
as regarded the troops at Candahar, and the
rumours of their approach to our assistance, he
would be sorry, in the absence of all authentic
information, to risk the sacrifice of the troops by
waiting for their arrival, when we were ignorant
even of their having commenced their march, and

were reduced to three days' supply of provisions
for our Sepoys at half rations, and almost without any forage for our horses and cattle : That
our number of sick and wounded in hospital ex-
ceeded 600, and our means for their transport were
far from adequate, owing to the death by starvation of so many of our camels, from which cause
also we should be obliged, at this inclement season, to leave their tents and bedding behind, with
such a march before us : That, as regarded the
King, he must be excused from entering upon
that point of the Envoy's letter, and leave its
consideration to his better knowledge and judgment; but he might be allowed to say that it
little became him, as commanding the British
troops in Affghanistan, to regard the necessity
of negotiation in any other light than as concerned *their* honour and welfare, for both of which
he should be answerable, by a further stay
here, after the sudden and universal rebellion
against His Majesty's authority which had taken
place throughout his dominions : That the
whole of the grain and forage in the vicinity was
exhausted, and the defence of the extensive and
ill-selected cantonment would not admit of distant expeditions, to obtain supplies from the
strongly fortified dwellings of an armed and hostile population ; our present numbers being in-

sufficient for its defence, and obliging the whole
of the troops to be almost constantly under arms.
In conclusion, he could only repeat his opinion
that the Envoy should lose no time in entering
into negotiations." This letter was counter-
signed by Brigadiers Shelton and Anquetil, and
Colonel Chambers, who entirely concurred in the
opinions it expressed. Meanwhile starvation
stared us in the face, and it became necessary to
adopt immediate measures for obtaining a further
supply of provisions. A consultation was accordingly held with this object at the General's
house, and it was determined that an attack
should be made on the neighbouring fort of
Khoja Ruwash at an early hour the following
morning.

December 9th. — The morning dawned, but no
signs of preparation appeared for the proposed
enterprise ; no bridge was laid down for the passage of the guns and cavalry ; no troops were in
readiness to march ; and it was plain that either
no orders had been given, or no attention had
been paid to them. Thus, notwithstanding the
importance of its object, the expedition was suffered
to die a natural death.

Upon this subject I shall only remark that
Brigadier Shelton commanded the garrison, and
that with him the necessary arrangements rested.

Intelligence having been this day received of a decisive victory gained over the enemy by Gen. Sale at Jellalabad, the Envoy conceived it might have the effect of modifying the General's opinion, regarding the immediate necessity of negotiating with the rebel chiefs, and addressed him a letter on the subject. The General, however, declared in reply, that, pleasing as the intelligence was, it could not in the slightest degree influence our position, so as to affect the expediency of our treating; in forming which opinion he was much influenced by the joint representations that had been just made to him by Capts. Boyd and Johnson, the respective heads of the Company's and Shah's commissariat, wherein they declared their utter inability to procure grain or forage within three or four miles, and that, although three days' supply of *atta* (ground wheat) might still be procurable from the Bala Hissar, yet every additional day's delay now crippled the cattle more and more, and rendered our position more perilous. Notwithstanding these apparently conclusive arguments, there existed strong grounds for believing that the Bala Hissar contained a much larger supply of provisions than was generally supposed.

December 10*th.* — Another convoy of military stores was despatched to the Bala Hissar this morning under command of Lieut. Le Geyt, by

whom a further supply of *atta* was brought back
in return.

December 11*th.* — The rebel chiefs having ma-
nifested an inclination to treat, the Envoy, ac-
companied by Capts. Lawrence, Mackenzie, and
Trevor, went out to meet them on the plain towards Seah Sung. There were present Mahomed
Akber Khan, Osman Khan, Mahomed Khan
Naib Ameer (commonly called Naib Ameer),
Barukzyes; — Mahomed Shah Khan, Humza
Khan, Khooda Bux Khan, Giljyes ; — Juayut
Oolol Khan, Populzye; — Khan Shereen Khan,
Kuzzilbash ; — and several others of inferior
note, but all heads of tribes. After the exchange of salutations, Sir William addressed
the assembled Khans, alluding to past times,
during which relations of perfect cordiality and
friendship had existed between them and the
English. He greatly lamented that feelings of
so pleasant and mutually beneficial a nature
should have been thus rudely interrupted; but
professed himself wholly ignorant of the causes of
such interruption. He proceeded to state that
sentiments of good-will towards the Affghan
nation had principally induced the British government to lend their aid, in restoring to the
seat of his ancestors a king, who, notwithstanding
his misfortunes, originating in causes to which he

would not then allude, had ever reigned in the hearts of the mass of his people ; that the restoration of their monarch had apparently given the utmost satisfaction to all classes throughout his dominions. If, however, that satisfaction had passed away, and given place to emotions of a wholly contrary nature (and he supposed that the assembled Sirdars and Khans might be considered the mouth-piece of the people), it no longer became the British Government to persist in a course so displeasing to those chiefly interested in the result. On this account he was willing to enter into negotiations, for the smoothing over of present difficulties, and for the adopting of such measures as were likely to be the most conducive towards the re-establishment of that mutual friendship between the British and Affghan governments, the maintenance of which, he felt assured, must be earnestly desired by both parties. — To all these propositions Mahomed Akber Khan and Osman Khan, as the principal personages present, expressed, with the hearty concurrence of the inferior chiefs, their entire assent, adding many expressions of their personal esteem for the Envoy himself, and their gratitude for the way in which the exiled Ameer had been used. The Envoy then requested permission to read to them a paper containing a general sketch of the

proposed treaty. This being agreed to, the
articles of the treaty were read and discussed.
Their general purport was to the effect—That the
British should evacuate Affghanistan, including
Candahar, Ghuznee, Cabul, Jellalabad, and all
the other stations absolutely within the limits of
the country so called; — that they should be
permitted to return not only unmolested to India,
but that supplies of every description should be
afforded them in their road thither, certain men
of consequence accompanying them as hostages;
—that the Ameer Dost Mahomed Khan, his
family, and every Affghan now in exile for political offences, should be allowed to return to
their country; — that Shah Shoojah and his
family should be allowed the option of remaining
at Cabul or proceeding with the British troops
to Loodiana, in either case receiving from the
Affghan government a pension of one lac of
rupees per annum; — that means of transport for
the conveyance of our baggage, stores, &c.,
including that required by the royal family, in
case of their adopting the latter alternative, should
be furnished by the existing Affghan government; — that an amnesty should be granted to
all those who had made themselves obnoxious on
account of their attachment to Shah Shoojah
and his allies, the British; — that all prisoners

should be released; — that no British force should
be ever again sent into Affghanistan, unless called
for by the Affghan government, between whom
and the British nation perpetual friendship
should be established on the sure foundation of
mutual good offices.

To all these terms the chiefs cordially agreed,
with the exception of Mahomed Akber, who
cavilled at several, especially that of the amnesty,
but was over-ruled by his coadjutors. He positively
refused to permit the garrison to be supplied with
provisions until it had quitted cantonments, which
movement he clamorously demanded should take
place the following morning. His violence caused
some confusion; but the more temperate of his
party having interfered, it was finally agreed that
our evacuation of the cantonments should take
place in three days — that provisions should be
supplied — and that to all the above-mentioned
articles of this new treaty a formal assent in writ-
ing should be sent, with all the usual forms of a
restored peace. The chiefs, on returning to the
city, took with them Capt. Trevor as a hostage
for the sincerity of the Envoy. During the whole
of this interview, which took place not far from
the bottom of the Seeah Sung hills, great anxiety
was felt in the cantonments from the apparent
danger to which the Envoy was exposed, — he

being accompanied only by a few troopers of the body-guard,—and from the circumstance of large bodies of the enemy's horse and foot being seen to pass towards the scene of conference from the city, their leaders evidently with much difficulty restraining their advance beyond a certain point. Sir William, however, although not unaware of the perfidious nature of those he had to deal with, nor insensible to the risk he ran, (a shot in fact, from the fanatic multitude, having whistled over the heads of the gentlemen in attendance on him, as they advanced towards the rendezvous,) wisely imagined that a display of confidence was the best mode of begetting good faith. It is, however, pretty certain that the tumultuary movements of the Affghan troops, whose presence was in direct violation of the stipulations under which the conference was held, were not without their cause, it having been the earnest desire of Mahomed Akber to seize upon the Envoy's person at that very meeting, from which step he was with difficulty restrained by the other Khans. But no sense of personal danger could have deterred a man of Sir William's truly chivalrous and undaunted character from the performance of any duty, private or public.

Would that he had been more alive to the apprehensions which influenced common men!

We might not then have to mourn over the untimely fate of one, whose memory must be ever cherished in the hearts of all who knew and were capable of appreciating him, notwithstanding the disastrous termination of his political career, as that of a good, and, in many essential points, a great man.

CHAP. VIII.

December 12th. — IT is undeniable that Sir
William Macnaghten was forced into this treaty
with men whose power he despised, and whose
treachery was proverbial, against his own judgment, by the pressing representations of our
military heads.   It is no less true that, whatever
may have been his political remissness or want of
foresight before the rebellion broke out, he had,
throughout the perils that afterwards beset us,
displayed a truly British spirit of unflinching
fortitude and indefatigable energy, calculated,
under more auspicious leaders, to have stimulated
the zeal and valour of the troops, and to have
cheered them under the trials and hardships they
were called on to endure; and I can safely add,
without fear of contradiction, that scarcely an
enterprise was undertaken throughout the siege,
but at the suggestion, and even the entreaties, of
the Envoy, he volunteering to take on himself
the entire responsibility.   Justice demands this

The Cast in the Tragedy.

Dost Mahomed

Sir William Macnaghten

Major Eldred Pottinger

Mahomed Akber Khan

Shah Shoojah Ul-Mulk

Alexander Burnes

tribute to the memory of one, whose acts, as they will assuredly undergo the severe scrutiny of his countrymen, it therefore becomes the duty of every eye-witness, who bears testimony on the subject, not only to shield from misrepresentation, but, where they are deserving of it, to hold up to public admiration. I am led to write this solely by my public knowledge of the man. If I could bring myself, on matters of such vital importance, to follow the dictates of mere private feeling, my bias would be altogether on the side of my late lamented military chief, who honoured me with his friendship, and for whose infirmities every allowance ought, in common justice, to be made. With a mind and talents of no ordinary stamp, and a hitherto unsullied fame, *he* committed the fatal error of transporting himself suddenly from a state of prolonged luxurious repose, at an advanced age, to undertake the fatigues and cares inseparable from high military command, in a foreign uncongenial climate; he thus not only ruined his already shattered health, but (which to a soldier was a far worse calamity) grievously damaged that high reputation which his early services had secured for him. His fate ought to serve as a warning to others of his class, who, priding themselves on a *Peninsular* fame of some thirty years' standing, are too apt to forget the inroads

that time may have meanwhile made on mind and
body; and who would do well to bear in remembrance that, of two of the most iron intellects of
their day — one of them was even the greatest
general of his age — it was written with too much
truth,—

" From *Marlborough's* eyes the tears of dotage flow,
And *Swift* expires a driveller and a show."

—The terms of the new treaty were immediately
made known to Shah Shoojah, by which that unfortunate monarch found himself once more
doomed to an old age of exile and degradation.
The first step towards its fulfilment was the
withdrawal of our troops from the Bala Hissar,
which was to have taken place this very day, but
was postponed for a short time longer, to admit of
the necessary preparations being made. A depu-
tation of chiefs had an interview in the close of
the day, who were the bearers of a most unexpected proposition, to the effect that Shah Shoojah should continue king, on condition of inter-
marrying his daughters with the leading Affghan
chiefs, and abandoning the offensive practice of
keeping the chief nobles of his kingdom waiting for hours at his gate, in expectation of
audience. The Affghans hate ceremony, which
Shah Shoojah carried at all times to an absurd

extent; hence much of his unpopularity. This arrangement was not intended to annul those parts of the treaty which related to our immediate evacuation of the country, for the fulfilment of which some married families were demanded as hostages.

December 13*th*. — Such was the inveterate pride of the King, that he yielded a most reluctant consent to the above-mentioned proposals, notwithstanding that the only alternative was the instant resignation of his kingdom. Little confidence was, however, placed by the Envoy in the sincerity of the chiefs, whose hatred of the Doranee ruler was notorious. As our retreat was now fully decided on, and our well-stocked magazine was shortly to fall a prey to our enemies, the General ordered that some ammunition should be distributed to certain of the camp-followers; and commanding officers were directed to indent for new arms and accoutrements, in exchange for such as were old and damaged. The reins of discipline had, however, by this time become so terribly relaxed, and so little attention was paid to superior orders by either officers or men, that many of the officers in command of companies rested content with sending their men to the magazine, to help themselves at will, the stores being unfortunately, in the absence of any

H

finished building for their reception, arranged under the trees of an orchard, in charge of a small guard. The consequence was, as might have been expected, a scene of disgraceful confusion and plunder, which was rendered worse by a rush of camp-followers, who, imagining that a licence had been given for every one to take whatever he pleased, flocked in hundreds to the spot, and terribly increased the tumult; insomuch that the authority of several officers, who, observing what was going on, exerted themselves to restore order, was for several minutes set at open defiance. At last, however, the place was cleared of the intruders, and the greater portion of the stolen articles was recovered the same evening. But this event may be taken as an instance of the unsteadiness of the troops, and of the recklessness that now began to extend itself amongst all ranks of the force.

At 2 P. M. the troops in the Bala Hissar, consisting of the 54th N. I., half of Capt. Nicholl's troop of horse artillery, and a detachment of the mountain train, with 2 howitzers, under Lieut. Green, commenced their evacuation of that fortress. They were also encumbered with an iron nine-pounder gun, and a twenty-four pounder brass howitzer, drawn by bullocks, which it was the General's wish should have been left behind, but his order to that effect had by some accident missed its destination. As the utmost scarcity of provisions prevailed in cantonments, Capt. Kirby, the commissariat officer, had zealously exerted himself to collect a supply of about 1600 maunds of wheat and flour to carry thither. Much delay, however, occurred in packing and loading ; and, the best part of the day being nearly spent ere above one third of that quantity was ready, Major Ewart deemed it advisable to move off without further loss of time. He found Mahomed Akber Khan in waiting with a small body of followers outside the gate, for the purpose of escorting him to cantonments ; and, as evening drew nigh, a dense crowd of armed Affghans had been observed to collect on the Seah Sung hill, along the base of which our troops must pass, giving rise to suspicions of some meditated treachery. While the rear-guard, with the mountain train gun and a portion of the baggage, was leaving the gate, some of Mahomed Akber's followers, pushing quietly past them, endeavoured to effect an entrance into the fort; but on their being recognized by the king's guard, the gates were immediately shut, and a round or two of grape fired upon the intruders, with so indiscriminate an aim as to endanger the lives of Capt. Conolly and several of the Sepoys, of whom some were severely wounded. It can scarcely be doubted that Mahomed Akber's intention was to have seized the gate with a few of his men, until a rush of the Affghans from the hill should have enabled him to carry the body of the place by storm. The vigilance of the garrison having defeated this plan, the wily chief, imagining that the gates would again be opened to re-admit our troops, informed Major Ewart that, owing to the lateness of the hour and the threatening attitude assumed by the crowd on the hill, it would be necessary to postpone his march until the following morning. In consequence of this sudden ill-timed announcement, Major Ewart applied to the King for the immediate readmission of his troops for shelter during the night; but the monarch, whose suspicions of foul play on the part of Mahomed Akber were now fully awakened, positively refused to accede to the request. The prospect of passing the night in the low marshy ground under the walls, without tents, bedding, firewood, or food, for officers or men, was sufficiently cheerless; while the fear of treachery on the part of Mahomed Akber, and the dangerous vicinity of an armed multitude, whose watch-fires already gleamed on the adjacent hills, tended but little to relieve the discomforts of such a situation. The cold was intensely bitter, and perhaps so miserable a night had never before been spent by Indian troops.

December 14*th*. — At an early hour this morning, Mahomed Akber having declared his readiness to proceed, the troops commenced their march. The advance-guard was suffered to proceed unmolested ; but the rear-guard, on reaching the base of the Seah Sung hill, was fired upon by the enemy, who crowned the ridge ; and the iron nine-pounder being for a few moments accidentally separated from the column in crossing a water-cut, an instantaneous rush was made upon it by a number of Affghans, and a poor sick European artillery-man, who, for want of a more suitable conveyance, had been lashed to the gun, was unmercifully butchered. The approach of the rear-guard, and a round or two of grape from the mountain train howitzer, drove off the assailants ; and they were restrained from offering any additional annoyance by the exertions of Mahomed Akber himself, who, galloping in amongst them with a few followers, threatened to cut down any who dared to be guilty of further opposition to the progress of the detachment, which accordingly reached cantonments safe at about 9 A. M.

December 16*th*. — Shah Shoojah having, for reasons best known to himself, withdrawn his consent to the arrangement which was to have

continued him in the possession of his rights, the
treaty resumed its original form; but the chiefs
positively refused to supply provisions or forage,
until we should further assure them of our sincerity by giving up every fort in the immediate
vicinity of cantonments. Forage had for many
days been so scarce, that the horses and cattle
were kept alive by paring off the bark of trees,
and by eating their own dung over and over again,
which was regularly collected and spread before
them. The camp-followers were destitute of other
food than the flesh of animals, which expired daily
from starvation and cold.   The daily consumption
of atta by the fighting men was about 150 maunds,
and not above two days' supply remained in store.
By giving up the forts in question, all of which
commanded the cantonment, we should place ourselves entirely at the mercy of the enemy, who
could at any time render our position untenable.
But our leaders now seemed to consider that we
had no other chance left than to concede to the
demands of the chiefs, however unreasonable; and
our troops were accordingly withdrawn from the
Rikabashee, Magazine, and Zoolfekar's forts, and
from the Musjeed opposite the western gate, all
of which were forthwith occupied by the Affghans, who, on their part, sent in Nussuroollah
Khan, a brother of Nuwab Zuman Khan, as a

hostage, and a supply of about 150 maunds of atta for the troops. They likewise promised us 2000 camels and 400 yaboos for the march to Jellalabad.

December 18*th*. — The delay of the chiefs in furnishing the necessary carriage, and the Shah's dilatoriness in deciding on his future course, compelled us from day to day to postpone our departure. Meanwhile the increasing severity of the winter rendered every hour's procrastination of the utmost consequence; and this morning our situation was rendered more desperate than ever by a heavy fall of snow, which covered the ground to the depth of five inches, and never afterwards disappeared. Thus a new enemy entered on the scene, which we were destined to find even more formidable than an army of rebels.

December 19*th*. — The Envoy wrote an order for the evacuation of Ghuznee, and it was arranged that the 27th N. I., which garrisoned the place, should march through the Zoormut valley, and pursue the route of Dera Ishmael Khan. The 22d was fixed for our departure.

December 20*th*. — The Envoy had an interview with the chiefs, who now demanded that a portion of our guns and ammunition should be immediately given up. They also required Brigadier Shelton as a hostage. It was proposed by Lieut.

Sturt to the General to break off the treaty, and march forthwith to Jellalabad, devoting all the means of transport we possessed to the service of the sick, and the conveyance of such public stores as were absolutely necessary. But neither the General nor his immediate advisers could bring themselves to adopt a course which would have saved the national honour, at the risk of sacrificing our whole force.

It has been truly said that a council of war never fights.—A door of hope had, until this day, still remained open to us in the approach of Col. Maclaren's force to our assistance from Candahar; we now heard with despair of its retreat from Tazee, in consequence of the snow.

December 21st. — The Envoy met Osman Khan and Mahomed Akber Khan on the plain, when four hostages were fixed upon, two of whom (Capts. Conolly and Airey) were at once given over. Brigadier Shelton, having expressed a decided objection to undertake the duty, was not insisted upon. In the evening Capts. Trevor and Drummond were permitted to return to cantonments, the latter officer having been concealed in the city since the 2d of November.

December 22d. — I was ordered to conduct an officer of Nuwab Zuman Khan over the magazine, that he might make choice of such stores as would be most acceptable to the chiefs. I recommended a large pile of 8-inch shells to his notice, which I knew would be of no use to the chiefs, as the mortars were with Capt. Abbott's battery at Jellalabad. He eagerly seized the bait, and departed in great glee, with his prize laden on some old ammunition-waggons.

The Envoy at the same time sent his carriage as a present to Mahomed Akber Khan. That same night the last-named chief spread the net into which Sir William Macnaghten was, on the following day, so miserably lured to his destruction. Capt. Skinner, at this time living under Mahomed Akber's protection, was made the bearer of proposals to the Envoy, of so advantageous a nature, as to prove, in his forlorn circumstances, irresistibly tempting.

Amenoollah Khan, the most influential of the rebels, was to be seized on the following day, and delivered up to us as a prisoner. Mahomed Khan's fort was to be immediately occupied by one of our regiments, and the Bala Hissar by another. Shah Shoojah was to continue king; Mahomed Akber was to become his wuzeer, and our troops were to remain in their present position until the following spring. — That a scheme like this, bearing impracticability on its very face, should have for a moment deceived a man of Sir

William's usual intelligence and penetration, is indeed an extraordinary instance of infatuation, that can only be accounted for on the principle that a drowning man will catch at a straw. Our fortunes were now at their lowest ebb; the chiefs were apparently delaying our departure until the snow should have formed an impassable barrier to the removal of our troops, who, even in the absence of an enemy, would but too probably perish from cold and famine. A treaty formed with men famed for falsehood and treachery, and who had already shown an utter disregard of some of its most important stipulations, could be regarded as little better than so much waste paper; added to which considerations, Sir William felt that his own fame was deeply involved in the issue of that policy*, of which he had from the very first been the prime advocate and upholder, and that with it he must stand or fall. The specious project of Mahomed Akber offered a solution to the difficulties that beset his path, at which he grasped with an eagerness engendered by despair. The strength of the rebels had hitherto lain in their unanimity; the proposed stroke of policy would at once dissolve the confederacy, and open a road by which to retrieve

* That of invading Affghanistan for the purpose of restoring Shah Shoojah as king.

our ruined fortunes. On either hand there was danger; and, miserable as Sir William's life had been for the past six weeks, he was willing to stake his all on the issue of a plan which seemed to offer a faint hope of recovering the ground we had lost.

In a fatal hour he signed his name to a paper consenting to the arrangement. — His doom was sealed. — The whole was a scheme got up by the chiefs, to test his sincerity.

December 23d. — At about noon Sir William Macnaghten, attended by Capts. Lawrence, Trevor, and Mackenzie, left the mission-house to attend a conference with Mahomed Akber Khan on the plain towards Seeah Sung. Previously to this he had requested the General that two regiments and two guns might be in readiness for secret service, and that, as the interview would be of a critical nature, the garrison might be kept well on the alert, and the walls strongly manned. In leaving the cantonments, Sir William expressed his disappointment at the paucity of men on the ramparts, and the apparent inertness of the garrison at such a critical moment, saying, " However, it is all of a piece with the military arrangements throughout the siege." On his leaving the gate only sixteen troopers of the body-guard were in attendance, but the remainder shortly afterwards joined, under Lieut. Le Geyt.

Sir William now for the first time explained to the officers who accompanied him the objects of the present conference ; and Capt. Lawrence was warned to be in readiness to gallop to the Bala Hissar, to prepare the King for the approach of a regiment.

Apprehensions being expressed of the danger to which the scheme might expose him, in case of treachery on the part of Mahomed Akber, he replied, " Dangerous it is ; but if it succeeds, it is worth all risks : the rebels have not fulfilled even one article of the treaty, and I have no confidence in them ; and if by it we can only save our honour, all will be well. At any rate, I would rather suffer a hundred deaths, than live the last six weeks over again."

Meanwhile crowds of armed Affghans were observed hovering near the cantonment and about Mahomed Khan's fort, causing misgivings in the minds of all but the Envoy himself, whose confidence remained unshaken. On arriving near the bridge, they were met by Mahomed Akber Khan, Mahomed Shah Khan, Dost Mahomed Khan, Khooda Bux Khan, Azad Khan, and other chiefs, amongst whom was the brother of Amenoollah

Khan, whose presence might have been sufficient to convince Sir William that he had been duped.

The usual civilities having passed, the Envoy presented Akber Khan with a valuable Arab horse, which had only that morning been purchased for 3000 rupees. The whole party then sat down near some rising ground, which partially concealed them from cantonments.

Capt. Lawrence having called attention to the number of inferior followers around them, with a view to their being ordered to a distance, Mahomed Akber exclaimed, " No, they are all in the secret;" which words had scarcely been uttered, when Sir William and his three companions found themselves suddenly grasped firmly by the hands from behind, whilst their swords and pistols were rudely snatched away by the chiefs and their followers. The three officers were immediately pulled forcibly along and compelled to mount on horseback, each behind a Giljye chief, escorted by a number of armed retainers, who with difficulty repelled the efforts of a crowd of fanatic Ghazees, who, on seeing the affray, had rushed to the spot, calling aloud for the blood of the hated infidels, aiming at them desperate blows with their long knives and other weapons, and only deterred from firing by the fear of killing a chief. The unfortunate Envoy was last seen struggling violently with Mahomed Akber, " consternation and horror depicted on his countenance."

On their nearing Mahomed Khan's fort, renewed attempts were made to assassinate the three captive officers by the crowd there assembled. Capt. Trevor, who was seated behind Dost Mahomed Khan, unhappily fell to the ground, and was instantly slain. Capts. Lawrence and Mackenzie reached the fort in safety, but the latter was much bruised in various parts of his body, and both were greatly exhausted from the excitement they had undergone.

At the entrance of the fort, a furious cut was aimed at Capt. Mackenzie's head by a ruffian named Moollah Momin, which was warded off by Mahomed Shah Khan, that chief receiving the blow on his own shoulder. Being taken into a small room, they found themselves still in continual jeopardy from repeated assaults of the Ghazees without, who were with the greatest difficulty restrained from shooting them through the window, where the hand of some recent European victim (afterwards ascertained to be that of the Envoy himself) was insultingly held up to their view. Throughout this trying scene they received repeated assurances of protection from the Giljye chiefs; but Amenoollah Khan coming in gave vent to a torrent of angry abuse, and even threatened to blow them from a gun. It is deserving of notice, that, amidst the congratulations which on all sides met the ear of Mahomed Shah Khan on the events of the day, the solitary voice of an aged Moollah was raised in condemnation of the deed, which he solemnly pronounced to be "foul," and calculated to cast a lasting disgrace on the religion of Mahomed. At midnight they were removed to the house of Mahomed Akber Khan. As they passed through the streets of Cabul, notwithstanding the excitement that had prevailed throughout the day, it resembled a city of the dead; nor did they meet a single soul.

By Akber Khan they were received courteously, and were now informed for the first time by Capt. Skinner of the murder of the Envoy and Capt. Trevor. That Sir William Macnaghten met his death at the hands of Mahomed Akber himself there can be no reasonable doubt. That chief had pledged himself to his coadjutors to seize the Envoy that day, and bring him into the city, when the chiefs hoped to have been able to dictate their own terms, retaining him as a hostage for their fulfilment. Finding it impossible, from the strenuous resistance Sir William offered, to carry him off alive, and yet determined not to disappoint the public expectation altogether, — influenced also by his tiger passions, and the remembrance of his father's wrongs, — Mahomed Akber drew a pistol, the Envoy's own gift a few hours before, and shot him through the body, which was immediately hacked to pieces by the ferocious Ghazees, by whom the dismembered trunk was afterwards carried to the city, and publicly exposed in the Char Chouk, or principal mart. The head was taken to the house of Nuwab Zuman Khan, where it was triumphantly exhibited to Capt. Conolly.

Such was the cruel fate of Sir William Macnaghten, the accomplished scholar, the distinguished politician, and the representative of Great Britain at the court of Shah Shooja-Ool-Moolk.

It cannot but be acceptable to my readers, if I here present entire the interesting and important letters of Capts. Mackenzie and Lawrence on this melancholy subject.

Letter addressed by CAPTAIN C. MACKENZIE *to* LIEUTENANT VINCENT EYRE.

MY DEAR EYRE,

YOU ask for a minute account of the circumstances attending the assassination of the late Sir William Macnaghten, and my own detention and imprisonment on that occasion. You may remember that, for many days previous to the fatal 23d December, the poor Envoy had been subjected to more wear and tear, both of body and mind, than it was possible for the most iron frame and the strongest intellect to bear without deeply feeling its effects. He had fulfilled all the preliminary conditions of the treaty which had been proposed between the British and the Affghan insurgents, whereas the Khans had in no one particular adhered to their engagements. Bad faith was evident in all their proceedings, and our condition was a desperate one; more especially as Sir William had ascertained, by bitter experience, that no hope remained in the energies and resources of our military leaders, who had formally rotested that they could do nothing more. Beset by this disgraceful imbecility on the one hand, and by systematic treachery on the other, the unfortunate Envoy was driven to his wits' end, and, as will be seen, forgot, in a fatal moment, the wholesome rule which he had theretofore laid down for himself, of refusing to hold communication with individuals of the rebel party, especially with him who was notorious, even amongst his villanous countrymen, for ferocity and treachery, to wit, Mahomed Akber Khan. Late in the evening of the 22d December, Captain James Skinner, who, after having been concealed in Cabul during the greater part of the siege, had latterly been the guest of Mahomed Akber, arrived in cantonments, accompanied by Mahomed Sudeeq Khan, a first cousin of Mahomed Akber, and by Sirwar Khan, the Arhanee merchant, who, in the beginning of the campaign, had furnished the army with camels, and who had been much in the confidence of Sir A. Burnes, being, in fact, one of our staunchest friends. The two latter remained in a different apartment, while Skinner dined with the Envoy. During dinner, Skinner jestingly remarked that he felt as if laden with combustibles, being charged with a message from Mahomed Akber to the Envoy of a most portentous nature.

Even then I remarked that the Envoy's eye glanced eagerly towards Skinner with an expression of hope. In fact, he was like a drowning man catching at straws. Skinner however referred him to his Affghan companions, and after dinner the four retired into a room by themselves. My knowledge of what there took place is gained from poor Skinner's own relation, as given during my subsequent captivity with him in Akber's house. Mahomed Sudeeq disclosed Mahomed Akber's proposition to the Envoy, which was, that the following day Sir William should meet him (Mahomed Akber) and a few of his immediate friends, viz. the chiefs of the Eastern Giljyes, outside the cantonments, when a final agreement should be made, so as to be fully understood by both parties; that Sir William should have a considerable body of troops in readiness, which, on a given signal, were to join with those of Mahomed Akber and the Giljyes, assault and take Mahmood Khan's fort, and secure the person of Ameenoollah. At this stage of the proposition Mahomed Sudeeq signified that, for a certain sum of money, the head of Ameenoollah should be presented to the Envoy; but from this Sir William shrunk with abhorrence, declaring that it was neither his custom nor that of his country to give a price for blood. Mahomed Sudeeq then went on to say, that, after having subdued the rest of the Khans, the English should be permitted to remain in the country eight months longer, so as to save their *purdah* (veil, or credit), but that they were then to evacuate Affghanistan, as if of their own accord; that Shah Shooja was to continue

king of the country, and that Mahomed Akber was to
be his wuzeer. As a further reward for his (Mahomed Akber's) assistance, the British Government were
to pay him 30 lacs of rupees, and 4 lacs of rupees per
annum during his life ! To this extraordinary and
wild proposal, Sir William gave ear with an eagerness
which nothing can account for but the supposition,
confirmed by many other circumstances, that his
strong mind had been harassed, until it had, in some
degree, lost its equipoise ; and he not only assented
fully to these terms, but actually gave a Persian paper
to that effect, written in his own hand, declaring as
his motives that it was not only an excellent opportunity to carry into effect the real wishes of government,
which were to evacuate the country with as much
credit to ourselves as possible, but that it would give
England time to enter into a treaty with Russia, de-
fining the bounds beyond which neither were to pass
in Central Asia. So ended this fatal conference,
the nature and result of which, contrary to his usual
custom, Sir William communicated to none of those
who, on all former occasions, were fully in his confidence, viz. Trevor, Lawrence, and myself. It seemed
as if he feared that we might insist on the impracticability of the plan, which he must have studiously
concealed from himself. All the following morning
his manner was distracted and hurried in a way that
none of us had ever before witnessed. It seems that
Mahomed Akber had demanded a favourite Arab
horse, belonging to Captain Grant, Assist-Adj.-Gen. of
force. To avoid the necessity of parting with the
animal, Captain Grant had fixed his price at the ex-
orbitant sum of 5000 rupees ; unwilling to give so

large a price, but determined to gratify the Sirdar, Sir William sent me to Captain Grant to prevail upon him to take a smaller sum, but with orders that if he were peremptory, the 5000 rupees should be given. I obtained the horse for 3000 rupees, and Sir William appeared much pleased with the prospect of gratifying Mahomed Akber by the present.

After breakfast, Trevor, Lawrence, and myself were summoned to attend the Envoy during his conference with Mahomed Akber Khan. I found him alone, when, for the first time, he disclosed to me the nature of the transaction he was engaged in. I immediately warned him that it was a plot against him. He replied hastily, " A plot ! let me alone for that, trust me for that ! " and I consequently offered no further remonstrance. Sir William then arranged with General Elphinstone that the 54th regiment, under Major Ewart, should be held in readiness for immediate service. The Shah's 6th, and two guns, were also warned. It is a curious circumstance, and betrays the unhappy vacillation of poor Elphinstone, that, after Sir William had actually quitted the cantonment in full expectation that every thing had been arranged according to his desire, he (the General) addressed a letter to him, which never reached him, remonstrating on the danger of the proposed attack, and strongly objecting to the employment of the two above regiments. About 12 o'clock Sir William, Trevor, Lawrence, and myself set forth on our ill-omened expedition. As we approached the Seeah Sung gate, Sir William observed with much vexation that the troops were not in readiness, protesting at the same time, however, that, desperate as the proposed attempt was, it was better that it should be made, and that a thousand deaths were preferable to the life he had lately led.

After passing the gate, he remembered the horse which he had intended as a present for Akber, and sent me back for it. When I rejoined him, I found that the small number of the body guard who had accompanied him had been ordered to halt, and that he, Trevor, and Lawrence, had advanced in the direction of Mahmood Khan's fort, being some 500 or 600 yards from the eastern rampart, and were there awaiting the approach of Mahomed Akber and his party, who now made their appearance. Close by were some hillocks, on the further side of which from the cantonment a carpet was spread where the snow lay least thick, and there the Khans and Sir William sat down to hold their conference. Men talk of presentiment; I suppose it was something of the kind which came over me, for I could scarcely prevail upon myself to quit my horse. I did so, however, and was invited to sit down among the Sirdars. After the usual salutations Mahomed Akber commenced business, by asking the Envoy if he was perfectly ready to carry into effect the proposition of the preceding night? The Envoy replied, "Why not?" My attention was then called off by an old Affghan acquaintance of mine, formerly chief of the Cabul police, by name Gholam Moyun-ood-deen. I rose from my recumbent posture, and stood apart with him conversing. I afterwards remembered that my friend betrayed much anxiety as to where my pistols were, and why I did not carry them on my person. I answered that although I wore my sword for form, it was not necessary at a friendly conference to be armed *cap-à-pee*. His discourse was also full of extravagant compliments, I suppose for the purpose of lulling me to sleep. At length my attention was called off from what he was saying, by observing that a number of men, armed to the teeth, had gradually approached to the scene of conference, and were drawing round in a sort of circle. This Lawrence and myself pointed out to some of the chief men, who affected at first to drive them off with whips; but Mahomed Akber observed that it was of no consequence, as they were in the secret. I again resumed my conversation with Gholam Moyun-ood-deen, when suddenly I heard Mahomed Akber call out, " Begeer! begeer!" (seize! seize!) and turning round, I saw him grasp the Envoy's left hand with an expression in his face of the most diabolical ferocity. I think it was Sultan Jan who laid hold of the Envoy's right hand. They dragged him in a stooping posture down the hillock, the only words I heard poor Sir William utter being, " Az barae Khooda" (for God's sake)! I saw his face however, and it was full of horror and astonishment. I did not see what became of Trevor, but Lawrence was dragged past me by several Affghans, whom I saw wrest his weapons from him. Up to this moment I was so engrossed in observing what was taking place, that I actually was not aware that my own right arm was mastered, that my urbane friend held a pistol to my temple, and that I was surrounded by a circle of Ghazees with drawn swords and cocked juzails. Resistance was in vain; so, listening to the exhortations of Gholam Moyun-ood-deen, which were enforced by the whistling of divers bullets over my head, I hurried through the snow with him to the place where his horse was standing, being despoiled *en route* of my sabre, and narrowly escaping divers attempts made on my life. As I mounted behind my captor, now my energetic defender, the crowd increased around us, the cries of "Kill the Kafir" became more vehement, and, although we hurried on at a fast canter, it was with the utmost difficulty Gholam Moyun-ood-deen, although assisted by one or two friends or followers, could ward off and avoid the sword-cuts aimed at me, the rascals being afraid to fire lest they should kill my conductor. Indeed he was obliged to wheel his horse round once, and, taking off his turban (the last appeal a Mussulman can make), to implore them for God's sake to respect the life of his friend. At last, ascending a slippery bank, the horse fell. My cap had been snatched off, and I now received a heavy blow on the head from a bludgeon, which fortunately did not quite deprive me of my senses. I had sufficient sense left to shoot ahead of the fallen horse, where my protector with another man joined me, and, clasping me in their arms, hurried me towards the wall of Mahmood Khan's fort. How I reached the spot where Mahomed Akber was receiving the gratulations of the multitude I know not, but I remember a fanatic rushing on me and twisting his hand in my collar until I became exhausted from suffocation. I must do Mahomed Akber the justice to say, that, finding the Ghazees bent on my slaughter, even after I had reached his stirrup, he drew his sword and laid about him right manfully, for my conductor and Meerza Bàoodeen Khan were obliged to press me up against the wall, covering me with their own bodies, and protesting that no blow should reach me but through their persons.

Pride, however, overcame Mahomed Akber's sense

of courtesy, when he thought I was safe, for he then turned round to me, and repeatedly said in a tone of triumphant derision, "Shuma moolk-i-ma me geered!" (*You'll* seize my country, will you!) he then rode off, and I was hurried towards the gate of the fort. Here new dangers awaited me; for Moollah Momin, fresh from the slaughter of poor Trevor, who was killed riding close behind me, — Sultan Jan having the credit of having given him the first sabre cut, — stood here with his followers, whom he exhorted to slay me, setting them the example by cutting fiercely at me himself. Fortunately a gun stood between us, but still he would have effected his purpose, had not Mahomed Shah Khan at that instant, with some followers, come to my assistance. These drew their swords in my defence, the chief himself throwing his arm round my neck, and receiving on his shoulder a cut aimed by Moollah Momin at my head. During the bustle I pushed forward into the fort, and was immediately taken to a sort of dungeon, where I found Lawrence safe, but somewhat exhausted by his hideous ride and the violence he had sustained, although unwounded. Here the Giljye chiefs, Mahomed Shah Khan, and his brother Dost Mahomed Khan, presently joined us, and endeavoured to cheer up our flagging spirits, assuring us that the Envoy and Trevor were not dead, but on the contrary quite well. They stayed with us during the afternoon, their presence being absolutely necessary for our protection. Many attempts were made by the fanatics to force the door to accomplish our destruction. Others spit at us and abused us through a small window, through which one fellow revelled a blunderbuss at us, which was struck up by our keepers and himself thrust back. At last Amee-noollah made his appearance, and threatened us with instant death. Some of his people most officiously advanced to make good his word, until pushed back by the Giljye chiefs, who remonstrated with this iniquitous old monster, their master, whom they persuaded to relieve us from his hateful presence. During the afternoon, a human hand was held up in mockery to us at the window. We said that it had belonged to an European, but were not aware at the time that it was actually the hand of the poor Envoy. Of all the Mahomedans assembled in the room discussing the events of the day, one only, an old Moollah, openly and fearlessly condemned the acts of his brethren, declaring that the treachery was abominable, and a disgrace to Islam. At night they brought us food, and gave us each a postheen to sleep on. At midnight we were awakened to go to the house of Mahomed Akber in the city. Mahomed Shah Khan then, with the meanness common to all Affghans of rank, robbed Lawrence of his watch, while his brother did me a similar favour. I had been plundered of my rings and every thing else previously, by the understrappers.

Reaching Mahomed Akber's abode, we were shown into the room where he lay in bed. He received us with great outward show of courtesy, assuring us of the welfare of the Envoy and Trevor, but there was a constraint in his manner for which I could not account. We were shortly taken to another apartment, where we found Skinner, who had returned, being on parole, early in the morning. Doubt and gloom marked our meeting, and the latter was fearfully deepened by the intelligence which we now received from our fellow-

I

captive of the base murder of Sir William and Trevor. He informed us that the head of the former had been carried about the city in triumph. We of course spent a miserable night. The next day we were taken under a strong guard to the house of Zeman Khan, where a council of the Khans was being held. Here we found Captains Conolly and Airey, who had some days previously been sent to the hurwah's house as hostage for the performance of certain parts of the treaty which was to have been entered into. A violent discussion took place, in which Mahomed Akber bore the most prominent part. We were vehemently accused of treachery, and every thing that was bad, and told that the whole of the transactions of the night previous had been a trick of Mahomed Akber, and Ameenoollah, to ascertain the Envoy's sincerity. They declared that they would now grant us no terms, save on the surrender of the whole of the married families as hostages, all the guns, ammunition, and treasure. At this time Conolly told me that on the preceding day the Envoy's head had been paraded about in the court yard; that his and Trevor's bodies had been hung up in the public bazar, or *chouk;* and that it was with the greatest difficulty that the old hurwah, Zuman Khan, had saved him and Airey from being murdered by a body of fanatics, who had attempted to rush into the room where they were. Also that previous to the arrival of Lawrence, Skinner, and myself, Mahomed Akber had been relating the events of the preceding day to the *Jeerga* or council, and that he had unguardedly avowed having, while endeavouring to force the Envoy either to mount on horseback or to move more quickly, *struck* him, and that, seeing Conolly's eye fastened upon him with an expression of intense indignation, he had altered the phrase and said, "I mean I *pushed* him." After an immense deal of gabble, a proposal for a renewal of the treaty, not however demanding all the guns, was determined to be sent to the cantonments, and Skinner, Lawrence, and myself were marched back to Akber's house, enduring *en route* all manner of threats and insults. Here we were closely confined in an inner apartment, which was indeed necessary for our safety. That evening we received a visit from Mahomed Akber, Sultan Jan, and several other Affghans. Mahomed Akber exhibited his double-barrelled pistols to us, which he had worn the previous day, requesting us to put their locks to rights, something being amiss. *Two of the barrels had been recently discharged*, which he endeavoured in a most confused way to account for by saying, that he had been charged by a havildar of the escort, and had fired both barrels at him. Now all the escort had run away without even attempting to charge, the only man who advanced to the rescue having been a Hindoo Jemadar of Chuprassies, who was instantly cut to pieces by the assembled Ghazees. This defence he made without any accusation on our part, betraying the anxiety of a liar to be believed. On the 26th, Capt. Lawrence was taken to the house of Ameenoollah, whence he did not return to us. Capt. Skinner and myself remained in Akber's house until the 30th. During this time we were civilly treated, and conversed with numbers of Affghan gentlemen who came to visit us. Some of them asserted that the Envoy had been murdered by the unruly soldiery. Others could not deny that Akber himself was the assassin. For two or three days we had a fellow-prisoner in poor Sirwar Khan, who had been deceived throughout the

whole matter, and out of whom they were then endeavouring to screw money.   He of course was aware
from his countrymen that, not only had Akber committed the murder, but that he protested to the Ghazees
that he gloried in the deed.   On one occasion a moonshee of Major Pottinger, who had escaped from Cha-
rekhar, named Mohun Beer, came direct from the
presence of Mahomed Akber to visit us.   He told us
that Mahomed Akber had begun to see the impolicy
of having murdered the Envoy, which fact he had just
avowed to him, shedding many tears either of pretended
remorse, or of real vexation, at having committed himself.   On several occasions Mahomed Akber personally, and by deputy, besought Skinner and myself to
give him advice, as to how he was to extricate himself
from the dilemma in which he was placed, more than
once endeavouring to excuse himself for not having
effectually protected the Envoy, by saying that Sir
William had drawn a sword stick upon him.   It seems
that meanwhile the renewed negotiations with Major
Pottinger, who had assumed the Envoy's place in cantonments, had been brought to a head, for on the night
of the 30th, Akber furnished me with an Affghan dress
(Skinner already wore one) and sent us both back
to cantonments.   Several Affghans, with whom I fell
in afterwards, protested to me that they had seen Mahomed Akber shoot the Envoy with his own hand;
amongst them Meerza Báoodeen Khan, who, being an
old acquaintance, always retained a sneaking kindness
for the English.

I am, my dear Eyre, yours very truly,

C. MACKENZIE.

Cabul, 29th July, 1842.

(True copy.)

Vint. Eyre, Lieut. Bengal Artillery.

Letter addressed by CAPTAIN G. ST. P. LAWRENCE,
late Military Secretary to the Envoy, to MAJOR
E. POTTINGER, C.B., *late in charge of the Cabul
Mission.*

SIR,

IN compliance with your request, I have the honour
to detail the particulars of my capture, and of the death
of my ever-to-be-lamented chief.

On the morning of the 23d December, at 11 A.M.,
I received a note from the late Sir W. H. Macnaghten,
warning me to attend, with Captains Trevor and
Mackenzie, an interview he was about to have with
Sirdar Mahomed Akber Khan. Accordingly, with
the above-named officers, at about 12, I accompanied
Sir William, having previously heard him tell Major-
General Elphinstone to have two regiments of infantry
and two guns ready for secret service. In passing
through cantonments, on my observing that there
were more Affghans in cantonments than usual, or
than I deemed safe, the Envoy directed one of his
Affghan attendants to proceed and cause them all to
leave, at the same time remarking, how strange it was
that, although the General was fully acquainted with
the then very critical state of affairs, no preparations
appeared to have been made, adding, " however, it is
all of a piece with the military arrangements throughout the siege." He then said, " There is not enough
of the escort with us," to which I replied, that he had
only ordered eight or ten, but that I had brought
sixteen, and that I would send for the remainder,
which I accordingly did, asking Lieut. Le Geyt to

bring them, and to tell Brigadier Shelton, who had expressed a wish to attend the next interview, that he might
accompany them.   On passing the gate, we observed
some hundreds of armed Affghans within a few yards
of it, on which I called to the officer on duty to get
the reserve under arms, and brought outside to disperse them, and to send to the General to have the
garrison on the alert.   Towards Mahmood Khan's
fort, were a number of armed Affghans, but we
observed none nearer.

The Envoy now told us that he, on the night
previous, had received a proposal from Sirdar Mahomed Akber Khan to which he had agreed, and
that he had every reason to hope it would bring our
present difficulties to an early and happy termination ;
that Mahomed Akber Khan was to give up Naib
Ameenoollah Khan as a prisoner to us, for which
purpose a regiment was to proceed to Mahmood
Khan's fort, and another corps was to occupy the Bala
Hissar.   Sir William then warned me to be ready to
gallop to the king with the intelligence of the approach
of the regiment, and to acquaint him with Akber's
proposal.   On one of us remarking that the scheme
seemed a dangerous one, and asking if he did not
apprehend any treachery, he replied : " Dangerous it
is, but, if it succeeds, it is worth all risks ; the rebels
have not fulfilled even one article of the treaty, and I
have no confidence in them, and if by it we can only
save our honour, all will be well ; at any rate, I would
rather suffer an hundred deaths, than live the last six
weeks over again."   We proceeded to near the usual
spot, and met Sirdar Mahomed Akber Khan, who was
accompanied by several Giljye chiefs, Mahomed Shah

Khan, Dost Mahomed Khan, Khoda Bux Khan, Azad Khan, &c. After the usual salutations, the Envoy presented a valuable horse which Akber had asked for, and which had been that morning purchased from Capt. Grant for 3000 rupees. The Sirdar acknowledged the attention, and expressed his thanks for a handsome brace of double-barrelled pistols which the Envoy had purchased from me, and sent to him, with his carriage and pair of horses, the day before.

The party dismounted, and horse clothes were spread on a small hillock which partially concealed us from cantonments, and which was chosen, they said, as being free from snow. The Envoy threw himself on the bank with Mahomed Akber and Captains Trevor and Mackenzie beside him; I stood behind Sir William till, pressed by Dost Mahomed Khan, I knelt on one knee, having first called the Envoy's attention to the number of Affghans around us, saying that if the subject of the conference was of that secret nature I believed it to be, they had better be removed. He spoke to Mahomed Akber, who replied, " No, they are all in the secret." Hardly had he so said, when I found my arms locked, my pistols and sword wrenched from my belt, and myself forcibly raised from the ground and pushed along, Mahomed Shah Khan, who held me, calling out, " Come along, if you value your life." I turned, and saw the Envoy lying, his head where his heels had been, and his hands locked in Mahomed Akber's, consternation and horror depicted in his countenance. Seeing I could do nothing, I let myself be pulled on by Mahomed Shah Khan. Some shots were fired, and I was hurried to his horse, on which he jumped, telling me to get up

behind, which I did, and we proceeded, escorted by
several armed men who kept off a crowd of Ghazees,
who sprang up on every side shouting for me to be
given up for them to slay, cutting at me with their
swords and knives, and poking me in the ribs with their
guns: they were afraid to fire, lest they should injure
their chief. The horsemen kept them pretty well off,
but not sufficiently so to prevent my being much
bruised. In this manner we hurried towards Mahomed Khan's fort, near which we met some hundreds
of horsemen who were keeping off the Ghazees, who
here were in greater numbers, and more vociferous for
my blood. We, however, reached the fort in safety, and
I was pushed into a small room, Mahomed Shah Khan
returning to the gate of the fort and bringing in Capt.
Mackenzie, whose horse had there fallen. This he did,
receiving a cut through his neencha (Scother coat)
on his arm, which was aimed at that officer, who was
ushered into the room with me much exhausted and
bruised from blows on his head and body. We sat
down with some soldiers who were put over us with
a view to protect us from the mob, who now surrounded
the house, and who till dark continued execrating and
spitting at us, calling on the men to give us up to be
slaughtered.

One produced a hand (European) which appeared
to have been recently cut off; another presented a
blunderbuss, and was about to fire it, when it was
knocked aside by one of our guard. Several of the
Sirdars came in during the day, and told us to be assured that no harm should befal us; that the Envoy
and Trevor were safe in the city (a falsehood, as will
be afterwards seen). Naib Ameenoollah Khan and his

sons also came. The former, in great wrath, said that we either should be, or deserved to be, blown away from a gun. Mahomed Shah Khan and Dost Mahomed Khan begged he would not so talk, and took him out of the room. Towards night food was given to us, and postheens to sleep on : our watches, rings, and silk handkerchiefs were taken from us ; but in all other respects we were unmolested. The followers of Mahomed Shah Khan repeatedly congratulated him on the events of the day, with one exception, viz. an old Moollah, who loudly exclaimed that " the name of the faithful was tarnished, and that in future no belief could be placed in them; that the deed was foul and could never be of advantage to the authors." At midnight we were taken through the city to the house of Mahomed Akbar Khan, who received us courteously, lamenting the occurrences of the day : here we found Captain Skinner, and for the first time heard the dreadful and astounding intelligence of the murder of the Envoy and Captain Trevor, and that our lamented chief's head had been paraded through the city in triumph, and his trunk, after being dragged through the streets, stuck up in the Char Chouk, the most conspicuous part of the town. Captain Skinner told us, that the report was, that on Mahomed Akbar Khan's telling Sir William to accompany him, he refused, resisted, and pushed the Sirdar from him ; that in consequence he was immediately shot and his body cut to pieces by the Ghazees ; that Captain Trevor had been conveyed behind Dost Mahomed Khan as far as Mahomed Khan's fort, where he was cut down, but that his body was not mangled, though carried in triumph through the city. On the following morning (24th)

we (Captain Skinner, Mackenzie, and self) were taken
to Nuwab Zuman Khan's house, escorted by Sultan
Jan and other chiefs, to protect us from the Ghazees;
there we met Captains Conolly and Airey (hostages)
and all the rebel Sirdars assembled in council.   The
Envoy's death was lamented, but his conduct severely
censured, and it was said that now no faith could be
placed in our words.   A new treaty however was discussed, and sent to the General and Major Pottinger,
and towards evening we returned as we came to Mahomed Akber's, where I remained a prisoner, but well
and courteously treated till the morning of the 26th.
when I was sent to Naib Ameenoollah Khan.   On
reaching his house I was ushered into his private
apartment.   The Naib received me kindly, showed me
the Envoy's original letter in reply to Mahomed Akber's
proposition, touching his being made Shah Shujah's
Wuzeer, receiving a lack of rupees on giving the Naib
a prisoner to us, thirty lacks on the final settlement
of the insurrection, &c.   To this the Naib added that
the Envoy had told Mahomed Akbar's cousin that a
lack of rupees would be given for his (Ameenoollah
Khan's) head.   I promptly replied " 'tis false," that
Sir William had never done so, that it was utterly
foreign and repugnant to his nature, and to British
usage.   The Naib expressed himself in strong terms
against the Envoy, contrasting his own fair and open
conduct with that of Sir William.   He told me that
General Elphinstone and Major Pottinger had begged
I might be released, as my presence was necessary to
enable them to prepare bills on India, which it had
been arranged the Sirdars were to get.   After some
delay, consequent on my asking for Captain Macken-

zie to be released with me, and Mahomed Akber's stoutly refusing the release of either of us, I was sent into cantonments on the morning of the 29th, escorted by the Naib's eldest son and a strong party of horse and foot, being disguised as an Affghan for my greater protection. I must here record that nothing could exceed the Naib's kindness and attention to me while under his roof.

I have, &c. &c.

(Signed)   G. St. P. LAWRENCE,

Military Secretary
to the late Envoy and Minister.

Camp Zoudah,
Ten miles south of Tezeen.
10*th May*, 1842.

(True copy.)
Vint. Eyre, Lieut. Bengal Artillery.

CHAP. IX.

BUT what were our troops about all this time? Were no steps taken to rescue the Envoy and his friends from their perilous position? Where was the body-guard which followed them from cantonments?— These questions will naturally occur to all who read the foregoing pages, and I wish it were in my power to render satisfactory answers.

The body-guard had only got a few hundred yards from the gate in their progress to the scene of conference, when they suddenly faced about and came galloping back, several shots being fired at them in their retreat. Lieut. Le Geyt, in passing through the gate, exclaimed that the Envoy had been carried off, and it was believed that, finding his men would not advance to the rescue, he came back for assistance. But the intelligence he brought, instead of rousing our leaders to instant action, seemed to paralyze their faculties; and, although it was evident that our Envoy had been basely entrapped, if not actually murdered,

before our very gate, and though even now crowds
of Affghans, horse and foot, were seen passing and
repassing to and fro in hostile array, between Mahomed's fort and the place of meeting, not a gun
was opened upon them; not a soldier was stirred
from his post; no sortie was apparently even
thought of; treachery was allowed to triumph in
open day; the murder of a British Envoy was
perpetrated in the face and within musket-shot
of a British army; and not only was no effort
made to avenge the dastardly deed, but the body
was left lying on the plain to be mangled and insulted, and finally carried off to be paraded in
the public market by a ruffianly mob of fanatical
barbarians.

Intense was the anxiety and wretched the
suspense felt by all during the rest of the day. A
number of Affghans, who were trafficking in cantonments at the time of the conference, on hearing
the report of fire-arms in that direction, endeavoured to escape, but were detained by the officer
at the gate. No certain tidings regarding the
Envoy could be obtained: many confidently
affirmed that he was alive and unharmed in Mahomed's fort; but Lieut. Warren stoutly maintained that he had kept his eye upon Sir William
from the moment of his leaving the gate, and had
distinctly seen him fall to the ground, and the

Affghans hacking at his body. The agony of his poor wife during this dread interval of suspense may be imagined.

December 24th. — The fate of the Envoy and his three companions remained a mystery, until the arrival of a note from Capt. Conolly notifying his death and that of Capt. Trevor, and the safety of Capts. Lawrence and Mackenzie.

The two latter officers had been that morning escorted to a conference of chiefs at the house of Nuwab Zuman Khan, where the late Envoy's conduct was severely commented on; but his death was nevertheless lamented. The treaty was again discussed; and, after a few alterations and additions had been made, it was sent to Gen. Elphinstone, with an explanation of the breach of faith which had cost the Envoy his life.

Gen. Elphinstone now requested Major Pottinger to assume the office of political agent and adviser, which, though still suffering greatly from his wound, and incapacitated from active bodily exertion, that gallant officer's strict sense of public duty forbade him to decline, although he plainly perceived our affairs to be so irretrievably ruined, as to render the distinction anything but enviable, or likely to improve his hardly-earned fame.

The additional clauses in the treaty now proposed for our renewed acceptance were — 1st. That we should leave behind all our guns, excepting six. 2nd. That we should immediately give up all our treasures. 3rd. That the hostages should be all exchanged for married men, with their wives and families. — The difficulties of Major Pottinger's position will be readily perceived, when it is borne in mind that he had before him the most conclusive evidence of the late Envoy's ill-advised intrigue with Mahomed Akber Khan, in direct violation of that very treaty, which was now once more tendered for consideration.

December 25th. — A more cheerless Christmas-day perhaps never dawned upon British soldiers in a strange land; and the few whom the force of habit urged to exchange the customary greetings of the season, did so with countenances and in tones indicative of anything but merriment. At night there was an alarm, and the drum beat to arms, but nothing occurred of any consequence.

December 26th. — Letters were received from Capt. Mackeson, political agent at Peshawur, announcing the march of strong reinforcements from India. An offer was made by Mahomed Osman Khan to escort us all safe to Peshawur for five lacs of rupees; and shortly after this the

Naib Ameer arrived, with a verbal agreement to certain amendments which had been proposed in the treaty by Major Pottinger. He was accompanied by a Cashmeer merchant and several Hindoo shroffs, for the purpose of negotiating bills to the amount of fourteen lacs of rupees, payable to the several chiefs on the promise of the late Envoy.

Major Pottinger being altogether averse from the payment of this money, and indeed strongly opposed to any treaty binding the Indian government to a course of policy, which it might find inconvenient to adopt, a council of war was convened by the General, consisting of himself, Brigadiers Shelton and Anquetil, Col. Chambers, Capt. Bellew, Assist. Qr.-Mast.-Gen., and Capt. Grant, Assist. Adjt.-Gen. In the presence of this council, Major Pottinger declared his conviction that no confidence could be placed in any treaty formed with the Affghan chiefs; that, under such circumstances, to bind the hands of government, by promising to evacuate the country, and to restore the deposed Ameer, and to waste moreover so much public money, merely to save our own lives and property, would be inconsistent with the duty we owed our country and the government we served; and that the only honourable course would be either to hold out to the

last at Cabul, or to force our immediate retreat
to Jellalabad.

This, however, the officers composing the
council, one and all, declared to be impracticable,
owing to the want of provisions, the surrender of
the surrounding forts, and the insuperable difficulties of the road at the present season ; they
therefore deemed it preferable to pay any sum
of money, rather than sacrifice the whole force in
a hopeless prolongation of hostilities. It was
accordingly determined, *nem. con.*, that Major
Pottinger should at once renew the negotiations
which had been commenced by Sir William
Macnaghten, and that the sums promised to the
chiefs by that functionary previous to his murder
should be paid.

Major Pottinger's objections being thus over-
ruled, the tendered treaty was forthwith accepted,
and a requisition was made for the release of
Capt. Lawrence, whose presence was necessary to
prepare the bills on India. Four married hostages, with their wives and children, being required by the chiefs, a circular was sent round, to
ascertain if that number would volunteer to remain, a salary of 2000 rupees per month being
guaranteed to each, as an inducement.

Such, however, was the horror entertained of
Affghan treachery since the late tragical occur-

rence, that some officers went so far as to say they would sooner shoot their wives at once, than commit them to the charge of men, who had proved themselves devoid of common honour and humanity. There were, in fact, but one or two who consented to stay, if the General considered that by so doing they would benefit the public service.

December 27th. — The chiefs were informed that it was contrary to the usages of war to give up ladies as hostages, and that the General could not consent to an arrangement, which would brand him with perpetual disgrace in his own country.

December 29th. — The Naib Ameer came in from the city with Capt. Lawrence and the shroffs, when the bills were prepared without farther delay. Capts. Drummond, Walsh, Warburton, and Webb, having been accepted as hostages, were sent to join Capts. Conolly and Airey at the house of Nuwab Zuman Khan. A portion of the sick and wounded, amongst whom was Lieut. Haughton of the Goorkha regiment, were likewise conveyed to the city, and placed under the protection of the chiefs. Three of the Shah's guns, with the greater portion of our treasure, were made over during the day, much to the evident disgust of the soldiery.

December 30th. — The remainder of the sick

went into the city, Lieut. Evans, H. M.'s 44th
foot, being placed in command, and Dr. Campbell, 54th N. I., with Dr. Berwick of the Mission,
in medical charge of the whole. Two more of
the Shah's guns were given up. It snowed hard
the whole day. A crowd of armed Giljyes and
Ghazees took up a threatening position close to
the eastern gate, and even attempted to force an
entrance into cantonments. Much annoyance
was daily experienced from these people, who
were in the habit of plundering the peaceable
dealers, who flocked in from the city with grain
and forage, the moment they issued from the cantonments; they even committed frequent assaults
on our Sepoys, and orders to fire on them on such
occasions were repeatedly solicited in vain, although it was well known that the chiefs themselves advised us to do so, and the General had
given Brigadier Shelton positive instructions to
that effect, whenever circumstances might render
it advisable. The consequence was that our
soldiers were daily constrained to endure the most
insulting and contemptuous taunts and treatment,
from fellows whom a single charge of bayonets
would have scattered like chaff, but who were
emboldened by the apparent tameness of our
troops, which they doubtless attributed to the
want of common pluck, rather than to the re-

straints of discipline.   Capts. Mackenzie and
Skinner obtained their release this evening, the
latter officer having, since the outbreak of the
rebellion, passed through some curious adventures,
in the disguise of an Affghan female.

January 5th. — Affairs continued in the same
unsettled state until this date.   The chiefs postponed our departure from day to day on divers
pretexts.   It had been agreed that Nuwab Jubbar
Khan should escort us to Jellalabad with about
2000 followers, who were to be entertained for
that purpose.

It is supposed that, up to the very last, the
majority of chiefs doubted the reality of our intention to depart : and many, fearful of the civil
discords for which our retreat would be the
signal, would have gladly detained us at Cabul.
Attempts were made continually by Akber Khan
to wean the Hindoostanees from their allegiance,
and to induce them to desert.   Numerous cau-
tions were received from various well-wishers, to
place no confidence in the professions of the
chiefs, who had sworn together to accomplish our
entire destruction.   Shah Shoojah himself sent
more than one solemn warning, and, finding we
were bent on taking our own course, used his
utmost endeavours to persuade Lady Macnaghten
to take advantage of his protection in the Bala

Hissar. He also appealed to Brigadier Anquetil, who commanded the Shah's force, " if it were well to forsake him in the hour of need, and to deprive him of the aid of that force, which he had hitherto been taught to consider as his own ?" All was however unavailing. The General and his council of war had determined that go we must, and go we accordingly did.

In the foregoing chapters I have offered what I honestly believe to be a faithful narration of the dismal train of events which preceded the evacuation of Cabul, and the abandonment of Shah Shoojah, by the British army. In taking a retrospective view of those unprecedented occurrences, it is evident that our reverses may be mainly attributed to a lack of ordinary foresight and penetration on the part of the chief military and civil authorities, on their first entering on the occupation of this country; a country whose innumerable fortified strongholds and difficult mountain passes, in the hands of a proud and war-like population, never really subdued nor recon-ciled to our rule, though unable to oppose the march of a disciplined army through their land, ought to have induced a more than common degree of vigilance and circumspection, in making adequate provision against any such popular outbreak as might have been anticipated, and did actually occur. But, instead of applying his undeniable talents to the completion of that conquest, which gained him an illustrious title and a wide renown, Lord Keane contented himself with the superficial success, which attended his progress through a country hitherto untraversed by an European army, since the classic days of Alexander the Great; he hurried off, with too great eagerness to enjoy the applause which awaited him in England, and left to his successors the far more arduous task of securing in their grasp the unwieldy prize, of which he had obtained the nominal possession.

On his return to India, Lord Keane took with him a large portion of the Bengal force, with which he had arrived at Cabul; the *whole* of the Bombay troops made a simultaneous homeward movement; and the army, with which he had entered Affghanistan, was thus reduced to a miserable moiety, before any steps had been taken to guard against surprise by the erection of a stronghold on the approved principles of modern warfare, or the establishment of a line of military posts to keep open our communications with India, on which country the army must ne-

cessarily for a long time have been entirely dependent for the munitions of war. The distance
from Cabul to Ferozepore, our nearest Indian
station, is about 600 miles. Between Cabul and
Peshawur occur the stupendous and dangerous
defiles of Khoord-Cabul, Tezeen, Purreedurrah,
Jugdulluk, and Kyber, throughout whose whole
extent food and forage are procurable only at
long intervals, and even then with much difficulty.

From Peshawur to Ferozepore is the Punjab,
or country of the Seiks, traversed by five great
rivers, and occupied by a powerful nation, on
whose pacific professions no reliance could be
placed. Along this extended line of communication Lord Keane established but one small solitary post, in the fort of Ali Musjed, in the heart
of the Khyber pass. He left behind him, in fact,
an army, whose isolated position and reduced
strength offered the strongest possible temptation
to a proud and restless race, to rally their scattered
tribes in one grand effort to regain their lost
independence.

In Lord Keane's successors may be seen the
same disposition to be too easily satisfied with the
outward semblance of tranquillity. Another
brigade was ere long withdrawn from a force
already insufficient for any great emergency ; nor

was their position for *holding* in subjection a
vanquished people much improved by their establishment in an ill-situated and ill-constructed
cantonment, with their commissariat stores separated from their lines of defence. To the
latter mentioned error may be mainly attributed
the evacuation of Cabul and the destruction
of the army; for there can be no doubt that,
notwithstanding all the difficulties of our position,
and the incompetence of our commanders, had the
cantonments been well supplied with provisions,
the troops could have easily held out until the
arrival of reinforcements from India. The real
cause of our retreat was, beyond all question,
famine. We were not *driven,* but *starved,* out of
Cabul; and although, in my relation of our military transactions, I have been compelled by a
regard to truth unwillingly to record proceedings
which must be condemned by all, I do not the
less feel most sensibly that every allowance ought
in common justice to be made for men, who
from the very commencement of the conflict, saw
the combined horrors of starvation and a rigorous
winter frowning in their face, — no succours within
reach, — their retreat cut off, — and all their
sanguinary efforts either altogether fruitless, or at
best deferring for a few short days the ruin which
on every side threatened to overwhelm them.

In connection with this subject, I may be excused for quoting, in conclusion, the powerful reasoning of a recent writer in the *Bombay Times* : —

" When a soldier finds that his every movement is directed by a master mind; that, when he is apparently thrust into the greatest danger, he finds, in truth, his greatest security; that his march to engage an apparently superior force is not a wild sacrifice, but the result of a well-calculated plan; when he knows that, however appearances may be, he is sure to come off with honour, for his brethren in arms are already in progress to assist him, and will not fail to be forthcoming at the hour appointed ; when he sees that there is a watchful eye over him, providing for all his wants, assisting him to overcome all his difficulties, and enabling him to reap the fruit of all his successes ; when he finds that even retreat is but a preparation for victory, and, as if guided by Providence, all his movements, though to him incomprehensible, are sure to prove steps to some great end ;— when the soldier finds this, he rises and lies down in security, and there is no danger which he will not brave. But when, in every thing they undertake, they find the reverse of the picture I have drawn; when they are marched, as they imagine to glory, but find it is only to slaughter; when even victory brings no fruit, and retreat they discover to be flight; when the support they hope for comes not, and they find their labours to be without end or purpose; when the provisions they look for daily are issued to them no more, and they see all their efforts paralysed; when an army of thousands finds itself delivered, bound hand and foot, into the hands of a man without system, foresight, or military knowledge enough for a sergeant of police, the stoutest heart will fail, the bravest sink; for the soldier knows that, do what he will, his efforts can only end in ruin and dishonour."

"The camp followers with the public and private baggage . . .
could not be prevented from mixing themselves up with the troops,
to the utter confusion of the whole column."

CHAP. X.

THE RETREAT OF THE ARMY, AND ITS ANNIHILATION.

January 6th.—AT last the fatal morning dawned, which was to witness the departure of the Cabul force from the cantonments, in which it had sustained a two months' siege, to encounter the miseries of a winter march through a country of perhaps unparalleled difficulty, where every mountain defile, if obstinately defended by a determined enemy, must inevitably prove the grave of hundreds.

Dreary indeed was the scene, over which, with drooping spirits and dismal forebodings, we had to bend our unwilling steps. Deep snow covered every inch of mountain and plain with one un-spotted sheet of dazzling white, and so intensely bitter was the cold, as to penetrate and defy the defences of the warmest clothing.

No signs of the promised escort appeared: but at an early hour the preparations commenced for our march. A cut was made through the eastern rampart, to open an additional passage for the troops and baggage, a sufficient number of gun-

waggons and platform planks were taken down
to the river for the formation of a temporary
bridge, and every available camel and yaboo (the
whole amounting to 2000) was laden with military stores, commissariat supplies, and such small
proportion of camp-equipage as was indispensably
necessary to shelter the troops in a climate of
extraordinary rigour.

The strength of the whole force at this time
was, so far as can now be ascertained, very nearly
as follows : —

1 troop of horse artillery - -	90	} 690 Europeans.
H. M.'s 44th foot - - -	600	
5th regt. light cavalry, 2 squad. -	260	
5th Shah's irreg. do. (Anderson's)	500	
Skinner's horse, 1 ressala -	70	} 970 cavalry.
4th irreg. do. 1 do. - -	70	
Mission escort, or body-guard -	70	
5th native infantry - - -	700	
37th do. - - - -	600	
54th do. - - - -	650	
6th Shah's infantry - - -	600	} 2840.
Sappers and miners - - -	20	
Shah's do. - - - -	240	
Half the mountain train - -	30	
Total -	4500 fighting men.	

6 horse artillery guns.
3 mountain train do.

Besides the above, the camp followers amounted,
at a very moderate computation, to about 12,000
men, besides women and children.   These proved

from the very first mile a serious clog upon our movements, and were, indeed, the main cause of our subsequent misfortunes. It is to be devoutly hoped that every future commander-in-chief of the Indian army will adopt decisive measures, to prevent a force employed on field service from being ever again afflicted with such a curse.

The order of march was as follows : —

H. M.'s 44th foot - - - -	The advance, under Brigadier Anquetil.
Sappers and miners - - -	
Irreg. horse, 1 squad. - - -	
3 mountain train guns - - -	
The escort, with the ladies - -	Main column, under Brigadier Shelton.
The invalids and sick - - -	
2 horse artillery guns - - -	
Anderson's irreg. horse - - -	
37th native infantry, with treasure -	
5th native infantry, with baggage -	
54th native infantry - - -	Rear-guard, under Col. Chambers.
6th Shah's infantry - - -	
5th light cavalry - - - -	
4 horse artillery guns - - -	

All being ready at 9 A. M., the advance commenced moving out. At this time not a single Affghan was to be seen in any direction, and the peaceable aspect of affairs gave rise to strong hopes that the chiefs intended to remain true to their engagements.

At 10 A. M. a message was brought from Nuwab Jubbar Khan, requesting us to defer our departure another day, as his escort was not yet ready to accompany us.   By this time, however, the greater part of the force was in motion, and a crowd of Affghans, who had issued from the village of Beymaroo, impatient for plunder, had forced their way into the northern cantonment, or mission compound (which, owing to some mistake, had been evacuated too soon by the Shah's 6th infantry), and were busily engaged in the work of pillage and destruction.   The advance was delayed for upwards of an hour at the river, having found the temporary bridge incomplete ; and it was noon ere the whole had crossed over, leaving a clear road for the main column to follow.

The order of march, in which the troops started, was, however, soon lost, and the camp followers with the public and private baggage, once out of cantonments, could not be prevented from mixing themselves up with the troops, to the utter confusion of the whole column.

The main body, with its long train of laden camels, continued to pour out of the gate until the evening, by which time thousands of Affghans, the majority of whom were fanatical Ghazees, thronged the whole area of cantonments, rending the air with their exulting cries, and committing every kind of atrocity.   The rear-guard, being unable to restrain them, was obliged to provide for its own safety by taking up a position outside, on the plain, where a great quantity of the baggage had been brought to a stand-still at the canal (within 150 yards of the gate), whose slippery sides afforded no safe footing for the beasts of burden. The bridge across the river, being by this time impracticable, occasioned additional delay.

The Affghans, who had hitherto been too busily engaged in the work of plunder and destruction to take much notice of the troops, now began to line the ramparts, and annoy them with a mischievous fire of juzails, under which many fell; and it became necessary, for the preservation of those who remained, to spike and abandon two of the horse artillery guns.

Night had now closed around; but the Ghazees, having fired the residency and almost every other building in the cantonment, the conflagration illuminated the surrounding country for several miles, presenting a spectacle of fearful sublimity. In the mad fervour of their religious zeal, these ignorant fanatics even set fire to the gun-carriages belonging to the various pieces of ordnance, which we had left in position round the works, of whose use the Affghan chiefs were thus luckily deprived. The General had been often urged to destroy these

guns, rather than suffer them to fall into the
enemy's hands, but he considered that it would
have been a breach of the treaty to do so. Before the rear-guard commenced its march, Lieut.
Hardyman of the 5th light cavalry, with fifty rank
and file, were stretched lifeless on the snow.
Much baggage was abandoned at starting, and
much was plundered on the road. Scores of worn-
out Sepoys and camp followers lined the way,
having sat down in despair to perish in the snow.
It was 2 A. M. ere the rear-guard reached camp
at Bygram, a distance of only five miles. Here
all was confusion. The tents had been pitched
without the slightest regard to regularity, those
of different regiments being huddled together in
one intricate mass, mixed up with baggage, camp-
followers, camels, and horses, in a way which
beggars description. The flimsy canvass of the
soldiers' tents was but a poor protection from the
cold, which towards morning became more and
more intense; and thousands of poor wretched
creatures were obliged to lie down on the bare
snow, without either shelter, fire, or food. Several
died during the night; amongst whom was an
European conductor of ordnance.

About twenty juzailchees, who still held faithfully by Capt. Mackenzie, suffered less than the
rest, owing to their systematic mode of pro-

ceeding. Their first step on reaching the ground was to clear a small space from the snow, where they then laid themselves down in a circle, closely packed together, with their feet meeting in the centre; all the warm clothing they could muster among them being spread equally over the whole. By these simple means sufficient animal warmth was generated to preserve them from being frost-bitten; and Capt. Mackenzie, who himself shared their homely bed, declared that he had felt scarcely any inconvenience from the cold. It was different with our Sepoys and camp followers, who, having had no former experience of such hardships, were ignorant how they might best provide against them, and the proportion of those who escaped, without suffering in some degree from frost-bites, was very small. Yet this was but the *beginning* of sorrows!

January 7th. — At 8 A.M. the force moved off in the reverse order of yesterday — if that could be called *order* which consisted of a mingled mob of soldiers, camp-followers, and baggage-cattle, preserving not even the faintest semblance of that regularity and discipline, on which depended our only chance of escape from the dangers which threatened us. Even at this early stage of the retreat scarcely one half of the Sepoys were fit for duty; hundreds had, from sheer inability to

K 5

keep their ranks, joined the non-combatants, and thus increased the confusion. As for the Shah's 6th inf., it was no where to be found; only a few straggling files were perceptible here and there; and it was generally believed that the majority of the regiment had absconded during the night to Cabul.

At starting, large clods of hardened snow adhered so firmly to the hoofs of our horses, that a chisel and hammer would have been requisite to dislodge them. The very air we breathed froze in its passage out of the mouth and nostrils, forming a coating of small icicles on our moustaches and beards.

The advance proceeded onward without molestation, though numerous small bodies of Affghan horse and foot were observed hanging about our flanks, and moving in a parallel direction with ourselves. These were at first supposed to form a part of our escort, but the mistake was soon discovered by their attacking the rear-guard, commanded by Brigadier Anquetil, consisting of H. M.'s 44th, Lieut. Green's mountain train guns, and a squadron of irregular horse. Much baggage fell into the enemy's hands, who, though in some degree kept in check by the guns, exhibited a bold front, and maintained a harassing fire on our troops, whose movements were terribly crip-

pled by the disorderly multitude that thronged
the road in front. The latter being for several
minutes brought to a stand-still by a deep water-
cut which intersected the road, the mountain-train
guns endeavoured to pass clear of them by making
a short detour, in doing which they got separated
from the infantry, and — one happening at this
unlucky moment to upset — the enemy seized the
opportunity to rush forward and capture them,
before H. M.'s 44th, who saw too late their
awkward predicament, could render effectual assistance.

Their re-capture might still have been effected,
could the soldiers have been prevailed upon to
make the attempt, a gallant example being shown
them by Lieut. Green and his few artillerymen,
who made a sudden charge upon the foe and
spiked the guns, but, not being supported, were
obliged a second time to abandon them. Lieut.
White, the Adjutant of H. M.'s 44th, received a
severe wound through the face on this occasion.

Brigadier Anquetil now sent to the front for
reinforcements, which, however, it was found impracticable to furnish, from the crowded state of
the road. The Affghan horse shortly after this
charged into the very midst of the column of
baggage, and carried off large quantities of plunder, creating the greatest confusion and dismay.

Numbers fell from wounds, and still greater numbers from mere bodily weakness produced by cold, fasting, and fatigue. It was found necessary to spike and abandon two more horse-artillery guns, which the horses were found perfectly incapable of dragging any further through the deep snow.

On the arrival of the advance at Bootkhak, the General, having been informed that the rear was in danger of being entirely cut off, ordered a halt, and sent back all the troops that could be spared, together with the two remaining guns, to drive off the enemy, who had now assembled in great numbers in the rear, and were proceeding to crown some heights on the right commanding the road. This was, however, prevented by our troops under Brigadier Shelton, who took possession of the nearer heights, and kept the enemy in check for upwards of an hour. On this occasion, Lieut. Shaw, of the 54th N. I., was wounded severely in the thigh. Meanwhile Capt. Skinner had fallen in with a follower of Mahomed Akber Khan, from whom having learned that the chief was encamped near at hand, he accompanied the man to his master's presence. Mahomed Akber now informed Captain Skinner that he had been sent by the chiefs to escort us to Jellalabad, and declared that we had been attacked in consequence of having marched contrary to their wishes. He insisted on our halting at Bootkhak till the following morning, in which case he would provide food, forage, and firewood for the troops ; but he said that he should expect six hostages to insure our not marching beyond Tezeen, before tidings should be received of Gen. Sale's evacuation of Jellalabad, for which an order had been already despatched to that officer, in compliance with the stipulations of the treaty.

These terms having been agreed to, the firing ceased for the present, and the force came to a halt on some high ground near the entrance of the Khoord-Cabul pass, having in two days accomplished a distance of only ten miles from Cabul.

Here, again, the confusion soon became indescribable. Suffice it to say that an immense multitude of from 14,000 to 16,000 men, with several hundred cavalry horses and baggage cattle, were closely jammed together in one monstrous, unmanageable, jumbling mass. Night again closed over us, with its attendant train of horrors, — starvation, cold, exhaustion, death ; and of all deaths I can imagine none more agonising than that, where a nipping frost tortures every sensitive limb, until the tenacious spirit itself sinks under the exquisite extreme of human suffering.

January 8th. — At an early hour the treacherous

Affghans again commenced to molest us with their fire, and several hundreds having assembled in hostile array to the south of the camp, the troops were drawn up in expectation of an attack. Major Thain, putting himself at the head of the 44th foot, and exhorting the men to follow him, led them boldly on to the attack; but the enemy did not think proper to await the shock of bayonets, and effected a hasty retreat. In this business it is satisfactory to be able to state that H. M.'s 44th foot behaved with a resolution and gallantry worthy of British soldiers, and plainly proved that, under an able and judicious leader, they could yet redeem their injured reputation.

Capt. Skinner again went to communicate with Mahomed Akber Khan, who demanded that Major Pottinger and Capts. Lawrence and Mackenzie should immediately be made over to him, which was accordingly done, and hostilities again ceased; the Sirdar promising to send forward some influential men to clear the pass from the Giljyes, who occupied it, and were lying in wait for our approach. Once more the living mass of men and animals was in motion. At the entrance of the pass an attempt was made to separate the troops from the non-combatants, which was but partially successful, and created considerable delay.

The rapid effects of two nights' exposure to the frost in disorganising the force can hardly be conceived. It had so nipped the hands and feet of even the strongest men, as to completely prostrate their powers and incapacitate them for service; even the cavalry, who suffered less than the rest, were obliged to be lifted on their horses. In fact only a few hundred serviceable fighting men remained.

The idea of threading the stupendous pass before us, in the face of an armed tribe of bloodthirsty barbarians, with such a dense irregular multitude, was frightful, and the spectacle then presented by that waving sea of animated beings, the majority of whom a few fleeting hours would transform into a line of lifeless carcasses to guide the future traveller on his way, can never be forgotten by those who witnessed it. We had so often been deceived by Affghan professions, that little or no confidence was placed in the present truce; and we commenced our passage through the dreaded pass in no very sanguine temper of mind. This truly formidable defile is about five miles from end to end, and is shut in on either hand by a line of lofty hills, between whose precipitous sides the sun at this season could dart but a momentary ray. Down the centre dashed a mountain torrent, whose impetuous course the

frost in vain attempted to arrest, though it succeeded in lining the edges with thick layers of ice,
over which the snow lay consolidated in slippery
masses, affording no very easy footing for our
jaded animals.   This stream we had to cross and
recross about eight-and-twenty times.   As we
proceeded onwards, the defile gradually narrowed,
and the Giljyes were observed hastening to crown
the heights in considerable force.   A hot fire was
opened on the advance, with whom were several
ladies, who, seeing their only chance was to keep
themselves in rapid motion, galloped forward at
the head of all, running the gauntlet of the
enemy's bullets, which whizzed in hundreds about
their ears, until they were fairly out of the pass.
Providentially the whole escaped, with the exception of Lady Sale, who received a slight
wound in the arm.   It ought, however, to be
mentioned, that several of Mahomed Akber's
chief adherents, who had preceded the advance,
exerted themselves strenuously to keep down the
fire; but nothing could restrain the Giljyes, who
seemed fully determined that nobody should in-
terfere to disappoint them of their prey.   Onward
moved the crowd into the thickest of the fire, and
fearful was the slaughter that ensued.   An universal panic speedily prevailed, and thousands,
seeking refuge in flight, hurried forward to the

front, abandoning baggage, arms, ammunition, women, and children, regardless for the moment of every thing but their own lives.

The rear-guard, consisting of H. M.'s 44th and 54th N. I., suffered severely; and at last, finding that delay was only destruction, they followed the general example, and made the best of their way to the front. Another horse-artillery gun was abandoned, and the whole of its artillerymen slain. Capt. Anderson's eldest girl, and Capt. Boyd's youngest boy, fell into the hands of the Affghans. It is supposed that 3000 souls perished in the pass, amongst whom were Capt. *Paton,* Assist.-Qr.-Mast.-Gen.; and Lieut. *St. George,* 37th N. I.—Majors *Griffiths,* 37th N. I., and *Scott,* H. M.'s 44th; Capts. *Bott,* 5th cavalry, and *Troup,* Brigadier-Major Shah's force, Dr. *Cardew* and Lieut. *Sturt,* engineers, were wounded, the latter mortally. This fine young officer had nearly cleared the defile when he received his wound, and would have been left on the ground to be hacked to pieces by the Ghazees, who followed in the rear to complete the work of slaughter, but for the generous intrepidity of Lieut. Mein of H. M.'s 13th light infantry, who, on learning what had befallen him, went back to his succour, and stood by him for several minutes, at the imminent risk of his own life, vainly entreating aid from the passers by. He was at length joined by Sergt. Deane of the Sappers, with whose assistance he dragged his friend on a quilt through the remainder of the pass, when he succeeded in mounting him on a miserable pony, and conducted him in safety to camp, where the unfortunate officer lingered till the following morning, and was the only man of the whole force who received Christian burial. Lieut. Mein was himself at this very time suffering from a dangerous wound in the head received in the previous October, and his heroic disregard of self, and fidelity to his friend in the hour of danger, are well deserving of a record in the annals of British valour and virtue.

On the force reaching Khoord-Cabul, snow began to fall, and continued till morning. Only four small tents were saved, of which one belonged to the General: two were devoted to the ladies and children, and one was given up to the sick; but an immense number of poor wounded wretches wandered about the camp destitute of shelter, and perished during the night. Groans of misery and distress assailed the ear from all quarters. We had ascended to a still colder climate than we had left behind, and were without tents, fuel, or food: the snow was the only bed for all, and of many, ere morning, it proved the *winding-sheet*.

It is only marvellous that any should have survived that fearful night!

January 9th. — Another morning dawned,
awakening thousands to increased misery; and
many a wretched survivor cast looks of envy at
his comrades, who lay stretched beside him in the
quiet sleep of death.   Daylight was the signal for
a renewal of that confusion, which attended every
movement of the force.   The General had intended us to march at 10 A. M., but a large portion
of the troops, with nearly all the camp, followers,
moved off without orders at 8 A. M., and had advanced about a mile from the camp, when they
were recalled by the General, in consequence of
a communication from Mahomed Akber Khan,
who promised to use every endeavour to furnish
us with supplies; but strongly recommended us
to halt until he could make some proper arrangements for escorting us down safely.   There can
be no doubt that the general feeling in camp
was adverse to a halt, there being scarcely even a
native soldier, who did not plainly perceive that
our only chance of escape consisted in moving on
as fast as possible.   This additional delay, therefore, and prolongation of their sufferings in the
snow, of which one more march would have carried them clear, made a very unfavourable impression on the minds of the native soldiery, who now

for the first time began very generally to entertain the idea of deserting ; nor is it at all as-
tonishing that these symptoms should have first
developed themselves amongst the Shah's native
cavalry, who were, for the most part, exceedingly
young soldiers, and foresaw full well the fatal
result of all these useless and pernicious delays.
The love of life is strong in every breast.

These men had hitherto behaved remarkably
well, notwithstanding the numerous efforts that
had been made to detach them from their duty ;
and, if their fealty at last gave place to the in-
stinct of self-preservation, be it remembered in
their favour, that it was not until the position of
the force, of which they formed a part, had become altogether desperate beyond the reach of
cure.

Towards noon Capt. Skinner arrived in camp
with a proposition from Mahomed Akber Khan
that all the widowed ladies and married families,
whose destitute situation in camp rendered them
objects of universal pity and sympathy, should at
once be made over to his protection, to preserve
them from further hardships and dangers ; in this
case he promised to escort them down safely,
keeping them one day's march in rear of the
army. The General, though not himself disposed
to place much confidence in Mahomed Akber's

friendly professions, was strongly recommended by Capt. Skinner to trust him on the present occasion, as he felt assured that such a mark of confidence would be attended with happy results to the whole force.　Anxious at all events to save the ladies and children from further suffering, the General gave his consent to the arrangement, and told Capt. Skinner to prepare all the married officers and ladies to depart immediately with a party of Affghan horse, who were in waiting to receive them.　His intention also was that all the wounded officers in camp should have had the option of availing themselves of the same opportunity to seek Mahomed Akber's protection; but the others were hurried off by the Affghans before this had become generally known, and only two were in time to join them.*

Up to this time scarcely one of the ladies had tasted a meal since leaving Cabul.　Some had infants a few days old at the breast, and were unable to stand without assistance.　Others were so far advanced in pregnancy, that, under ordinary cir-

---

* Capt. Troup, Brigadier-major Shah's force, and Lieut. Mein, H. M.'s 13th Light Inf., who went as Lady Sale's protector.

Lieuts. Waller and Eyre were likewise suffering from severe and painful wounds received in action at Cabul, which totally disabled them from active service.

cumstances, a walk across a drawing-room would have been an exertion; yet these helpless women, with their young families, had already been obliged to rough it on the backs of camels, and on the tops of the baggage yaboos : those who had a horse to ride, or were capable of sitting on one, were considered fortunate indeed. Most had been without shelter since quitting the cantonment — their servants had nearly all deserted or been killed — and, with the exception of Lady Macnaghten and Mrs. Trevor, they had lost all their baggage, having nothing in the world left but the clothes on their backs ; *those,* in the case of some of the invalids, consisted of *night dresses* in which they had started from Cabul in their litters. Under such circumstances a few more hours would probably have seen some of them stiffening corses. The offer of Mahomed Akber was consequently their only chance of preservation. The husbands, better clothed and hardy, would have infinitely preferred taking their chance with the troops ; but where is the man who would prefer his own safety, when he thought he could by his presence assist and console those near and dear to him?

It is not therefore wonderful that, from persons so circumstanced, the General's proposal should have met with little opposition, although it was a matter of serious doubt whether the whole were not rushing into the very jaws of death, by placing themselves at the mercy of a man, who had so lately imbrued his hands in the blood of a British Envoy, whom he had lured to destruction by similar professions of peace and good-will.

But whatever may have been the secret intent of Akber's heart, he was at this time our professed friend and ally, having undertaken to escort the whole force to Jellalabad in safety. Whatever suspicions, therefore, have been entertained of his hypocrisy, it was not in the character of an *enemy* that he gained possession of the married families; on the contrary, he stood pledged for their safe escort to Jellalabad, no less than for that of the army to which they belonged; and by their unwarrantable detention as prisoners, no less than by the treacherous massacre of the force, he broke the universal law of nations, and was guilty of an unpardonable breach of faith. Shortly after the departure of the married families, it was discovered that the troopers of the Shah's irregular cavalry and of the mission escort were deserting in great numbers, having been enticed away, as was supposed, by Mahomed Akber, to whom a message of remonstrance was in consequence sent. He assured the General, in reply, that not only would he refrain from enticing the men away, but

that every future deserter from our camp should
be shot.

Meanwhile a large body of Affghan horse had
been observed in the vicinity of camp, in company
with the cavalry deserters; and, fears being entertained that it was their design to attack the camp,
a general parade of the troops was ordered for the
purpose of repelling them. The 44th foot at this
time was found to muster 100 files, and the native
infantry regiments, on an average, about 60 files
each. Of the Irregular Horse not above 100
effective troopers remained, and the 5th Light
Cavalry, though more faithful to their salt, had
been reduced by casualties to about 70 fighting
men. On the arrival of Mahomed Akber's answer
to the General's message, the opportunity was
taken of the troops being paraded, to explain to
them its purport, and to warn them that every
man, who might be discovered deserting, would be
shot. At this very time, a Chuprassie of the
mission, being caught in the act, was instantly
shot, as an example to the rest, by order of the
General, and the crime thus received a salutary
check. Capt. Mackay, having been chosen to
convey to Gen. Sale a fresh order for the evacuation of Jellalabad, was sent over in the evening
to the Sirdar with that view. The promises of
Mahomed Akber to provide food and fuel were

unfulfilled, and another night of starvation and cold consigned more victims to a miserable death.

January 10*th.* — At break of day all was again confusion, the troops and camp-followers crowding promiscuously to the front, so soon as the orders for a march were given, every one dreading, above all things, to be left in the rear.   The European soldiers were now almost the only efficient men left, the Hindoostanees having all suffered more or less from the effects of frost in their hands and feet; few were able even to hold a musket, much less to pull a trigger.; in fact, the prolonged delay in the snow had paralysed the mental and bodily powers of the strongest men, rendering them incapable of any useful exertion.   Hope seemed to have died in every breast.   The wildness of terror was exhibited in every countenance.

The advanced guard (consisting of H. M.'s 44th foot, the sole remaining horse-artillery gun, and about fifty troopers of the 5th cavalry) having managed, with much difficulty, to push their way to the front, proceeded a couple of miles without molestation, as far as a narrow gorge between the precipitous spurs of two hills, through which flowed a small stream.   Towards this point numbers of Affghan foot had been observed hurrying, with the evident intention of opposing the passage

L

of the troops, and were now found to occupy the
height on the right in considerable force. No
sooner did the advance approach within shot, than
the enemy, securely perched on their post of vantage, commenced the attack, pouring a destructive fire upon the crowded column, as it slowly
drew nigh to the fatal spot. Fresh numbers fell
at every volley, and the gorge was soon choked
with the dead and dying : the unfortunate Sepoys,
seeing no means of escape, and driven to utter
desperation, cast away their arms and accoutrements, which only clogged their movements without contributing to their defence, and along with
the camp-followers fled for their lives. The Affghans now rushed down upon their helpless and
unresisting victims sword in hand, and a general
massacre took place. The last small remnant of
the Native Infantry regiments were here scattered
and destroyed; and the public treasure, with all
the remaining baggage, fell into the hands of the
enemy. Meanwhile, the advance, after pushing
through the Tungee with great loss, had reached
Kubbur-i-Jubbar, about five miles ahead, without more opposition. Here they halted to enable
the rear to join, but from the few stragglers who
from time to time came up, the astounding truth
was brought to light, that, of all who had that
morning marched from Khoord-Cabul, they were

almost the sole survivors, nearly the whole of the main and rear columns having been cut off and destroyed. About 50 horse artillerymen, with one twelve-pounder howitzer, 70 files H.M.'s 44th, and 150 cavalry troopers, now composed the whole Cabul force ; but, notwithstanding the slaughter and dispersion that had taken place, the camp-followers still formed a considerable body.

The approach of a party of Affghan horse induced the General to draw up his little force in line, preparatory to an expected attack ; but on its being ascertained to be Mahomed Akber Khan and his followers, Captain Skinner was despatched to remonstrate with him on the attack on our troops, after a treaty had been entered into, and their safety guaranteed.

In reply, he expressed his regret at what had occurred, but said that, notwithstanding all his endeavours, he found it impossible to restrain the Giljyes, who were in such a state of excitement as to be beyond the control even of their own chiefs. As a last resource, he recommended that the few remaining troops should lay down their arms, and place themselves entirely under his safeguard, in which case he could ensure their safe escort to Jellalabad ; but that as the camp-followers still amounted to some thousands, and far outnumbered his own people, there was no alternative but to leave them to their fate. To these terms the General could not bring himself to consent, and the desperate march was resumed. Here Captain Mackay rejoined the troops, as the Sirdar considered it impossible for him at present to make his way safe to Jellalabad.

About five more miles led down the steep descents of the Huft Kotul, into a narrow defile, or confined bed of a mountain stream.

A ghastly sight here met the eye, the ground being strewn with the bodies of a number of camp-followers, with whom were several wounded officers and soldiers, who, having gone on ahead of the column, were attacked on reaching the foot of the hill, and massacred. The heights commanding the defile (which was about three miles long) were found crowned with the enemy. Mahomed Akber and his train had taken a short cut over the hills to Tezeen, and were followed by the few remaining troopers of the Irregular Cavalry. Dr. Magrath, seeing them take, as he thought, a wrong direction, hastened to recall them, and was taken prisoner by a Giljye chief. In their passage down the defile, a destructive fire was maintained on the troops from the heights on either side, and fresh numbers of dead and wounded lined the course of the stream. Brigadier Shelton commanded the rear with a few Europeans, and but for his persevering energy and unflinching fortitude in repelling the assailants, it is probable the whole would have been there sacrificed.

The diminished remnant reached the encamping ground in the Tezeen valley at about 4 P. M., having lost since starting from Cabul, inclusive of camp-followers, about 12,000 men ; no less than 15 officers were killed and wounded in this day's disastrous march.

Although it was now sufficiently plain that Mahomed Akber either could not or would not act up to his friendly professions, the General endeavoured to renew his worse than useless negotiation with that chief, in the faint hope that something might still be done to better the situation of the troops; but Capt. Skinner, who was deputed on the occasion, returned with precisely the same answer as before ; and as the General could not in honour accede to his proposal, all hope of aid from that quarter was at an end.

It was now determined to make an effort, under cover of darkness, to reach Jugdulluk, a distance of twenty-two miles, by an early hour on the following morning, the principal object being to get through the strong and dangerous pass of that place, before the enemy should have sufficient notice of their intention, to occupy it in any force. As there existed a short cut from Tezeen to Jugdulluk over the hills, the success of the attempt was very doubtful; but the lives of all depended on the issue; and at 7 P. M. the little band renewed its forlorn and dismal march, word having been previously sent to Mahomed Akber that it was the General's intention to move only as far as Seh Baba, distant seven miles. On moving off, the last gun was abandoned, and with it Dr. Cardew, who had been lashed to it in the hope of saving him. This gentleman had rendered himself conspicuous from the commencement of the siege for his zeal and gallantry, and had become a great favourite with the soldiery in consequence, by whom his hapless fate was sincerely lamented. Dr. Duff, the superintending surgeon of the force, experienced no better fortune, being left in a state of utter exhaustion on the road midway to Seh Baba. Little or no molestation was experienced by the force until reaching Seh Baba, when a few shots being fired at the rear, there was an immediate rush of camp-followers to the front, and the main body of the 44th European soldiers, who had hitherto been well in advance, getting mixed up in the crowd, could not be extricated by withdrawing them to the rear, owing to the narrowness of the road, which now traversed the hills to Burik-àb. Bodies of the neighbouring tribes were by this time on the alert, and fired at random from the heights, it being fortunately too dark for them to aim with precision; but the panic-stricken camp-followers now resembled a herd of startled deer, and fluctuated backwards and forwards, *en masse*, at every shot, blocking up the entire road, and fatally retarding the progress of the little body of soldiers who, under Brigadier Shelton, brought up the rear.

At Burik-àb a heavy fire was encountered by the hindmost from some caves near the road-side, occasioning fresh disorder, which continued all the way to Kutter-Sung, where the advance arrived at dawn of day, and awaited the junction of the rear, which did not take place till 8 A. M.

January 11*th*. — The distance from Jugdulluk was still ten miles; the enemy already began to crown the surrounding heights, and it was now evident that the delay occasioned by the camp followers had cut off the last chance of escape.

From Kutter-Sung to Jugdulluk it was one continued conflict; Brigadier Shelton, with his brave little band in the rear, holding overwhelming numbers in check, and literally performing wonders. But no efforts could avail to ward off the withering fire of Juzails, which from all sides assailed the crowded column, lining the road with bleeding carcasses. About 3 P. M. the advance reached Jugdulluk, and took up its position behind some ruined walls that crowned a height by the road-side. To show an imposing front, the officers extended themselves in line, and Capt. Grant, Asst.-Adjt.-Gen., at the same moment received a wound in the face. From this eminence they cheered their comrades under Brigadier Shelton in the rear, as they still struggled their way gallantly along every foot of ground, perseveringly followed up by their merciless enemy, until they arrived at their ground. But even here rest was denied them; for the Affghans, immediately occupying two hills which commanded the position, kept up a fire from which the walls of the enclosure afforded but a partial shelter.

The exhausted troops and followers now began to suffer greatly from thirst, which they were unable to satisfy. A tempting stream trickled near the foot of the hill, but to venture down to it was certain death. Some snow that covered the ground was eagerly devoured, but increased, instead of alleviating, their sufferings. The raw flesh of three bullocks, which had fortunately been saved, was served out to the soldiers, and ravenously swallowed. At about half past three

a message having been brought from Mahomed
Akber to Capt. Skinner requesting his presence, that officer promptly obeyed the call,
hoping thereby, even at the eleventh hour, to
effect some arrangement for the preservation of
those who survived.   The harassed and worn-out
troops, in the expectation of a temporary truce
during his absence, threw themselves down to
snatch a brief repose; but even this much-needed
luxury was denied them by their vigilant foes,
who now, from their commanding position,
poured into the crowded enclosure death-dealing
volleys in rapid succession, causing the utmost
consternation among the terrified followers, who
rushed wildly out in the vain hope of finding
shelter from the fire.   At this perilous juncture
Capt. Bygrave, with about fifteen brave Europeans, sallied forth in the full determination to
drive the enemy from the heights, or perish in
the attempt.   Unflinchingly they charged up the
hill, the enemy retreating before them in the
greatest trepidation.   The respite, however, thus
signally gained was of but short duration, for the
heroic little band had no sooner returned, than the
enemy reoccupied their posts of vantage, and
resumed their fatal fire.   Thus passed the time
until 5 P.M., when Capt. Skinner returned from
his interview with Mahomed Akber, bringing a

message to the General from that chief, who requested his presence at a conference, and demanded Brigadier Shelton and Capt. Johnson as
hostages for the evacuation of Jellalabad. The
General, seeing no alternative, made over temporary command to Brigadier Anquetil, and departed with the two above-named officers under
the escort of Mahomed Shah Khan. The troops
witnessed their departure with despair, having
seen enough of Affghan treachery, to convince
them that these repeated negotiations were mere
hollow artifices, designed to engender confidence
in their victims, preparatory to a fresh sacrifice of
blood. The General and his companions were
received by the Sirdar with every outward token
of kindness, and no time was lost in supplying
them with the bodily sustenance they so greatly
needed ; they were likewise assured that immediate arrangements should be made for the supply
of food to the famishing troops, and for their safe
escort to Jellalabad, after which they were shown
into a small tent, to enjoy, for the first time since
leaving Khoord-Cabul, a quiet and refreshing
sleep.

January 12th. — Numerous Giljye chiefs, with
their attendant clansmen, flocked in from the
neighbouring parts to pay their homage to Mahomed Akber ; and about 9 A. M. a conference

was held, at which the three British officers and
all the influential chiefs were present. All the
latter were loud and profuse in their expressions
of bitter hatred against the English, and for a
long time the Sirdar's efforts to conciliate them
seemed to be unsuccessful; but the offer of two
lacs of rupees appeared at last in some measure
to appease them, of which sum Mahomed Akber
promised to advance one lac himself, and to be
security for the other. The day nevertheless
wore on without anything decisive having been
agreed upon. The General became impatient to
rejoin his force, and repeatedly urged the Sirdar
to furnish him with the necessary escort, informing him at the same time that it was contrary to British notions of military honour, that a
general should be separated from his troops in
the hour of danger; and that he would infinitely
prefer death to such a disgrace. The Sirdar put
him off with promises, and at 7 P. M., firing being
heard in the direction of the pass, it was ascertained that the troops, impatient of further delay,
had actually moved off. From the time of the
General's departure the situation of the troops
had been in truth one of dark and cruel suspense,
unenlightened by one solitary ray of hope. At
an early hour in the morning, before the enemy

had yet made their appearance on the hills, Major Thain, accompanied by Capt. Skinner, rode out a few hundred paces in the direction of Mahomed Akber's camp, in expectation of meeting a messenger from the Sirdar to the last-named officer; a Giljye soldier suddenly made his appearance, and, passing Major Thain, who was several yards in advance, went close up to Capt. Skinner, and shot him with a pistol through the face. Major Thain instantly returned to camp, and announced this act of treachery. The unfortunate officer was carried inside the enclosure, and lingered in great pain till 3 P. M. In him the state lost an officer of whose varied merits as a soldier and a man it is difficult to speak too highly. A deep feeling of anguish and despair now pervaded the whole assemblage. The extremes of hunger, thirst, and fatigue were suffered alike by all; added to which, the Affghans again crowned the heights and recommenced hostilities, keeping up a galling fire the whole day with scarcely half an hour's intermission. Sally after sally was made by the Europeans, bravely led on by Major Thain, Capt. Bygrave, and Lieuts. Wade and Macartney; but again and again the enemy returned to worry and destroy. Night came, and all further delay in such a place being useless, the whole sallied forth, determined to pursue the route to Jellalabad at all risks.

The sick and wounded were necessarily abandoned to their fate. Descending into the valley of Jugdulluk, they pursued their way along the bed of the stream for about a mile and a half, encountering a desultory fire from the Giljyes encamped in the vicinity, who were evidently not quite prepared to see them at such an hour, but were soon fully on the alert, some following up the rear, others pressing forward to occupy the pass. This formidable defile is about two miles long, exceedingly narrow, and closed in by lofty precipitous heights. The road has a considerable slope upwards, and, on nearing the summit, further progress was found to be obstructed by two strong barriers formed of branches of the prickly holly-oak, stretching completely across the defile. Immense delay and confusion took place in the general struggle to force a passage through these unexpected obstacles, which gave ample time for the Giljyes to collect in force.

A terrible fire was now poured in from all quarters, and a massacre even worse than that of Tunga Tareekee commenced, the Affghans rushing in furiously upon the pent-up crowd of troops and followers, and committing wholesale slaughter. A miserably small remnant managed to clear

the barriers. Twelve officers*, amongst whom was
Brigadier Anquetil, were killed. Upwards of
forty † others succeeded in pushing through, about
twelve ‡ of whom, being pretty well mounted,
rode on ahead of the rest with the few remaining
cavalry, intending to make the best of their way
to Jellalabad. Small straggling parties of the
Europeans marched on under different officers ;
the country became more open, and they suffered
little molestation for several miles, most of the
Giljyes being too busily engaged in the plundering of the dead to pursue the living. But much
delay was occasioned by the anxiety of the men
to bring on their wounded comrades, and the rear
was much harassed by sudden onsets from parties
stationed on the heights, under which the road
occasionally wound. On reaching the Sourkab
river, they found the enemy in possession of the
bridge, and a hot fire was encountered in crossing
the ford below it, by which Lieut. Cadet, H. M.'s
44th, was killed, together with several privates.

January 13th.—The morning dawned as they
approached Gundamuk, revealing to the enemy,
who had by this time increased considerably in
their front and rear, the insignificance of their
numerical strength. To avoid the vigorous as-

---

* Appendix.   † Ibid.   ‡ Ibid.

saults that were now made by their confident foe, they were compelled to leave the road, and take up a defensive position on a height to the left of it, where they made a resolute stand, determined to sell their lives at the dearest possible price. At this time they could only muster about twenty muskets.

Some Affghan horsemen, approaching from the direction of Gundamuk, were now beckoned to, and an attempt was made by Lieut. Hay to enter upon some pacific arrangement. Hostilities were for a few minutes suspended, and, at the invitation of a chief, Major Griffiths, the senior officer, accompanied by Mr. Blewitt to act as interpreter, descended the hill to a conference.

Several Affghans now ascended the height, and assumed a friendly tone towards the little party there stationed; but the calm was of short duration, for the soldiers, getting provoked at several attempts being made to snatch away their arms, resumed a hostile attitude, and drove the intruders fiercely down. The die was now cast, and their fate sealed; for the enemy, taking up their post on an opposite hill, marked off man after man, officer after officer, with unerring aim. Parties of Affghans rushed up at intervals to complete the work of extermination, but were as often driven back by the still dauntless handful of invincibles. At length, nearly all being wounded more or less, a final onset of the enemy, sword in hand, terminated the unequal struggle, and completed the dismal tragedy. Major Griffiths and Mr. Blewitt had been previously led off to a neighbouring fort, and were thus saved. Of those whom they left behind, Captain Souter alone, with three or four privates, was spared, and carried off captive, having received a severe wound in the shoulder; he had tied round his waist before leaving Jugdulluk the colours of his regiment, which were thus miraculously preserved.

It only remains to relate the fate of those few officers and men, who rode on ahead of the rest after passing the barriers. Six of the twelve officers, Capts. Bellew, Collier, Hopkins, Lieut. Bird, Drs. Harpur and Brydon, reached Futtehabad in safety, the other six having dropped gradually off by the way and been destroyed. Deceived by the friendly professions of some peasants near the above-named town, who brought them bread to eat, they unwisely delayed a few moments to satisfy the cravings of hunger; the inhabitants meanwhile armed themselves, and, suddenly sallying forth, cut down Capt. Bellew and Lieut. Bird; Capts. Collyer and Hopkins, and Drs. Harpur and Brydon, rode off, and were

"In the conflict my posteen flew open
and exposed the Colour. They thought I was
some great man."
(Lieut. T. A. Souter in a letter to his wife.)

pursued; the three former were overtaken and slain within four miles of Jellalabad; Dr. Brydon by a miracle escaped, and was the only officer of the whole Cabul force, who reached that garrison in safety.

Such was the memorable retreat of the British army from Cabul, which, viewed in all its circumstances, — in the military conduct which preceded and brought about such a consummation, the treachery, disaster, and suffering which accompanied it, — is, perhaps, without a parallel in history.

"The only officer of the whole Cabul force who reached that garrison in safety."

ROUGH NOTES

DURING

IMPRISONMENT IN AFFGHANISTAN.

EDITOR'S NOTICE.

THE following " rough notes " will be found a very interesting sequel to the foregoing narrative. They are strictly what they profess to be — penned in haste, to be despatched when opportunity should serve, as perhaps the last proof of his existence, which the writer might give his friends for many a day. How narrowly the Cabul prisoners did at last escape an indefinitely prolonged captivity, is known to all. And now that a gracious Providence has so restored them, it is hoped that the Author will, at a future opportunity, be enabled to add *more particulars* of an every-day life with such a party in an Affghan prison, and to fill up the gap which necessarily now remains between the 29th of June, when these Notes break off, and the 21st of September, on which happy day they again breathed the air of freedom.

ROUGH NOTES

DURING

IMPRISONMENT IN AFFGHANISTAN,

1842.

January 9th.—IN my notes on the retreat of the British force from Cabul, I have already mentioned the departure, from Gen. Elphinstone's camp at Khoord-Cabul, of the ladies, with their husbands and other officers, to the proffered protection of Mahomed Akber Khan; but it may be expedient briefly to remind the reader of the mode in which this event was brought about. I have been assured by Major Pottinger that, on the night of the 8th, the Sirdar, having spontaneously entered on the subject, expressed to that officer his serious apprehensions of the peril to which the ladies and children would be exposed by remaining in camp (it being impossible to restrain the Giljyes from a continuance of hostilities), and that, with a view to prevent further misery and suffering to the individuals in question, he should lose no time in proposing to the General that all the ladies and married families might be made over to his care, for safe escort to Jellalabad, keeping one march in rear of the army. Major Pottinger having declared his entire approval of the Sirdar's humane intentions, advantage was taken of Capt. Skinner's return to camp on the following morning, to make known the proposal to Gen. Elphinstone ; and a small party of Affghan horse was sent with him, to escort all such as might be able to avail themselves of the offer. The General, hoping that so signal a mark of confidence in Mahomed Akber's good faith, might be attended with beneficial results to the army, and anxious at all events to save the ladies from a prolongation of the hardships they had already endured, readily consented to the arrangement ; and, under the peculiar circumstances of the case, deemed it incumbent on him to send their husbands also, more especially as some were helpless from severe wounds. The whole [a] were

[a] Lady Macnaghten,
Lady Sale *,
Mrs. Sturt, her daughter,
Capt. Boyd, wife, and child,
Capt. Anderson, ditto, ditto,

accordingly ordered to depart immediately with the Affghan escort, by whom we were impatiently hurried off, before the majority had been made clearly to comprehend the reason of their being so suddenly separated from their companions in trouble. At that time so little confidence was placed by any of us in Mahomed Akber's plausible professions, that it seemed as though we were but too probably rushing from a state of comparative safety into the very jaws of destruction; but, placing our dependence on a watchful Providence, we bade a hasty, and as it proved to many, an eternal, farewell to our friends, and mournfully followed our conductors to the place allotted for our reception, about two miles distant from camp. The road lay through ravines and wilds of the most savage description, one universal garb of snow clothing the dreary and uninviting scene. On the way we passed seve-

---

Lieut. Waller *, ditto, ditto,
Lieut. Eyre *, ditto, ditto,
Mr. Ryley, ditto, ditto,
Mrs. Trevor and seven children,
Mrs. Mainwaring and child,
Capt. Troup *,
Lieut. Mein *,
Serjt. Wade and family.

N.B. Those marked thus * were wounded.

M

ral hundred Giljye horse drawn up in line, as if in readiness for an attack on the camp. Half an hour's ride brought us to a small fort perched on the edge of a precipitous bank, which we ascended by a slanting slippery path, and entered the gate with a mistrust by no means diminished by the ferocious looks of the garrison, amidst a circle of whom some of us were kept standing for several minutes, during which our sensations were far from agreeable. At last, however, we were shown into a small inner court, where, to our great relief, we found our three countrymen, Major Pottinger, and Capts. Mackenzie and Lawrence, who had been made over as hostages at Bootkhak, and in the midst of whom sat, to the inexpressible joy of his parents, the youngest boy of Capt. and Mrs. Boyd, who, having been picked up in the Khoord-Cabul pass on the previous day by one of Mahomed Akber's followers, had been committed by that chief to Major Pottinger's protection. The accommodation provided for us, though the best the place afforded, was of the most humble description, consisting of three small dark hovels, into which ladies and gentlemen were promiscuously crowded together, the bachelors being, however, separate from the married families. But even this state of things was heaven itself compared with the cold and misery we had been suffering in camp on the bare snow, and we felt most thankful for the change. The courtyard was all day crowded with the friends and relations of Mahomed Akber, whose bearing towards us was exceedingly kind and courteous; but their presence obliged the ladies to remain closely immured in their dark cells. In the course of the afternoon the chief himself made his appearance, and, having requested an interview with Lady Macnaghten, expressed to that lady his sorrow at having been instrumental to her present misfortunes, and his desire to contribute to her comfort as long as she remained his guest. But an Affghan nobleman's ideas of comfort fall very far short of an English peasant's; and we soon learned to consider spoons, forks, and other table gear as effeminate luxuries, and plunged our fingers unhesitatingly into the depths of a greasy pilao, for which several of us scrambled out of one common dish. The warmth of a wood * fire, though essential to protect us from the severe extremes of cold, could only be enjoyed at the expense of being blinded

---

* The Affghans are in many parts of the country almost entirely dependent for fuel on a species of *Artemisia*, or southernwood, which grows everywhere in the greatest profusion, and scents the whole atmosphere with its powerful fragrance.

and half stifled by the smoke; the bare ground
was our only bed, and postheens (or sheepskin
cloaks) our only covering; but these and various
other inconveniences were indeed of small moment, when weighed in the balance against the
combination of horrors we had escaped, and which
still encompassed our unhappy countrymen and
fellow soldiers in camp.

January 11th.—At about 11 A. M. we started,
under an escort of about 50 horse, for Tezeen,
having been previously cautioned to use our
swords and pistols in case of need, as an attack
might be expected from the bloodthirsty Ghazees,
who thronged the road. The retreating army had
marched over the same ground on the previous
day, and terrible was the spectacle presented to
our eyes along the whole line of road: the snow
was absolutely dyed with streaks and patches of
blood for whole miles, and at every step we
encountered the mangled bodies of British and
Hindoostanee soldiers, and helpless camp-followers,
lying side by side, victims of one treacherous un-
distinguishing fate, the red stream of life still
trickling from many a gaping wound inflicted by
the merciless Affghan knife. Here and there
small groups of miserable, starving, and frost-
bitten wretches, among whom were many women
and children, were still permitted to cling to life,

perhaps only because death would in their case have been a mercy. The bodies of Majors Scott and Ewart, and of Dr. Bryce, were recognized. Numerous parties of truculent Ghazees, the chief perpetrators of these horrors, passed us laden with booty, their naked swords still reeking with the blood of their victims. They uttered deep curses and sanguinary threats at our party, and seemed disappointed that so many of the hated Feringhees should have been suffered to survive. We reached Tezeen, a distance of sixteen miles, at close of day, where the fort of Mahomed Khan received us for the night. Here we found Lieut. Melville of the 54th N.I., who had delivered himself up to Mahomed Akber on the previous day, having received some slight sword cuts in defending the colours of his regiment. We were also sorry to see no less than 400 of our irregular Hindoostanee horse encamped outside the fort, having deserted to the enemy on the 9th and 10th. They belonged chiefly to Anderson's horse and the bodyguard.

January 12th.—At 10 A. M. we again proceeded on our journey down the Tezeen valley preceded by the cavalry deserters. At Seh Baba, striking off from the high road, which here crosses some hills to the right, we kept our course along the stream *, to the fort of Surroobee, a distance of sixteen miles. Between Tezeen and Seh Baba we encountered the same horrifying sights as yesterday; we passed the last abandoned horse-artillery gun, the carriage of which had been set on fire by the Ghazees, and was still burning; the corpse of poor Cardew lay stretched beside it, with several of the artillery men. A little further on we passed the body of Dr. Duff, the superintending surgeon to the force, whose left hand had suffered previous amputation with a *penknife* by Dr. Harcourt! Numbers of worn-out and famished camp-followers were lying under cover of the rocks, within whose crevices they vainly sought a shelter from the cold. By many of these poor wretches we were recognized, and vainly invoked for the food and raiment we were unable to supply. The fate of these unfortunates was a sad subject of reflection to us, — death in its most horrid and protracted form stared them in the face; and the agonies of despair were depicted in every countenance. The fort of Surroobee belongs to Abdoolah Khan, Giljye. Near Seh Baba we were overtaken by Dr. Macgrath of the 37th N. I., who had been taken prisoner

* I have not particularised the features of such portions of the high road as we traversed, because they were already well known.

on the 10th, and was now sent to join our party; we were thus unexpectedly furnished with medical assistance, of which the sick and wounded had sorely felt the want.

January 13th. —Resuming our march at 10 A. M., we crossed the hills in a south-east direction towards Jugdulluk. The road in many places was very steep, and for several miles traversed a high table-land, presenting no signs of cultivation or human propinquity. Within about five miles of Jugdulluk, we again entered the high road, along which our army had recently passed; and the first sight that presented itself was the body of a fine European soldier: — Again our path was strewed with the mangled victims of war. — We reached Jugdulluk late in the evening; and, passing by the ruined inclosure within which the remnant of the force had so hopelessly sought shelter, we beheld a spectacle more terrible than any we had previously witnessed, the whole interior space being one crowded mass of bloody corpses. The carnage here must have been frightful. The body of Capt. Skinner was recognized, and an Affghan was persuaded by Capt. Lawrence to inter it during the night, Mahomed Akber's consent having been previously procured. About two hundred yards below this fatal spot we found three ragged tents pitched for our reception, Mahomed Akber Khan being encamped hard by ; and we now learned for the first time that Gen. Elphinstone, Brigadier Shelton, and Capt. Johnson, were *hostages* in his hands, the rest of the force having been annihilated.   Mr. Fallon, an assistant in one of the public offices, had also been taken prisoner at the same time.

January 14*th.* — Shortly after sunrise we pursued our journey, accompanied by Akber Khan, with his hostages, or rather *prisoners,* and about 600 horse, of whom the Hindoostanee deserters formed a part.   The road took a northerly direction up a gorge in the hills, and thence proceeded for five or six miles up a narrow defile, through which runs a small stream whose upper surface was covered with ice.   Throughout these regions of snow the cold was intense, and we passed several springs whose waters, arrested by the frost, hung suspended in long glittering icicles from the rocks, exhibiting a spectacle whose brilliancy would, under less depressing circumstances, have called forth exclamations of wonder and admiration, which we had not now the heart to utter. After clearing this defile, our course became somewhat easterly, through a more open country, and over a tolerably good road, for four or five miles, when we entered another short defile leading over a rocky ghat, after surmounting which the road again improved, until we reached the steep and difficult pass of Udruk-budruk. The ascent was about 1000 feet, up a narrow winding path, which, from the sharp and jagged nature of the rocks, scarcely afforded a practicable footing for our horses and camels. From the summit we had an extensive view of the country to the north, bounded by lofty snow-clad hills, the intervening space being broken up into innumerable ravines, whose barren surface was unrelieved by a single tree, the only signs of vegetable life being confined to the banks of the Cabul river, which partially fertilised the narrow valley immediately below us. The descent into this plain, down the rugged mountain side, was infinitely more tedious, and attended with greater peril, than the previous ascent, our jaded beasts threatening to cast their riders with violence on the rocks at every step. It was dark ere we reached the fort of Kutz, after a fatiguing journey of twenty-four miles, which had occupied no less than ten hours. This place belongs to Mahomed Ali Khan, Giljye, and is situated near the right bank of the Punjsheer river. Although the clouds threatened rain, we were refused admittance within the walls, and were consequently obliged to repose in the open air, exposed the whole night to a high cutting wind. Fortunately we had now descended into a milder climate, or the poor ladies and children must have suffered severely. At midnight we were roused up by the arrival of our daily meals, consisting of half-baked cakes of unleavened bread, and untempting lumps of tough mutton; but our servants had by this time prepared us some hot tea, which was far more satisfactory to wearied travellers than the solid fare of Affghan cooks.

January 15*th.* — At an early hour we were again on the move, and a few hundred yards brought us to the Cabul river, which at the ford was divided into two branches, the last extremely rapid, and the water reaching up to our saddle-girths; many of the ladies, being mounted on ponies, were obliged to dismount, and ride astride on the chargers of their Affghan acquaintance, to avoid getting wet. Nothing could exceed the politeness and attention of Mahomed Akber on this occasion, who manifested the greatest anxiety until all had crossed over in safety. Several men and ponies were swept down by the violence of the current and drowned; a whole host of camp dogs, whose masters had been slain, and who had attached themselves to us, remaining on the other side, to our great relief. — Our course was now north-easterly, over a barren undulating country, for about ten miles, until we reached the fertile valley of Lughmanee, at the border of which we crossed a wide and rapid stream; the whole plain beyond was thickly studded with small high-walled forts and villages, by whose inhabitants we were greeted, *en passant*, in no measured terms of abuse, in which exercise of speech the fair sex, I am sorry to say, bore a conspicuous part, pronouncing the English ladies not only immoral in character, but downright " scarecrows" in appearance, and the gentlemen, " dogs," "base-born," " infidels," " devils," with many other unpronounceable titles equally complimentary, the whole being wound up with an assurance of certain death to our whole party ere many hours should elapse.

We also passed within a mile of a plain white building on our left, which was pointed out as the tomb of Lamech the father of Noah, and a favourite place of pilgrimage with the Affghans. At about 3 P. M. we reached the walled town of Turghurree, within which we found lodging, after a march of about sixteen miles. We found the Affghan gentry most agreeable travelling companions, possessing a ready fund of easy conversation and pleasantry, with a certain rough polish and artless independence of manner, which, compared with the studied servility and smooth-tongued address of the Hindoostanee nobles, seldom fails to impress our countrymen in their favour.

January 16*th*. — We were well pleased to find that a day's halt had been determined upon, which was no less acceptable for the needful rest it secured for man and beast, than for the opportunity it afforded us of performing our Sabbath devotions, which, under present circumstances, could not fail to be a source of more than ordinary comfort. Some disturbance was occasioned during the day by a party of Giljyes threatening to attack the town, and a few shots were exchanged from both sides, by which two or three men were said to have been killed. The affray was believed to have originated in discontent at the division of the spoil of our army. This place has a small bazar, and many poor wanderers from our camp were permitted to take refuge within the walls, where a meal was dealt out to them daily by some charitable Hindoo residents.

January 17*th*. — The Sirdar's intention had been to keep us at Turghurree for several days; but, owing to the hostile spirit evinced towards us by the populace, he was obliged to hurry us away. At 11 A. M. we accordingly resumed our journey, under a guard of about 200 Juzailchees, whom it had been necessary to collect for our protection. Crowds of Affghans lined the walls to witness our departure, and some of our small remains of baggage fell a prey to the insatiable love of plunder, for which the Giljyes are notorious. Many of our Hindoostanee servants, who had hitherto followed our fortunes, now left us, under the idea that the Sirdar had decided upon our destruction. We pursued a north-easterly course along the valley, passing numerous forts, and at 2 A. M. reached Buddeeabad, a distance of eight miles, where one of the chief strongholds of Mahomed Shah Khan, Gyljye, had been vacated for our reception. The accommodation provided for us here was better than we had hitherto experienced. The fort was of a square form, each face about 80 yards long, with walls 25 feet high, and a flanking tower at each corner. It was further defended by a faussebray and deep ditch all round, the front gate being on the south-west face, and the postern on the north-east, each defended by a tower or bastion. The Zuna-Khaneh, or private dwelling, occupied two sides of a large square space in the centre, shut in by a high wall, each wing containing three apartments raised about eight feet from the ground, and the outer side of the principal room, consisting entirely of a wooden framework, divided into five compartments, with ornamented panels in each, made to slide up and down at pleasure. All the better sort

of houses in the country have the chief rooms
constructed in this manner, which is better
adapted for the summer than the winter season,
as it admits of a free circulation of air, but is an
insufficient barrier against the cold.   There was
no supply of water inside the fort, but a small
river ran past, at the distance of half a mile on
the south-east side, and a little stream or canal
about 100 yards outside the walls.   It is singular
that few Affghan forts have wells, notwithstanding the general abundance of water near the
surface in all the cultivated valleys; and it would,
generally speaking, be very easy to cut off the
external supply of that necessary element, thus
forcing the garrison to surrender without expend-
ing a shot.   This fort is quite new, having been
built since our occupation of the country.   The
owner, Mahomed Shah Khan, is father-in-law of
Mahomed Akber Khan, and is one of the few
chiefs who never deigned to acknowledge Shah
Shooja.   Insatiable avarice and ambition are his
ruling passions, and, as our conquest put an end
to his promising schemes of aggrandisement, his
hatred towards us is intense.   Unhappily he ex-
ercised great influence over his son-in-law, of
whose cause in fact he was the chief supporter;
and he was generally admitted to have been the
principal instigator to the treacherous seizure of

our envoy, for whose murder, however, which was committed in the heat and impulse of the moment, he is not answerable. Mahomed Akber and his cousin Sultan Mahomed Khan, familiarly called Sultan Jan, accompanied us to Buddeeabad, where they endeavoured to arrange matters for our comfort to the utmost of their power. Sultan Jan is eminently handsome, proportionately vain, and much given to boasting. Both he and the Sirdar were equally kind and courteous; but the latter is in manner a more perfect gentleman, and never, like his cousin, indulges in comparisons to the disadvantage of the English, of whom he invariably speaks with candour and respect.

The Sirdar has been completely baulked in his plans by the refusal of Gen. Sale to vacate Jellalabad, on which he had by no means calculated; even now he could not be persuaded that an order from Major Pottinger would not be obeyed by Capt. Macgregor, the political authority there, although the Major constantly assured him that with us a prisoner, however exalted his rank, not being considered a free agent, has no power or control over any public officers of government, however much his inferiors in rank and station. I have no doubt his hope was that General Sale, yielding to the apparent necessities of the case, would have vacated the town and forthwith retreated to Peshawur, in which case he made pretty sure of the assistance of the Khyberries, in completing the annihilation of the British force.

January 18th. — Mahomed Akber and Sultan Jan departed, with the professed object of attempting the reduction of Jellalabad, and apparently very confident of success. — As we remained immured in the fort of Buddeeabab until the 11th of April, I can scarcely expect that a minute detail of daily occurrences during that period would interest the reader. It would be equally idle to note down the various reports that reached us from time to time of passing events. The Affghans excel all the world in the ready fabrication of falsehoods, and those about us were interested in keeping us in the dark as much as possible. Nevertheless the truth could not always be concealed, and we managed, notwithstanding all their vigilance, to obtain pretty accurate intelligence of what was passing in the world without, though of course it was difficult entirely to separate the wheat from the chaff. On our first arrival we suffered some inconvenience from the want of clean linen, having in our transit from fort to fort been much pestered by vermin, of which, after they had once established a footing, it was by no means an easy matter to rid ourselves. The first discovery of a real living l-o-u-s-e was a severe shock to our fine sense of delicacy; but custom reconciles folk to anything, and even the ladies eventually mustered up resolution to look one of these intruders in the face without a scream. The management of our household matters, as well as the duty of general surveillance, was committed to a Mehmandar, who generally took advantage of his temporary authority to feather his own nest, by defrauding us in respect to the quality and quantity of our needful supplies. Moossa Khan was the first agent of this kind with whom we had to deal; and he was so little restrained by scruples, as to pass for a most consummate rogue even among Affghans. For mere ordinary civility the unfortunate widow of the murdered envoy found it her interest to repay him with costly presents of Cashmere shawls, &c., and was twice induced to pay twenty rupees for the recovery of a favourite cat, which Moossa Khan had actually stolen from her himself, for the sake of the expected reward. This man was, nevertheless, much trusted by Mahomed Akber, who valued him no less for his capacity for intrigue, than for his unscrupulous zeal in the performance of the meanest or wickedest purposes. Such a coadjutor could not long be spared from his master's side in attendance upon us, and he was accord-

ingly relieved on the 20th January, for the purpose of carrying on intrigues against the British
with the leading chieftains of the Punjab. His
successor was an old acquaintance of Capt.
Troup, named Meerza Bawndeen Khan, who in
peaceful times styled himself Syud, but now for
a time sunk his religious distinction in the more
warlike title of Khan. This man had, at the
outbreak of the rebellion, been imprisoned on
suspicion of favouring the English, but was released immediately on the arrival of Mahomed
Akber, whom he had befriended during that
chief's confinement at Bokhara, and to whose
fortune he now attached himself. His manners
were exceedingly boorish, and he took little
pains to render himself agreeable, though, from
his previous conduct, there was reason to believe
that, under all his roughness of exterior, there
lurked a secret preference for our cause. In
most respects we certainly benefited by the
change.

On the 21st we had rain, and on the 22d snow
fell on the neighbouring hills.

On the 23d there was snow in the fort itself, a
proof of the unusual severity of the winter, being
quite a rare occurrence in this valley.

We had hitherto received our food at the hands
of Affghan cooks, who little consulted the delicacy

of the European palate. Our daily diet consisted of boiled rice, mutton boiled to rags, and thick cakes of unleavened dough ; which, for ladies and children, was not the most enviable fare, whilst the irregular hours at which it was served up interfered greatly with our own comforts. It was now arranged, however, greatly to the satisfaction of all concerned, that our meals should be prepared by our own Hindoostanee servants, the Affghans furnishing materials.

We had a visit from the Sirdar and Sultan Jan on the 23d, the chief having his head quarters at present at Trighurree, where he was making preparations for the siege of Jellalabad. Major Pottinger, at his request, wrote a letter to Capt. Macgregor, explaining all that had occurred since the army left Cabul.

On the 24th, the Sirdar, having heard that we were much in want of money, sent 1000 rupees to be distributed among us.

On the 27th, he paid us another visit, his principal object being to induce Major Pottinger to make some alterations in the letter for Capt. Macgregor.

January 29th. — This day was rendered a joyous and eventful one to us, by the arrival from Jellalabad of a budget of letters and newspapers from our brother officers there garrisoned, who had likewise generously subscribed a quantity of clothes and other comforts from their little store for our use.   It was truly gratifying to receive these proofs of sympathy from our countrymen, and to have a door of communication opened once more with the civilised world.   Some of our friends managed to inform us of all that was going on, by dotting off letters of the alphabet in the newspapers, which is an easy mode of carrying on secret correspondence, and not likely to be detected by an Asiatic.   In this manner we became acquainted with Brigadier Wild's failure in the Khyber pass, and with General Pollock's march from India : we also heard now for the first time that Dr. Brydon had reached Jellalabad alive, being the only officer who escaped out of the whole army which had left Cabul.   Captains Collyer and Hopkins, with Dr. Harpur, were found dead within four miles of the town of Jellalabad.   It is said that, one of the ill-fated trio having been wounded, the remaining two went back to his assistance ; but for which act of charity they would probably have been saved.   It is singular that Dr. Brydon was mounted on a miserable pony, and seemed, humanly speaking, one of the most unlikely persons of the whole force to effect so wonderful an escape.   Capt. Bellew, Lieut. Bird, and 2 or 3 other officers, with several European soldiers, were killed near Futtehabad, having imprudently delayed at a village to satisfy the cravings of hunger, and thus given the inhabitants time to arm themselves and overpower them.

February 15*th.*—The tedium of a prison life was again relieved to-day by the arrival of Abdool Guffoor Khan and Dost Mahomed Khan from the Sirdar, bringing with them Major Griffiths of 37th N. I. and Mr. Blewitt, a clerk of the pay office, both of whom, with the Sergt.-Major of the 37th N. I., were taken prisoners at Gundamuk, after witnessing the massacre of almost all the officers and men who reached that place. Capt. Souter, H. M. 44th regiment, was led off at the same time by another chief, having preserved the colours of his regiment by tying them round his waist. The Sergt.-Major was so fortunate as to be set at liberty on the payment of certain rupees as a ransom, and a similar arrangement was on the point of being made for the release of Major Griffiths and Mr. Blewitt, when they were demanded by Mahomed Akber, and unwillingly delivered up by their captor. Major Griffiths had received a severe wound in the arm from a bullet. We were also delighted to learn that Capt. Bygrave, paymaster to the force, was safe, and would soon join us.

By command of Mahomed Akber we were this

day ordered to deliver up our arms, which we had hitherto been permitted to retain. The cause of this was declared to be the discovery of a clandestine correspondence, carried on between Major Pottinger and Capt. Macgregor, which had so much displeased the Sirdar, that he sent a solemn warning to the Major to desist from such practices in future, significantly reminding him of the tragical fate of Sir William Macnaghten. Major Pottinger boldly acknowledged the fact of his having written privately to Jellalabad, and justified it on the plea that he had given no promise to the Sirdar to refrain from so doing. By Abdool Guffoor Khan we again enjoyed the gratification of receiving letters from our friends at Jellalabad. This chief was supposed to be friendly to our interests, having materially assisted Gen. Sale with supplies for his force. He was evidently much suspected by the Affghans about us, who maintained a strict watch over every word he uttered during his visit.

February 15*th.* — Captain Souter joined us to-day, having been made over to the Sirdar by the chief who captured him.

February 19*th.* — On the 6th, we had a heavy fall of rain, since which the weather had become exceedingly close. This morning it was remarked that an unusual degree of heat and stillness pervaded the air. Whether these were premonitory symptoms of what was shortly to happen it is impossible to determine; but at 11 A. M. we were suddenly alarmed by a violent rocking of the earth, which momentarily increased to such a degree that we could with difficulty maintain our balance. Large masses of the lofty walls that encompassed us fell in on all sides with a thundering crash; a loud subterraneous rumbling was heard, as of a boiling sea of liquid lava, and wave after wave seemed to lift up the ground on which we stood, causing every building to rock to and fro like a floating vessel. After the scenes of horror we had recently witnessed, it seemed as if the hour of retribution had arrived, and that Heaven designed to destroy the blood-stained earth at one fell swoop, The dwelling in which we lodged was terribly shaken, and the room inhabited by Lady Sale fell in, — her lady-ship, who happened to be standing on the roof just above it, having barely time to escape. Most providentially, all the ladies, with their children, made a timely rush into the open air at the commencement of the earthquake, and entirely escaped injury. Gen. Elphinstone, being bedridden, was for several moments in a precarious position, from which he was rescued by the intrepidity of his servant *Moore*, a private of H. M. 44th, who rushed into his room and carried him forth in his arms. — The poor General, notwithstanding all that had occurred to cloud his fame, was greatly beloved by the soldiery, of whom there were few who would not have acted in a similar manner to save his life. — The quaking continued for several minutes with unabated violence, and a slight tremor in the earth was perceptible throughout the remainder of the day. The Affghans were, for the time being, overwhelmed with terror ; for, though slight shocks of earthquake are of common occurrence every year during the cold season, none so fearful as this had visited the country within the memory of the present generation. We shortly learned that our fort had been singularly favoured, almost every other fort in the valley having been laid low, and many inhabitants destroyed in the ruins. The town of Turghurree especially seems to have suffered severely, scarcely a house being left standing, and several hundreds of people having been killed in the fall.

The first idea that struck the Affghans, after their fears had subsided, was, that the defences of Jellalabad must have been levelled to the ground, and a high road made for the Sirdar and his followers to walk in. Elevated by this hope, they confidently attributed the late phænomenon to a direct interposition of the Prophet in their favour.

We all passed the night in the open air, being afraid to trust the tottering walls of our habitation, especially as shocks of earthquake continued to occur almost every hour, some of which were rather severe.

February 21st. — The swords of Gen. Elphinstone and Brigadier Shelton were this day returned to them by order of the Sirdar.

February 23d. — Capt. Bygrave joined us in a very weak state, having suffered much from frost in one foot, and having entirely lost the ends of his toes. His adventures, after leaving Jugdulluk, were perilous, and his ultimate escape wonderful. After starting from Jugdulluk on the night of the 12th January, he was one of the first to surmount the strong barriers of prickly holly-oak which choked the pass. Collecting a small party of the men, who were similarly fortunate, he harangued them on the absolute necessity of their holding firmly together in the bond of discipline, for the preservation of their lives, declaring his willingness to lead them, if they would only obey orders, and act with spirit adequate to the emergency. The men, thus addressed, set up a loud cheer, and protested their intention to be guided solely by his commands

N

and wishes. For three or four miles they steadily kept their ranks, and held the pursuing enemy at bay; but at length the repeated onsets of the Affghan horsemen, who every moment increased in number in their rear, threw the little band into confusion, which Capt. Bygrave exerted himself in vain to remedy. The men would neither hold together, nor pursue their march with that steadiness of purpose, on which hung their only chance of safety. Capt. Bygrave, at length finding all his efforts to save them unavailing, and foreseeing the inevitable destruction of the whole party, determined, as a last resource, to strike off the high road and endeavour to make his way over the hills to Jellalabad. Mr. Baness, an enterprising merchant, who had become involved in the difficulties that beset our army, was induced to accompany him in this hazardous undertaking. Their course for the first few miles was altogether north, in order to get as far as possible from the track of the pursuing Giljyes: by day they sought close cover — now among long rushes in the low bed of a mountain stream, and now under the thick foliage of evergreen shrubs on the summit of some lofty snow-clad peak. Their sole subsistence was a few dry grains of coffee, of which Mr. Baness had a small supply in his pocket, with an occasional bit of wild liquorice root, which they fortunately discovered growing in the bed of the Soorkab river. Travelling entirely at night, they experienced great difficulties in steering a direct course among the tortuosities of the innumerable ravines, which everywhere intersected their desultory track; on one occasion they found themselves suddenly upon the high road, where the first sight that offered itself was the mangled body of an European soldier; and, fearing to proceed along a path so lately beset with enemies, they were obliged to avoid the danger by retracing their steps for many miles. Thus passed four wearisome nights and days, during which time Capt. Bygrave, with frost-bitten feet, and worn-out shoes, had suffered so much from lameness, as to become more and more incapable of progressing; until at last, in the extreme of weakness and misery, having declared to Mr. Baness his inability to proceed further, he endeavoured to persuade that gentleman to seek with him the nearest village, and throw themselves on the protection of a chief. Mr. Baness would not, however, consent to run such hazard, and declared his intention to pursue his course to Jellalabad, if possible. Loth, however, to forsake his companion, he urged him unavailingly to fresh exertion; and at length, declaring that for the sake of his large family he was bound to proceed onward without delay, he took a mournful leave of his fellow-traveller, and, after twice returning in the forlorn hope of prevailing on him to move, departed on his solitary way. Left to himself, under such helpless circumstances, Capt. Bygrave almost yielded to despair,— but, after a prolonged slumber, found himself strong enough to walk, or rather crawl, a few miles further. The second night after Mr. Baness's departure brought him to a Giljye village*, where, lying concealed till morning under some straw in a cave, he gave himself up to the first person who came near, who, being easily conciliated by the offer of some gold, conducted him to a neighbouring hut; — hence, after partaking of some refreshment, he was led to the residence of the chief of the village, Nizam Khan, who received him hospitably, and treated him with the utmost kindness for several days, when he was delivered up to the Sirdar, then encamped at Charbagh, in the neighbourhood of Jellalabad. There he found the chief actively employed in preparing gun-ammunition for the proposed siege; several of our captured guns were there, from which the Affghan smiths managed to extract the spikes in a very few hours.

March 3d. — Severe shocks of earthquake every

---

* Kutch Soorkab, four miles north of Gundamuk.

day. The Meerza, professing to have received an order from the Sirdar, insisted on searching the boxes of Lady Macnaghten and Capt. Lawrence. Unfortunately, the former had a great number of valuable Cashmere shawls, all of which were critically examined in order to ascertain their probable worth : but much disappointment was evinced that no jewels were forthcoming, as it was generally believed that her ladyship possessed a large assortment. Nothing was taken from her on this occasion; but it might easily be foreseen that such booty would ere long prove an irresistible temptation to our Giljye friends.

A cruel scene took place after this, in the expulsion from the fort of all the unfortunate Hindoostanees, whose feet had been crippled by the frost. The limbs of many of these poor wretches had completely withered, and had become as black as a coal ; the feet of others had dropped off from the ancle ; and all were suffering such excruciating torture as it is seldom the lot of man to witness. Yet the unmerciful Giljyes, regardless of their sufferings, dragged them forth along the rough ground, to perish miserably in the fields, without food or shelter, or the consolations of human sympathy. The real author of these atrocities was generally believed to be the owner of the

N 3

fort, Mahomed Shah Khan. The Meerza, however, though compelled to carry the order into effect, re-admitted several of the unfortunate victims at night.

March 10*th.* — In consequence of the repeated earthquakes, we deserted the house, and took up our abode in some small wooden huts constructed by our servants. To-night our slumber was broken by loud cries of " Murder !" which were found to proceed from Lady Sale's Hindoostanee ayah, whom one of her admirers, in a fit of jealousy, had attempted to strangle in her sleep. The wretch, failing in his purpose, jumped over the wall, which was about twenty feet high, and, being discovered in the morning, narrowly escaped a hanging by Lynch law at the hands of the Meerza, who was with difficulty persuaded to alter his sentence to banishment from the fort.

March 11*th.* — Dost Mahomed Khan, accompanied by Imam Verdi, arrived from the Sirdar, and held a long private conference with Major Pottinger. It was generally supposed that Mahomed Akber had made some overtures to the Indian government relative to the return of the Ameer his father. Reports were in circulation of the fall of Ghuznee, which afterwards proved too true. We also learned on good authority that Khoda Bux Khan, a powerful Giljye chief, had left the Sirdar, whose cause seemed on the decline.

March 12*th.* — Very heavy rain. Heard of Gen. Sale's sortie from Jellalabad in consequence of a supposed attempt on the part of the Affghans to mine the walls; — many of the enemy killed.

March 13*th.* — A report abroad, which turned out true, that the Sirdar was wounded in the left arm by one of his own followers, who had been bribed with a lac of rupees by Shah Shooja. The assassin was ripped open, according to Affghan custom in such cases.

March 18*th.* — The Meerza was this day recalled by the Sirdar, and his place filled by the Nazir of Mahomed Shah Khan, Saleh Mahomed. We heard of the murder of Shah Shooja by the hand of Shooja Dowla, eldest son of Nuwab Zeman Khan, who shot the unfortunate old king with a double-barrelled gun, as they were proceeding together to the royal camp at Seah Sung. It is a curious fact that Shah Shooja was present at the birth of his murderer, to whom he gave his own name on the occasion.

March 21*st.*—The inhabitants of this valley are said to be removing their families and property to the hills for safety. The Safees, a mountain tribe in the neighbourhood, were said to have

N 4

created much alarm, having been bought over by Capt. Macgregor.

March 24th.—The Nazir endeavoured to find out what amount of ransom was likely to be paid for us, and gave out that two lacs of rupees would be accepted. This, however, seemed to us all a mere *ruse* to fathom our purses, and he was referred to Capt. Macgregor for the information he required.

March 29th.—Sooltan Jan is said to have gone to oppose General Pollock with 1000 horse.

April 1st.—We received letters from Jellalabad, by which we learned that Gen. Pollock had authorised Capt. Macgregor to ransom us. A severe thunder storm at night.

April 3rd.—Heard of the destruction of the 27th N. I. at Ghuznee, and of another successful sortie made by Gen. Sale at Jellalabad, by which he obtained a large supply of cattle.

April 9th.—Tidings brought of Mahomed Akber's camp at Char Bagh having been surprised by Gen. Sale, when his whole force was completely routed, three guns recaptured, and the Sirdar himself and friends barely managed to save themselves by flight. The arrival of Mahomed Shah Khan this evening confirmed this joyful intelligence. It had been reported to us this morning that at a council of chiefs held at Tirghurree on the previous night, much debate had taken place regarding the disposal of their prisoners, when it was proposed by some to destroy us at once : our anxiety was, therefore, intense all day, until the Khan by his friendly manner somewhat reassured us. He had a long interview with Major Pottinger, who endeavoured to propose terms for our release ; to which, however, the Khan would not listen for a moment, but said we must follow the Sirdar's fortune, who would start for the hills early next morning.

April 10*th.* — We were all ready for a start at an early hour, but no camels came till 3 P. M. ; meanwhile a scene of pillage went on, in which Mahomed Shah Khan acted the part of robber-chief. His first act was to select all our best horses for himself, after which he deliberately rummaged Lady Macnaghten's baggage, from which he took shawls to the value of 5000*l*. He next demanded her jewels, which she was obliged reluctantly to give up, their value being estimated at 10,000*l*., or a lac of rupees. Not satisfied even with this rich plunder, he helped himself freely out of Capt. Lawrence's boxes to every thing that took his fancy ; after which, being well aware of the poverty of the rest, he departed. Fortunately my own riding horse was spared, through the kind interference of the Meerza who accompanied the Khan. This characteristic little drama having been acted, the signal was given for our departure, the European soldiers being left behind, with a promise of release on the payment of a ransom.

It was a treat to get free of the dismal high walls, within which we had been so long immured; and as we had arrived in the depth of winter, when all was bleak and desolate to the eye, the universal verdure with which returning spring had now clothed the valley struck us with all the force of magic. We had proceeded about four miles on the road towards Alishung, when our progress was arrested by a few horsemen, who galloped up waving their hands joyfully, and crying out " Shabash!" " Bravo!" " All is over! the Feringhee army has been cut up in the Khyber Pass, and all their guns taken by Sultan Jan!" The mutual joy of the Affghans seemed so perfectly sincere, that, notwithstanding the im-probability of the story, we felt almost compelled to believe it, especially when the order was given to return forthwith to our old quarters at Bud-deeabad. On the way back the new comers entered into full-length particulars regarding the alleged defeat of our army. The Ensofzyes, they said, had agreed to take three lacs of rupees for the free passage of our troops through the

Khyber, of which half was paid in advance. They had no sooner fingered the cash, than they laid a trap with Sultan Jan for the simultaneous attack of the front and rear of the army in the narrowest part of the pass, which had proved entirely successful.—We found the poor soldiers delighted to see us again; for, having heard several shots fired after our departure, they imagined we had all been killed. We were not long in discovering that the story we had heard was all a hoax, the real cause of our sudden return being some dispute among the chiefs, in consequence of which an attack on our party was anticipated; but we were told to hold ourselves in readiness for a fresh start on the following morning.

The whole population of the valley are in the greatest consternation for fear of an attack from the English force, and are bundling their families up to the hills for safety.

April 11*th.*—We were off again at 12 A. M. The first three miles were along the Tirghurree road, after which we struck off to the hills to the right. Our course now became westerly, and skirting the base of the hills for four or five miles, we crossed a low ridge into the cultivated valley of Alishung; where, after crossing a rapid, we passed close by Mahomed Akber Khan on the opposite bank, seated in a nalkee on a knoll by the road side. He looked ill and careworn, but returned our salutes politely. A little further in we found three tents pitched for our reception, on which we had scarcely time to take shelter ere the rain fell in torrents, and continued all night. A very indifferent dish of tough mutton constituted our meal for the day. In the course of the evening Sultan Jan arrived in camp, with only about thirty horsemen left of the thousand with whom he went forth to battle; the rest had all fled. He seemed grievously crest-fallen, and, unlike the Sirdar, exhibited his malice and spleen by cutting our acquaintance. Mahomed Akber, with the liberality which always marks the really brave, invariably attributes his own defeat to the fortune of war, and loudly extols the bravery exhibited by our troops led on by the gallant Sale. The guard around our camp consisted entirely of Seiks, under a Musulman Rajah, who, having been banished many years ago by Runjeet Sing, was befriended by Dost Mahomed Khan, the then ruler of Cabul, to whose family he has ever since attached himself. He was a splendid looking fellow, with very prepossessing manners, and expressed himself much disgusted with the Affghans, who took advantage of his going out to fight at Char Bagh to plunder his camp. Altogether, he seemed well disposed towards us, which, under our present circumstances, was cheering.

April 12th.—At our first starting this morning the bachelors were separated from the married families and ladies, and we went off by different roads. This sudden separation being very disagreeable to us all, Capt. Lawrence besought the Sirdar to permit us to proceed together as before. He also remonstrated with him for dragging the ladies and children with him all over the country, when they were so ill able to bear up against fatigue and exposure, representing that it would redound more to his honour to release them at once. Mahomed Shah Khan, who was present, upon this flew into a rage, and declared that "wherever he went we must all follow; that if our horses failed, we must trudge on foot; and that if we lagged behind, he would drag us along by force." He is the greatest enemy we have, and seems at present to govern the Sirdar completely. He was, however, taken to task by Mahomed Akber for his rudeness, and we were allowed to proceed all together, as heretofore. The road lay among low hills over a sandy soil, with several slight ascents and descents, one ascent being rather steep and long. About half way we crossed a small stream, and, after travelling about twelve miles, found the camp pitched in a narrow ravine, through which flowed a rivulet, the ground being covered with bunches of tall reeds, to which the Affghans set fire at night. Two old goats were sent us for dinner, which, not being fit to eat, we returned, and were afterwards supplied with an awfully tough old sheep in exchange.

April 13*th.*—The road again lay over steeps. On the left we saw the pass of Udruk-budruk in the distance. We gathered quantities of a curious herbaceous plant, the under surface of whose leaves was covered with a beautiful crimson dewy-looking substance, which the Affghan ladies use as rouge. About twelve miles brought us to a small scantily-cultivated valley, in which were two small forts partially ruined by the earthquake. The inhabitants enjoy the credit of being the greatest thieves in the whole country, so they must be bad indeed. Our whole march was about fourteen miles.

April 14*th.*—At starting we crossed the pass of Bad-push, the ascent up which was not less than 1600 feet over a very steep and rocky road. The descent was less abrupt and comparatively short. On these hills grew the hollyoak, wild almond, and a terebinthaceous tree called Khinjuck, yielding a fragrant medicinal gum, which I imagined might be the myrrh or balsam of commerce. It is, at all events, in great repute among the Affghans, who find it efficacious for sabre wounds. A species of mistletoe grew in great profusion on its branches; the flower somewhat resembled that of the mango, and the young leaves were oblong, lanceolate, opposite, and slightly serrate. An evergreen shrub, with a jasmine-like flower, was very abundant.

Following the course of a stream about six miles, we reached the left bank of the Cabul river, which here issued from between some precipitous hills with an exceedingly rapid current. About a hundred yards from the bank stood a small fort. We crossed on a raft of inflated bullock hides, the motion of which we found exceedingly pleasant. The horses crossed by a ford some distance higher up and about four miles round. On the right bank we found Mahomed Akber in his *nalkee*, to whom we paid our respects. The stream is about a hundred yards broad, and a few Affghans swam their horses over, though with some difficulty. The river is not navigable from this to Jellalabad, owing to the number of rapids and whirlpools.

April 15th.—We were kept waiting until noon for our horses, and in the mean time were amused by seeing a herd of cattle swim over the river; in attempting which they were all carried violently

down a rapid, and several, failing to effect a land-
ing, were obliged to return along the bank and
make a second effort. No camels were brought
with kujawurs for the weak ladies and the sick,
who were accordingly forced to ride on horseback.
Poor Gen. Elphinstone, who left Buddeeabad in
a most precarious state of health, was much shattered by the fatigues of travelling, and seemed to
be gradually sinking to the grave. The road ran
for a mile along the bank of the river, and then
suddenly turned up a ravine to the right. Two
miles more led to a valley communicating with
that of Tezeen, about a mile up which we encamped outside the fort of Surroobee, where we
had previously halted on the 12th of January.
Here was one of the mountain-train guns which
had been captured on the retreat. We found
that our Hindoostanee servants, who remained
behind here, had been well treated by Abdoolah
Khan, but the majority had died from the effects
of frost-bites.

April 16*th*.—Mahomed Akber fortunately found
it convenient to halt here, which proved seasonable both to man and beast; but we were told to
expect a long journey unto the hills in the neighbourhood of Tezeen, where it is the Sirdar's intention to conceal us. An Affghan, lately arrived
from Cabul, informed us that the city was divided

into two great parties, of whom the Dooranees and Kuzzilbashes formed one, and the Barukzies and Giljyes the other.

April 17*th.* — Another halt enabled us to enjoy a quiet Sunday. The Sirdar and a portion of his followers paid a visit to some neighbouring chiefs, but his people were deserting him fast. The Giljyes have been trying hard to excite the fears of the peasantry against the English by tales of our cruelty and oppression.

April 18*th.* — Having been warned last night to be ready for a march at dawn of day, we were all on the alert; but, after waiting a long time for orders to mount, we received a message from Mahomed Akber that we should await his return.

April 19*th.* — It rained hard all night and continued to pour the whole day, but we were obliged, nevertheless, to march sixteen miles to Tezeen. The road was up a narrow valley the whole way, crossing a stream twice before reaching Seh Baba, which we passed half way, after which we crossed the stream continually. At Seh Baba we encountered a putrid smell from the decomposed bodies of those who fell on the retreat, which lined the whole road. In some places we passed high piles of human bodies still fresh, the remains probably of those unfortunate beings who, having escaped the knives of the Ghazees, had struggled for existence until they sunk under the combined miseries of famine and exposure. The Affghans informed us that many had been driven to the miserable expedient of supporting life by feeding off the flesh of their deceased comrades ! — From Seh Baba to Tezeen is one continued rise, the valley being about half a mile broad and shut in by lofty heights on both sides. The stream is at this season a perfect torrent from the melting snow. We passed several encampments of the wandering Giljyes, whose flocks browsed on the neighbouring hills. We were all wet to the skin in spite of our *posteens*, or sheep-skin cloaks, and, on arriving at Mahomed Khan's fort at Tezeen, we found it so much dilapidated by the earthquake as to afford only the most scanty accommodation. The poor ladies were at first crammed into a small dirty room, filled with Affghan women, where they sat in their dripping clothes until, after much delay and trouble, they were accommodated with a separate apartment. As for the gentlemen, they had to scramble for shelter in a dark confined hovel, Capt. Mackenzie and myself preferring to pass the night in a stable with our horses, the rain dripping over us until morning.

This day's exposure decided the fate of Gen.

Elphinstone, who reached the fort in a dying state.

Captain Mackenzie received an intimation this night of the Sirdar's intention to send him on a mission to Gen. Pollock's camp at Jellalabad.

April 20th.—It rained the whole day, and, having nothing dry to put on, we were more uncomfortable than ever. Mrs. Waller was delivered of a daughter. This was the fourth addition to our number of captives ; Mrs. Boyd, Mrs. Riley, and a soldier's wife named Byrne, having been confined during our sojourn at Buddeeabad. A peculiar Providence seemed on all occasions to watch over the ladies, and nothing surprised us more than the slight nature of their sufferings on *these* occasions.

There was a severe shock of earthquake again to-day. These shocks have always appeared to me to be in some way connected with heavy rain beforehand.

April 21st.— Some tents having been pitched outside the fort, the whole of our party removed into them, with exception of the Wallers, ourselves, Gen. Elphinstone, Major Pottinger, Capt. Mackenzie, and Dr. Magrath, to all of whom permission was given to remain for the present in the fort. Atta Mahomed Khan, the owner of the place, expressed to us much annoyance at the

conduct of his kinsman Mahomed Shah Khan in
stirring up the rebellion, and hinted at his own
desire to be on friendly terms with our government. It seems he was promised remuneration
by Capt. Macgregor for the damage done to his
property by Gen. Sale's force in October 1841,
to the fulfilment of which pledge he still looked
forward.

The Sirdar was holding a levée to-day, at which
Major Pottinger was present, when he burst into
a violent passion, and declared that his own
countrymen had basely deserted and betrayed
him, although he had all along acted entirely at
the instigation of the chiefs at Cabul, especially
in the murder of the Envoy and the destruction
of our army ; yet these very men now refused to
support him ; and he solemnly swore that, if ever
he had the power, a severe example should be
made of them.

A part of the outer wall fell to-day from the
effects of yesterday's earthquake. At night the
ladies of Mahomed Shah Khan, and other chiefs
who were travelling in our company, invited Mrs.
Eyre to dinner. She found them exceedingly
kind in manner and prepossessing in outward appearance, being both well dressed and good looking. They asked her the old question as to the
gender of the Company Sahib, and were greatly

wonderstruck to learn that England was governed by a woman. They expressed the utmost dread of Capt. Macgregor, whom they regard in the same formidable light in which a child does the giant of a nursery tale.

April 22d.—A great bustle was created at an early hour this morning by the arrival of a messenger from the Sirdar to Dost Mahomed Khan, who was awakened from his slumbers in the General's room and immediately hurried away. Our fellow-captives in camp marched shortly afterwards for the Zanduk valley, near the Aman Koh, about eight miles south of Tezeen. There was apparently some apprehension entertained of a surprise from Cabul, as we ourselves were hurried off at about 9 A. M. to a small fort two miles higher up the valley, whither the Sirdar had preceded us. This sudden movement was a deathstroke to the General, who, though so weak as to be unable to stand, was made to ride on horseback the whole way.

April 23d.—Mahomed Akber received about 6000 rupees from Cabul, probably sent by his uncle, Nuwab Jubbar Khan. Futty Jung, the eldest son of the murdered monarch, retained possession of the Bala Hissar, and demanded from the Sirdar that all the European prisoners should be rendered up to him. The residents of

Cabul, we learned, were deserting the city in great numbers, from dread of our army, and all efforts to induce the people to oppose Gen. Pollock's advance were fruitless. This information at once decided the Sirdar to send Capt. Mackenzie to treat with Gen. Pollock without further delay, and that officer was warned to be in readiness to start at a moment's notice.

Some one having told the Sirdar that I could draw faces, he sent for me on that pretence; but to my surprise pumped me for half an hour on artillery matters, being very inquisitive as to the manufacture of fuses and port-fires, the mode of throwing shells from mortars and howitzers, and the mode of regulating the length of fuze for different distances, on all which subjects I enlightened him just enough to render his darkness visible. Before I went, he requested me to take the likeness of one of his followers, and of a favourite Arab horse, and, though my performance was very indifferent, he expressed himself pleased. I was afterwards called to examine a sextant which had been just brought to him: it was greatly damaged, but I explained its uses; after which, finding he could make no better use of it, he made me remove the coloured glasses, which he proposed to convert into spectacles to preserve his eyes from the glare.

The Fort near Tezeen where General Elphinstone died
on the 23 April 1842.
(After a water colour by Lieut. Vincent Eyre.)

About 7 p. m. Major-Gen. Elphinstone breathed his last, — a happy release for him from suffering of mind and body. Deeply he felt his humiliation, and bitterly regretted the day when he resigned the home-born pleasures of his native land, to hazard the high reputation of a proud name in a climate and station, for which he was constitutionally unfit. Of his merits I have already spoken at large in another place ; but it is due no less to the memory of the dead than to the large circle of living friends and relatives, who, I feel assured, will mourn his loss, that I should record how, to the very last moment of his being, he exhibited a measure of Christian benevolence, patience, and high-souled fortitude, which gained him the affectionate regard and admiring esteem of all who witnessed his prolonged sufferings and his dying struggles, and who regarded him as the victim less of his own faults, than of the errors of others, and the unfathomable designs of a mysterious Providence, by whom the means are always adapted to the end. The Sirdar seemed to have been unconscious of the General's extreme danger until this morning, when he offered, too late, to grant him his release. Had he listened to the advice of those who wished him well, he would have adopted this generous course at Buddeeabad ; but his chief supporters were interested

in keeping him in the dark, and in frustrating
every scheme that tended to reconcile him to the
British nation; so the timely counsel was unheeded.
His eyes at last were opened to the truth; and he
now endeavoured to make all the amends in his
power by offering to send the remains for honourable interment at Jellalabad.   At 8 A. M. Capt.
Mackenzie departed on his mission, which related
principally to the release of the ladies and
children.

April 25th. — A rude framework having been
constructed by an Affghan carpenter, the General's body, after being well covered up in felt
blankets, was packed in it, and the vacant spaces
filled with the highly scented leaves of wormwood.
At 2 P. M., all being ready, it was slung across the
back of a camel, and sent off under a small guard
of Giljyes, accompanied by one of the European
soldiers who attended the deceased, whom the
Sirdar thought likely to pass unnoticed in the
common costume of the country.   The Sirdar
afterwards invited us all to sit with him outside
the fort.   Whilst we were engaged in conversation, a messenger arrived with letters from Loo-
dianah, informing him that his family had been
starved for a whole week.   On being told the
contents, we all immediately pronounced the
whole a mischievous fabrication; upon which the

Sirdar somewhat bombastically proclaimed his disregard whether it were true or false, for that the destruction of his whole family should not alter his resolutions. He then resumed the previous conversation as if nothing had occurred, in the course of which he told me that the daily loss of life, by the fire of the cantonment guns during the siege, was between thirty and forty, but he declared that the shells fired from the Bala Hissar into the city did little or no damage to life or property.

April 26th. — Sad to say, the poor General's body was interrupted on its journey near Jugdulluk. It seems that the party in charge, on approaching the camp of some wandering Giljyes, were challenged, and thought that the best way to avoid discovery would be to assume confidence, and come to a halt there for the night. The European soldier was covered up with blanket⸵, and warned to remain quiet until morning. About 10 P. M., however, he was roused by a tumult of angry voices, in which the words " Feringhee " and " Kafir " were frequently repeated. A rush was shortly after made to where he was lying, and the covering being snatched from off his head, he was immediately attacked, and wounded in the arm with a sword, nothing saving his life but the thick blanket of felt which covered his body, and

o

the interposition of a chief who hurried him off
to his tent. The bigotted savages next stripped
the body of the General, which they pelted with
stones, and would have burned, but for the remon-
strances of the Sirdar's men, who threatened them
with the vengeance of their master. Mahomed
Akber's annoyance was great on receiving these
awkward tidings, but he lost no time in despatch-
ing as large a party as he could spare, to rescue
the European and re-pack the body.

In the course of conversation with Major Pottinger, the Sirdar asked him whether he would
take his oath that he had never written anything
to Jellalabad, but what had come to his (the
Sirdar's) knowledge. The Major maintained a
significant silence, but shortly afterwards, having
occasion to remark that, if the treaty had been
fulfilled, not a British soldier would now have
remained in Affghanistan, the Sirdar emphatically
asked him if he would swear to the truth of what
he uttered, to which the Major readily consenting,
the Sirdar seemed now for the first time to believe
what he had before utterly discredited, and looked
around upon his followers with an expression of
face which seemed to say, " What a miserable
fool then have I been ! "

April 27th. — The Sirdar started with Major
Pottinger to visit our fellow-prisoners in the

Zanduh valley. Lieut. Waller and myself, in the course of our evening stroll, amused ourselves in observing some Juzailchees firing at a mark about 100 yards distant: almost every shot was well directed, but they were all so dilatory in loading, that a British soldier could have fired four or five shots to their one.

The European soldier who accompanied the General's body returned this evening, having been rescued by the Sirdar's men from the savages who had detained him, and who now professed great contrition for having offended the Sirdar. The body, after being re-packed, had been forwarded on its way to Jellalabad.

April 28th. — A cossid, bearing a letter from Capt. Conolly to Gen. Pollock, was intercepted and severely beaten by the Sirdar's men, and detained a prisoner until his return.

April 29th. — A wild sheep was brought in, having been shot in the neighbouring hills. Its horns resembled those of a common ram, but its face and general outline were not unlike an antelope, though more coarse and clumsy.

April 30th. — The Sirdar and Major Pottinger returned from their excursion. Whilst at Zanduh, Ameenoollah Khan and other chiefs sent to demand that Major Pottinger should be delivered up to him, or twelve lacs of rupees in his stead.

The bills given by the Major on the Indian Government, payable on the safe arrival of the Cabool force at Jellalabad, having been dishonoured, the chiefs have been endeavouring to extort the money from the Hindoo shroffs.

May 1st. — To-night the Sirdar sent us a large supply of English letters and newspapers which had just come from Jellalabad, where Capt. Mackenzie had arrived safe. These were the first letters we had received for eight months, and we sat up the greater part of the night devouring their contents.

May 2d. — I was sent for by the Sirdar to examine a cavalry saddle, as he was anxious to know whether it was made of hog's skin. I told him it was a difficult question to decide, as both hog and cow skins were used, and could not easily be distinguished. As he gave me some knowing winks, and was evidently most unwilling that a good saddle should be sacrificed to the religious scruples of his moolah, who was seated in the room, I voted in favour of the cow; and, as Lieut. Waller afterwards declared himself on the same side, the Sirdar, considering that two witnesses decided the point, determined to hold his own: and I believe in his heart he cared little about the natural history of the hide, so long as it suited his purposes.

Late at night I was roused from bed by a message from the Sirdar, who pressed me hard to go and fight for him at Cabul against Ameenoollah Khan and Futty Jung. He was perfectly aware, he said, that no Englishman would serve against his own countrymen, but that in this case his enemies were equally hostile to the British; so that, in fighting for him, I should be serving my own country. I replied that I was already badly wounded and tired of fighting for the present; that I was quite incompetent, from my ignorance of Affghan politics, to form an opinion as to the rights and merits of the case; and that, even were I ever so much disposed to embrace his cause, no English officer or soldier could legally take arms under a sovereign power, without having first obtained the consent of his own Sovereign. My refusal apparently annoyed him a good deal, and I was obliged to repeat it several times before he would allow me to return to rest.

May 3d.—The Wallers and ourselves started for the Zanduh valley after breakfast, and had just mounted our horses, when Capt. Mackenzie made his appearance on his return from Jellalabad. His mission had not opened any immediate prospect of release for us, though the negotiation was, on the whole, of a friendly nature. After the exchange of a few words, he was hurried off

to the Sirdar, and we pursued our way to Zanduh. The road ascended the hills in a south-
easterly direction, and was very steep and undulating for about three miles, when it descended
into the narrow bed of a stream, one of the rami-
fications of the Tezeen valley, up which our
course was southerly for the rest of the march.
Four or five miles further brought us to camp,
where the valley was a little wider, with cultivated steppes of land, on which the tents were
pitched. Snow was still lying on the neighbour-
heights, and about four miles further south the
lofty mountain peak of Aman Koh reared its
pine-clad crest. On our way we noticed the
juniper, which universally prevails in these hills,
attaining in some spots the size of a goodly tree.
Here and there we passed a few stunted pines,
which might be considered as mere stragglers
from the neighbouring forests of Suffed Koh.
The wild almond, a showy and fragrant species of
Edwardsia; a shrubby cratægus-looking plant,
covered with blossoms; the yellow dog-rose, the
sweet-brier, the artemisia, the white tulip, and a
very pretty iris, constituted the prominent bota-
nical features of the road over which we travelled.
We found our friends enjoying themselves during
the heat of the day, in shady bowers formed of
juniper : the climate seemed delightful.

May 4th.—The Sirdar sent for Capt. Troup to accompany him and Major Pottinger to Cabul. Capt. Mackenzie was to start immediately on a second mission to Jellalabad.

May 5th. — The English hostages at Cabul were said to be under the protection of a Syud, son of the chief moolah; and Ameenoollah Khan, having endeavoured to seize them, had been driven into the Bala Hissar by Nuwab Zeman Khan, and his house in Cabul burned to the ground.

May 7th.—A hard frost this morning! the shrubs and herbs within reach of the spray of the stream being covered with large icicles. Our keeper now was Mahomed Rufeek, whose family resides at Candahar. From his pleasing manners, and constant civility and kindness, he soon became a general favourite. I took a long walk with him to-day among the hills south of camp; we saw nothing but juniper trees, anemones, and wild geraniums, the spring having only just commenced in that elevated region. The rocks were chiefly of limestone, with vertical strata.

May 8th.—This morning I was agreeably surprised by an Affghan bringing some of my own books and sketches for sale, of which I immediately possessed myself. In the forenoon a few drops of snow fell! The last three days were

o 4

bitterly cold, and we enjoyed a blazing fire at night.

May 9th.—Enjoyed another walk in the hills, with a fine bracing air, and a magnificent view in the direction of Hindoo Khoosh, whose everlasting snows and jagged peaks bounded the scene. On our return we heard the cheerful note of the cuckoo. I found a curious parasite on the juniper.

May 10th.—Capt. and Mrs. Anderson were agreeably surprised by the arrival of their eldest girl from Cabul. It will be remembered that she was lost in the Khoord-Cabul pass during the retreat on the 8th of January; since which she had been an inmate of Nuwab Zeman Khan's family, where she was treated with the greatest possible kindness. She had been taught to say " My father and mother are infidels, but I am a Mussulman." Capt. Troup, who had obtained her release, wrote word that he and Major Pottinger were in Nuwab Jubbar Khan's house at Cabul; that the city was in a most unquiet state, and the opposite parties fighting every day, the Cabulees siding alternately with whichever side paid them best. At night, a note was received from Major Pottinger, who had just witnessed an engagement between the Barukzyes and Dooranees, in which the former were victorious; but he described the affair as more ludicrous than tragical, having been a forcible representation of the " battle of spurs."

May 12*th.*— Capts. Boyd, Waller, and myself, accompanied by two Affghans, ascended some lofty hills to the west. Some Giljyes of the Jubbar Khail overtook us, and offered to escort us to Jellalabad. Our attendants, instantly taking alarm, hurried us away homewards. We had a fine view of Hindoo Koosh to the north, and Suffeed Koh to the south. At the height of 2000 feet above our camp, the husbandmen were only now ploughing the ground, whilst in the Zandu valley, immediately below, the crops were green. We descended by the bed of a stream, on whose steep sides a species of wild onion grew abundantly. A beautiful fritillaria was also common; and an asphodelous plant bearing a gigantic spadix of yellow flowers, which I took for an ornithogalum. On our return, Dost Mahomed Khan, who was encamped near us, rated Mahomed Rufeek severely for allowing us to stray so far. This chief is a thorough boor in his ideas and manners, and is always exhibiting some mean and silly suspicion of our intentions : had it depended on him, we should all have been shut up in dark cells or narrow cages long ago.

May 16*th.* — Capt. Mackenzie returned from

his second trip to Jellalabad, where Gen. Elphinstone's body had arrived safe and been interred with due military honour. It does not appear that much was done towards effecting our release. The terms the Sirdar proposed to Gen. Pollock for our release were, — that he should be made governor of the Lughman province, and be exempted from attendance at court, and uncontrolled by our political officers. Of this proposal Gen. Pollock very properly took not the smallest notice. It seems that a despatch from the Sirdar, in which an offer was made to release the ladies and children unconditionally, which was sent after Capt. Mackenzie, did not reach him, having been intercepted, as was supposed, by Mahomed Shah Khan. Gen. Nott was expected to march for Cabul from Candahar on the 17th instant.

May 17th. — Capt. Mackenzie left for Cabul, to communicate the result of his mission to the Sirdar.

May 18th. — Dost Mahomed Khan was much struck by hearing Mahomed Rufeek read a Persian translation of the " Sermon on the Mount " out of Gladwain's " Moonshee." He was fervent in his admiration of the Lord's Prayer, as well as of several other passages ; and the injunction to pray in private seemed to throw light on our apparent neglect of outward observances. Cor-

poral Lewis of H. M. 44th, who had been kept
a prisoner at Tezeen in the fort of Khooda Bux-
khan, was allowed to visit our camp to-day. The
poor fellow had been starved and illtreated by his
savage captors, until he made an outward pro-
fession of Mahomedanism, when he received the
name of Deen Mahomed, and was made to attend
prayers daily with the faithful.

May 20th.— A beacon-light was burning all
night on the hill above us, and pickets were
thrown out in all directions. It was supposed
that a chuppāo, or night surprise, was expected.

May 22d. — Our horses arrived from Cabul,
for which city we received notice to march next
morning.

May 23d. — Marched about 9 A. M.   Three of
us obliged to walk for want of horses. Ladies
travelled in kujawurs, laden on mules. We
retraced our former track down the bed of the
stream, and across the hills, to the fort where
Gen. Elphinstone died. A few miles of descent
made a great difference in the climate and the
progress of vegetation ; the wild roses were every
where in full bloom, and, with other gay flowers,
scented the air and enlivened the scene. We
crossed a branch of the Tezeen valley ; a short cut
over the hills led us to the foot of the Huft
Kotul, or hill of seven ascents. Here we once

o 6

more encountered the putrid bodies of our
soldiery, which thenceforward strewed the road as
far as Khoord Cabul, poisoning the whole atmosphere. A little beyond Kubbur-i-jubbar we
passed two caves, on opposite sides of the road,
full as they could hold of rotten carcasses. Thence
to Tungee Tureekee the sight became worse and
worse. Mahomed Rufeek asked me whether all
this would not excite the fury of Gen. Pollock's
army; I told him he need not be surprised if
every house in Cabul were levelled to the ground.
From the last-mentioned spot we turned off the
high road to the left, and, passing a large ruined
village, arrived at the fort of Khoord Cabul,—
where we had previously lodged on the 9th of
January,—after a fatiguing march of twenty-two
miles. The contrast between the summer and
winter aspect of the valley immediately below the
fort was striking : the whole now presenting one
red field of cultivation.

May 24th. — Again on the move at 9 A. M.
The Khoord Cabul pass being now absolutely
impassable from the stench of dead bodies, we
took the direct road towards Cabul, having
Alexander the Great's column in view nearly the
whole way. The first three or four miles were
over a barren plain, when the road entered among
hills crossing a ghat of moderate height into a

valley about three miles in width, in the middle of which we halted for half an hour at a deliciously cool and clear spring, which supplied a small tank or pond: just above this, crowning the hill to the left, stood a ruined Grecian tope. Resuming our way, we again entered some hills, the road making a continuous ascent for about a couple of miles to Alexander's pillar, one of the most ancient relics of antiquity in the East, and conspicuously situated on the crest of a mountain range which bounds the plain of Cabul on the south-east. It stands about seventy feet high; the shaft is of the Doric order, standing on a cubic pedestal, and surmounted by a sort of urn. As we reached this classic spot, a view of almost unrivalled magnificence burst suddenly upon our sight. At the distance of some two thousand feet below, the whole picturesque and highly cultivated valley of Cabul was spread before us like a map: the towering mountain ranges of Kohistan and Hindoo Khoosh, clad in a pure vesture of snow, bounded the horizon, at the distance of nearly a hundred miles. The Bala Hissar was dimly discernible in the distance, from whose battlements the roar of cannon broke ever and anon upon the ear, betokening the prolongation of the strife between hostile tribes and ambitious chiefs. The descent was very long and tedious, and the road

about midway very steep and bad. On the way
down another Grecian pillar was discernible
among the hills on the left. The rocks were
chiefly of micaceous schist, and a dark stone resembling basalt. The gum-ammoniac plant grew
here; the young flower was clustered together
not unlike a small cauliflower. It is an um-
belliferous plant, growing to the height of six
feet, and in its general appearance and mode of
growth resembling an heracleum. It has a strong
disagreeable scent, which reminded me slightly of
assafœtida. The gum exudes plentifully, and is
at first milky, but afterwards turns to yellow, and
has a bitter nauseous taste. The plant is called
by the Affghans *gundĕlē,* and the gum is sold in
the Cabul bazar under the name of *feshook.*

At the foot of the hill we rested at a tank or
pond supplied by a large spring which gushes
from under the rock; another ruined Grecian
tope crowned a small eminence at a few hundred
yards' distance. The road now skirted the base
of the hills to the left for about four miles, when
we reached the fort of Ali Mahomed, Kuzzilbash,
distant three miles from Cabul, and close to the
Logur river, where we were accommodated for
the night, having marched altogether about
twenty miles.

May 25th.—The ladies of Ali Mahomed having

removed to a neighbouring fort, we occupied their apartments, which lined two sides of an inclosed square, and were very commodious, and decidedly the best quarters we have yet enjoyed. The valley about here is thickly studded with forts, and very highly cultivated.

May 26th.—Captain Troup paid us a visit. He told us the Sirdar was living in the outskirts of the city about two miles from us, that Amen-oollah Khan had joined him, but that Futty Jung still held out in the Bala Hissar, in hopes of being soon relieved by the arrival of our army. Mahomed Akber is desirous to obtain possession of the citadel principally on account of the treasure within it, as he never professed to dream of resisting our arms. He earnestly desired to be on friendly terms with the British government, and often said that he wished he had been so fortunate as to become acquainted with the English in early life, as he had been filled with prejudices against them which had greatly influenced his conduct, but which he now saw to be unfounded. It seems that Gen. Pollock offered on his own responsibility to release the ladies and children of his family from their confinement, but in his present precarious state of life the Sirdar has declined the offer.

Hundreds of Hindostanees crowded the streets

of Cabul begging for bread, which was daily served out to them by Nuwab Jubbar Khan and Zeman Khan. The civility of all classes to the European hostages and prisoners in and about Cabul was remarkable.

May 27th.—We all received permission to walk in the adjacent garden, and the gentlemen were allowed to bathe in a running canal near the fort, which, now that the weather had become sultry, were real luxuries.

May 29th.— Shuja Dowlah, the assassin of Shah Soojah, paid us a visit. He was a handsome quiet-looking man, whom few would have guessed to be the perpetrator of such a deed. He tried hard to persuade us that the Shah had played us false, and that he had committed a praiseworthy action in getting rid of him. The murder was committed at the instigation of Dost Mahomed Khan, Giljye, by way of retribution for the attempt on Mahomed Akber's life at Charbagh by an agent of Shah Soojah; but the act is much reprobated by all classes at Cabul, and by no one more than than the Nuwab Zuman Khan, who has banished Shuja Dowlah from his house ever since.

May 30th. — Shah Dowla, another son of Nuwab Zuman Khan, paid us a visit, and inquired particularly if we were well treated by the

Sirdar. We were informed that, in consequence of the Sirdar having demanded the persons of the Naib Shereef Mohun Loll and the late wuzeer, the Kuzzilbash had risen in a body against him, and declared their intention to hold their part of the city until the arrival of our troops. We heard a great deal of firing to-night, and the extreme vigilance of our guard led us to suppose that the Sirdar's affairs were not prospering. Dost Mahomed Khan arrived in the fort at night.

May 31st. — Guns were heard all night, and we were refused permission to leave the fort, as usual, to-day. Mahomed Rufeek, we were sorry to learn, had incurred suspicion, from his family having aided Gen. Nott at Candahar. He determined to throw up the Sirdar's service in consequence.

June 1st. — Dost Mahomed Khan departed for the city accompanied by Mahomed Rufeek. Permission was again given us to go into the garden, and to bathe in the canal as before.

June 2d. — Intelligence was brought us that Gen. Nott had obtained a victory at Kelat-i-Giljye, in which 2000 of the enemy were killed.

June 3d. — It was reported that Futty Jung had offered a large reward to any one who would seize and escort us all to the Bala Hissar. The

Sirdar made a fierce attack on the Bala Hissar in the evening, and a brisk cannonade was kept up on both sides for several hours, but without any decisive result.

June 4th. — Capt. Troup paid us a visit, bringing with him several necessaries, for which we had previously written to the Sirdar. It was believed in the city that one of the bastions of the Bala Hissar had been mined, but that the Sirdar was deferring its explosion in the hope that he might succeed without it, being unwilling to injure the defences of the place. But this report was probably set abroad for the purpose of intimidating the defenders, of whom only two men had been wounded during the whole siege up to this date.

A messenger arrived this morning from Jellalabad with letters for Futty Jung and Lady Sale. From the latter we learned that Gen. Pollock had written to Mahomed Akber, declaring it to be contrary to the laws of nations to make war against women and children, which it was hoped might shame him into the release of that portion of his prisoners, who came under the benefit of the rule.

Hopes began to be entertained of the safety of Dr. Grant of the Goorkha regiment, who was supposed to be concealed in Cabul. A shock of earthquake felt to-day.

June 6th. — About 5 P. M. a good deal of firing

was heard, and our garrison was in a state of great excitement. Futty Jung said to have sallied from the Bala Hissar and carried off a quantity of Mahomed Akber's military stores and camels. At night we heard that the Sirdar had seized Amenoolah Khan, whom he suspected of intriguing with Futty Jung, probably with good foundation. The Khan said to be worth 18 lacs of rupees, which it was the Sirdar's intention to make him disgorge. Amenoolah Khan was originally the son of a camel-driver, but by dint of his talents, bravery, and cunning, rose to be one of the most powerful nobles in the country. The late Ameer Dost Mahomed Khan feared and suspected him so much as to forbid him to enter Cabul. He possessed the whole of the Logur valley, and could bring 10,000 men into the field. The accession of such a man to his cause was of much importance to Mahomed Akber, and his seizure was a dangerous step, being likely to provoke the hostility of his sons. Amenoolah Khan was the chief instigator of the rebellion, and of the murder of Sir Alexander Burnes; after which he lent the weight of his influence to each party alternately, as it suited his purpose. Such a vacillating wretch was not long likely to escape retributive justice.

June 7th. — Contradictory reports were in cir-

culation all day. Some affirm the Bala Hissar to
have been taken ; others that the Sirdar had sustained a ruinous defeat, and that he was engaged
in plundering the city, prior to taking flight. That
something extraordinary had occurred was evident
from the mysterious deportment of the Affghans,
and their anxiety to prevent our receiving any
communication from without. A parcel of useful
articles arrived for us from our good friends at
Jellalabad, but every thing was opened by the
guard at the gate, who gave us only what they
chose, and seized all the letters, to send to the
Sirdar. There was no firing from the Bala Hissar
to-day as usual. The climate in this part of the
valley we found delightfully cool and pleasant,
which may have arisen in part from the luxuriant
cultivation round about. The most common trees
are the poplar, willow, mulberry, and oleaster, or
sinjut, the bright silvery foliage of the latter contrasting strikingly with the deep green of the rest,
and its flowers scattering a powerful and delicious
perfume through the surrounding air. Purple
centaurias adorned the corn fields, and a handsome
species of hedysarum, with a lupin-like flower,
enlivened the border of every field and watercourse ; whilst a delicate kind of tamarisk ornamented the banks of the neighbouring river.
In the garden I found a very beautiful oro-

banche growing parasitically from the roots of the melon.

June 9th. — Capt. Mackenzie paid us a visit. From him we learned positively that the Sirdar sprung a mine under one of the towers of the Bala Hissar, near the Shah Bazar, on the 6th ; that the storming party was driven back with a loss of sixty men killed, and that much damage was done in the adjacent part of the town by the explosion. On the following day, Futty Jung, finding his people disinclined to support him any longer, made terms with Mahomed Akber and the other chiefs, giving up a tower in the Bala Hissar to each, and himself retaining possession of the royal residence. Thus the citadel was now divided between the Dooranees, Barukzyes, Gilgyes, and Kuzzilbashes, represented by Futty Jung, Mahomed Akber, Nuwab Zeman Khan, Mahomed Shah Khan, and Khan Shereen Khan. A curious arrangement, truly ! and calculated to facilitate the union of parties already jealous of each other, and each of whom had, doubtless, an eye to the rich treasure of money and jewels still in Futty Jung's possession. The story of Amenoolah Khan's seizure turned out to be untrue. There was a violent quarrel a few days back between the two old Nuwabs, Zeman Khan and Jubbar Khan, when the former seized hold of the latter's beard, exclaiming, " You are the fellow who first brought the Feringhees into the country, and to whom, therefore, all our troubles may be attributed." Abdool Glujas Khan, the son of Jubbar Khan, being present, drew a pistol and threatened to shoot Zeman Khan for the indignity offered to his father. Mahomed Akber sat by the whole time, laughing heartily at the scene.

June 10*th.* — A smart shock of earthquake during the night.

June 11*th.* — Capt. Mackenzie returned to the city. It was supposed he would start in a day or two on a fresh mission to Jellalabad.

June 20*th.* — Heard from Capt. Mackenzie that Mahomed Akber was waging war with Nuwab Zeman Khan; also that Gen. Nott had seized the person of Sufter Jung, the rebel son of Shah Shooja-ool-moolk. Ali Mahomed assured us that it was the Sirdar's intention shortly to march to Jellalabad, to pay his respects to Gen. Pollock! From other quarters we heard that he meditated carrying us all off to the banks of the Oxus.

June 21*st.* — We were told by Ali-Mahomed that the Sirdar had taken Nuwab Zeman Khan and his two sons prisoners, and, after seizing all his guns, treasure, and ammunition, had released them again.

June 25th. — Capts. Mackenzie and Troup paid us a visit. Mahomed Akber's late successful conflict with Nuwab Zeman Khan had rendered him, for the time being, supreme in Cabul. The Kuzzilbashes had tendered their unwilling submission, and had delivered up Mohun Loll, who was immediately put to the torture. Jan Fishan Khan, the laird of Purghman, a staunch friend of the British, had been obliged to fly for his life, his two sons having been slain in the fight. Khoda Bux Khan, and Atta Mahomed Khan, Giljyes, fought against Mahomed Akber on this occasion. Both Capt. Troup and Capt. Mackenzie had since been allowed to visit the hostages, whom they found in the house of the Meer Wyze, the chief moollah of the city, to whose protection they had been committed by Zeman Khan, in consequence of the desperate efforts of the Ghazees to slay them. During their stay in the good Nuwab's house, their lives were in constant danger from those fanatics, who on one occasion actually forced their way into the building to accomplish their purpose, and were only hindered by the Nuwab falling on his knees, casting his turban on the ground, and entreating them not to dishonour his roof by committing violence to those under its protection. Before sending them to the Meer Wyze, which was done at night, he took the precaution to line the streets with his own followers, with strict orders to fire upon every one who should so much as poke his head out of a window; and he not only accompanied them himself, but sent his own family on ahead. Capt. Conolly had obtained convincing proof that Shah Shoojah originated the rebellion with a view to get rid of Burnes, whom he detested, and of several chiefs, whom he hoped to see fall a sacrifice to our vengeance; little anticipating the ruinous result to himself and to us. Poor Burnes had made but few friends among the chiefs, who now never mention his name but in terms of the bitterest hatred and scorn. He seems to have kept too much aloof from them; thus they had no opportunity of appreciating his many valuable qualities, and saw in him only the traveller, who had come to spy the nakedness of the land, in order that he might betray it to his countrymen. The King considered him as a personal enemy, and dreaded his probable succession to the post of Envoy on the departure of Sir W. Macnaghten.

Of Mahomed Akber Khan, I have been told from an authentic source that, on the morning of the departure of the army from Cabul on the 6th of January, he and Sultan Jan made their appearance booted and spurred before the assembly of chiefs, and being asked by Nuwab Zeman Shah where they were going, Mahomed Akber replied, " I am going to slay all the Feringhee dogs, to be sure." Again: on the passage of our troops through the Khoord-Cabul pass on the 8th, he followed with some chiefs in the rear, and in the same breath called to the Giljyes in *Persian* to desist from, and in *Pushtoo* to continue, firing. This explains the whole mystery of the massacre, and clears up every doubt regarding Mahomed Akber's treachery.

June 27th.—To our surprise, the European soldiers whom we left in the fort at Buddeeabad, and whom we believed to have been ransomed, made their appearance. They all agreed in stating that they had been ill-treated and starved ever since our departure, which they mainly attributed to the evil influence of their own countrywoman, Mrs. Wade, who had disgraced her country and religion by turning Mahommedan, and, having forsaken her husband, had become the concubine of an Affghan in Mahomed Shah Khan's service, and had taken every occasion to excite prejudice and hostility against the English captives, who were plundered of the little money and the few clothes they possessed, and exposed to continual insult and savage threats. She actually was so base as to betray her own husband, in whose boot two pieces of gold had been sewn up with her

P

own hands, of which he was deprived at her suggestion. On their arrival at Cabul, she had gone
off to Mahomed Shah Khan's fort, taking• with
her a little orphan child named Staker, of which
she had charge.

June 27th. — Capt. Mackenzie having been
taken ill, Capt. Troup returned to the city without him. The Sirdar, we learned, had made preparation for a flight to Bameean, in anticipation
of the advance of our troops; whither, of course,
the prisoners would accompany him. His ultimate place of refuge, it was supposed, would be
Herat.

June 29th. — A shock of earthquake. Capt.
Troup came to see us again before starting to
Jellalabad on a mission from the Sirdar. Futty
Jung was this day proclaimed king by Mahomed
Akber, who contented himself for the present
with the title of wuzeer. Capt. Mackenzie still
very ill. * * * *

The Author's autograph manuscript breaks off
here; but, as there remain still to be noted the
events of three months, including those critical
movements by which Mahomed Akber's captives
were so nearly hurried beyond the hope of freedom, it is hoped that he will yet tell, in his own
words, the remainder of the tale. In the mean

time his private letters will make the conclusion less abrupt.

—" Our real foe is Mahomed Shah Khan, but for whose baneful influence the Sirdar would have released the ladies long ago. The latter has many good points, and, but for *one* act, would be more worthy of clemency than the chiefs at whose instigation he did everything, and who would fain make him their scape-goat." * * * *

" *July* 29th. — We have had a good deal of sickness amongst us, and Mackenzie had a narrow escape of his life from a malignant fever. All the invalids are, however, recovering, thank God! I fear, however, that our prospects are blacker than ever. We had hopes, a few days ago, that a fair exchange would be agreed upon between Mahomed Akber and Gen. Pollock, of the Ameer and all the other Affghan prisoners for us poor wretches. But the General has since received instructions to advance on Cabul; and Mahomed Akber declared to-day to Troup, with an expression of savage determination in his countenance, that so surely as Pollock advances, he will take us all into Toorkistan, and make presents of us to the different chiefs. And depend upon it he will carry his threats into execution, for he is not a man to be trifled with." * * * *

The public are aware how well Mahomed Akber

would have kept this pleasant promise; but the next and last communication is from Cabul, announcing the happy deliverance of the whole party, whose varied fortunes have for the last twelve months excited such universal interest.

" Camp, Cabul, 22d Sept. 1842.

" *Cabul, Sept. 22d.* — Heaven be praised! we are once more free. Our deliverance was effected on the 20th, and we arrived safe in Gen. Pollock's camp yesterday evening. On the 25th of August we were hurried off towards *Toorkistan*, and reached *Bameean* on the 3d of September, every indignity being heaped upon us by the way. There we awaited fresh orders from Mahomed Akber. Meanwhile Pollock's army advanced on Cabul, carrying all before them. About the 10th of September an order came to carry us off to *Koorloom*, and to butcher all the sick, and those for whom there was no conveyance. Fortunately discontent prevailed among the soldiers of our guard, and their commandant began to intrigue with Major Pottinger for our release. A large reward was held out to him, and he swallowed the bait. The Huzarah chiefs were gained over; and on the 16th we commenced our return towards Cabul, expecting to encounter the defeated and now furious Akber on the way. On the 17th we were reinforced by Sir R. Shakespeare, who had ridden out from Cabul with 600 Kuzzilbash horsemen to our assistance. His aid was most timely; for Sultan Mahomed Khan, with 1000 men, was hastening to intercept us. On the 20th, after forced marches, we met a brigade of our troops, and our deliverance was complete."

LIST OF PRISONERS RELEASED ON GENERAL POLLOCK'S ARRIVAL AT CABUL.

Major-Gen. Shelton, Her Majesty's 44th foot.
Lieut.-Col. Palmer*, 27th Bengal native infantry.
Major Griffiths, 37th Bengal native infantry.
Capt. Troup, Shah's service.
— Anderson, ditto.
— Bygrave, paymaster.
— Boyd, commissariat.
— Johnson, ditto S. S. F., 26th native infantry.
— Burnett, 54th native infantry.
— Souter, Her Majesty's 44th foot.
— Waller, Bengal horse artillery.
— Alston*, 27th native infantry.
— Poett*, ditto.
— Walsh, 52d Madras native infantry.
— Drummond, 3d Bengal light cavalry.
Lieut. Eyre, Bengal artillery.
— Airey, Her Majesty's 3d buffs.
— Warburton, Bengal artillery, S. S. F.
— Webb, 38th Madras native infantry, S. S. F.
— Crawford, Bengal 3d native infantry, S. S. F.
— Mein, Her Majesty's 13th light infantry.
— Harris*, 27th Bengal native infantry.

* Those marked thus * were of the Ghuznee garrison.

Lieut. Melville, 54th Bengal native infantry.
— Evans, Her Majesty's 44th foot.
Ensign Haughton, 31st Bengal native infantry.
— Williams, 37th Bengal native infantry.
— Nicholson,   ditto.
Conductor Ryley, ordnance commissariat.
Doctor Campbell.
Surgeon Magrath.
Assistant-Surgeon Berwick, left in charge.
— Thomson.

LADIES.

Lady Macnaghten.
— Sale.
Mrs Trevor, 8 children.
— Anderson, 3 ditto.
— Sturt and 1 child.
— Mainwaring, ditto.
— Boyd, 3 children.
— Eyre, 1 child.
— Waller, 2 children.
Conductor Ryley's wife, Mrs. Ryley, 3 children.
Private Bourne's (13th light infantry) wife, Mrs. Bourne.
Mrs. Wade, wife of Sergeant Wade.

Major Pottinger, Bombay artillery.
Captain Lawrence, 11th light cavalry.
— Mackenzie, 48th Madras native infantry.
Mr. Fallon, clerk ⎫ not in the service.
— Blewitt, do. ⎭

HER MAJESTY'S 44TH FOOT.

Sergeant Wedlock.
— Weir.
— Fair.
Corporal Sumpter.
— Bevan.
Drummer Higgins.
— Lovell.

Drummer Branagan.
Private Burns.
— Cresham.
— Cronin.
— Driscoll.
— Deroney.
— Duffy.

Private Matthews.
— M'Dade.
— Marron.
— M'Carthy.
— M'Cabe.
— Nowlan.
— Robson.
— Seyburne.
— Shean.
— Tongue.
— Wilson.
— Durant.

Private Arch.
— Stott.
— Moore.
— Miller.
— Murphy.
— Marshall.
— Cox.
— Robinson.
— Brady.
— M'Glyn.
Boys Grier.
— Milwood.

HER MAJESTY'S 13TH LIGHT INFANTRY.

Private Binding.
— Murray.
— Magary.
— Monks.

Private Maccullar.
— M'Connell.
— Cuff.

BENGAL HORSE ARTILLERY.

Sergeant M'Nee.
— Cleland.
Gunner A. Hearn.
— Keane.

Gunner Dalton.
Sergeant Wade, baggage-sergeant to the Cabul mission.

(Signed)   G. PONSONBY, Captain,
Assistant-Adjutant-General.

(True copy.)   (Signed)   R. C. SHAKESPEAR,
Military Secretary.

(True copies.)   (Signed)   T. H. MADDOCK,
Secretary to the Government of India
with the Governor-General.

(True copies.)   J. P. WILLOUGHBY,
Secretary to the Government.

P 4

APPENDIX.

APPENDIX.

List of Civil and Military Officers killed during
the Rebellion, at and near Cabul,
Between 12*th October* 1841, *and* 6*th January* 1842, *the
day of leaving Cabul.*

Political.

Sir W. H. Macnaghten, Bart.	Murdered at a conference on	23d Dec.
Sir Alexander Burnes	Ditto in his own house in the city on - -	2d Nov.
Capt. Broadfoot, 1st Eng. Regt.	Ditto in Sir A. B.'s house in the city on - -	2d "
Lieut. Burnes, Bombay Infty.	Ditto in Sir A. B.'s house in the city on - -	2d "
Lieut. Rattray -	- Ditto at a conference at Lughmanee in Kohistan -	3d "

H. M. 44th.

Lieut. Col. Mackrell -	- Killed in action at Cabul	- 10th Nov.
Capt. Swayne - -	- Ditto	Ditto	- 4th "
Capt. M Crea -	- Ditto	Ditto	- 10th "
Capt. Robinson -	- Ditto	Ditto	- 4th "
Lieut. Raban - -	- Ditto	Ditto	- 6th "

5th N. I.

Lieut. Col. Oliver -	- Ditto	Ditto	- 23d Nov.
Capt. Mackintosh -	- Ditto	Ditto	- 23rd "

37th N. I.

Capt. Westmacott -	- Ditto	Ditto	- 10th Nov
Ensign Gordon -	- Ditto	Ditto	- 4th "

35th N. I.

Lieut. Jenkins -	- Ditto at Khoord-Cabul	- 12th Oct.
Capt. Wyndham -	- Ditto at Jugdulluk	- 12th "

H. M. 13th Light Infantry.

Lieut. King -   -   -   Killed at Tezeen   - 12th Oct.

Local Horse.

Capt. Walker, 1st N. I.   -   Ditto at Cabul -   - 23d Nov.

27th N. I.

Lieut. Laing -   -   -   Ditto   Ditto   - 23d Nov.

Shah's Service.

Capt. Woodburn, 44th N. I. -   Ditto   Ditto   - 23d Nov.
Capt. Codrington, 49th N. I. -   Ditto at Chareeker   - 23d ”
Ensign Salisbury, 1st V. Regt.   Ditto   Ditto   - 23d ”
Ensign Rose, 54th N. I.   -   Ditto   Ditto   - 23d ”
Doctor Grant, Bombay Estab. -   Ditto   Ditto   - 23d ”
Lieut. Maule, Artillery   -   Ditto in his camp at Kah-
                                 darrah   -   - 3d   ”
Capt. Trevor, 3d Light Cav. -   Ditto at a conference   - 23d Dec.
Local Lieut. Wheeler   -   Ditto in his camp at Kah-
                                 darrah   -   - 3d Nov.

From 6th January up to the 12th January 1842 inclusive on the retreat.

Staff.

Dr. Duff, Superin.-Surgeon - Killed between Tezeen and
                                 Seh Baba   -   - 10th Jan.
Capt. Skinner, 61st N. I.   -   Ditto at Jugdulluk   - 12th ”
Capt. Paton*, 58th N. I.   -   Ditto Khoord-Cabul pass 8th ”
Lieut. Sturt *, Engineers   -   Ditto   Ditto   - 8th ”

Horse Artillery.

Dr. Bryce   -   -   -   Ditto on march to Tezeen 10th Jan.

5th Light Cavalry.

Lieut. Hardyman   -   -   Ditto outside the canton-
                                 ment   -   - 6th Jan.

H. M. 44th.

Major Scott -   -   -   Ditto on march to Tezeen 10th Jan.
Capt. Leighton   -   -   Ditto   Ditto   - 10th ”
Lieut. White   -   -   Ditto Junga Fareekee   - 10th ”
Lieut. Fortye *   -   -   Ditto Jugdulluk   - 10th ”

* These officers had been previously wounded at Cabul. Captain
Paton's left arm had been amputated.

5th N. I.

Major Swayne *	-	-	Killed at Junga Fareekee - 10th Jan.
Capt. Miles	-	-	Ditto Ditto - 10th ”
Lieut. Deas *	-	-	Ditto Ditto - 10th ”
Lieut. Alexander	-	-	Ditto Ditto - 10th ”
Lieut. Warren	-	-	Ditto Ditto - 10th ”

54th N. I.

Major Ewert	-	-	Ditto on march to Tezeen 10th Jan.
Capt. Shaw *	-	-	Ditto Ditto - 10th ”
Lieut. Kirby	-	-	Ditto Ditto - 10th ”

37th N. I.

Lieut. St. George - - Ditto Khoord-Cabul pass 8th Jan.

H. M. 44th.

Lieut. Wade - - Ditto Jugdulluk - 12th Jan.

27th N. I.

Dr. Cardew * - - Ditto Tezeen - - 10th Jan.

After leaving Jugdulluk on the 12th to the final massacre.

Staff.

Major Thain* H. M. 21st Ft. a. d. c.	Jugdulluk Pass -	- 12th Jan.
Capt. Bellew, 56th N. I.	- Futtehabad -	- 13th ”
Capt. Grant, 27th N. I.	- Gundamuk -	- 13th ”
Capt. Mackay, Assist. P. M. †	- Doubtful.	

Horse Artillery.

Capt. Nicholl	- Jugdulluk Pass -	- 12th Jan.
Lieut. Stewart	- Gundamuk -	- 13th ”

5th Light Cavalry.

Lieut.-Col. Chambers -	- Jugdulluk Pass -	- 12th Jan.
Capt. Blair	- Ditto -	- 12th ”
Capt. Bott	- Ditto -	- 12th ”
Capt. Hamilton	- Gundamuk -	- 13th ”
Capt. Collyer	- near Jellalabad -	- 14th ”
Lieut. Bazett -	- Jugdulluk Pass -	- 12th ”
Dr. Harpur	- near Jellalabad -	- 14th ”
Veterinary Surgeon Willis	- Doubtful.	

* These officers had been previously wounded at Cabul.

† Capt. Mackay, Assist. P. M. Shah's Staff, being mentioned in the text twice (pp. 216. 220.), I insert his name thus. It is not in the original list. — Editor.

H. M. 44th.

Capt. Dodgin - -	- Jugdulluk pass -	- 12th Jan.
Capt. Collins - -	- Gundamuk -	- 13th "
Lieut. Hogg - -	- Ditto -	- 13th "
Lieut. Cumberland -	- Ditto -	- 13th "
Lieut. Cadett - -	- Soorkab -	- 12th "
Lieut. Swinton -	- Gundamuk -	- 13th "
Ensign Gray - -	- Doubtful.	
Paymaster Bourke -	- Jugdulluk -	- 12th "
Qr.-Master Halaban* -	- Jugdulluk pass -	- 12th "
Surgeon Harcourt -	- Ditto -	- 12th "
Assist. Surgeon Balfour	- Doubtful.	
Assist. Surgeon Primrose	- Gundamuk -	- 13th "

5th N. I.

Capt. Haig - -	- Doubtful.	
Lieut. Horsbrough -	- Gundamuk -	- 13th Jan.
Lieut. Tombs - -	- Doubtful.	
Ensign Potenger -	- Ditto.	
Lieut. Burkinyoung -	- Ditto.	
Dr. Metcalfe - -	- Gundamuk -	- 13th Jan.

37th N. I.

Capt. Rind - -	- Gundamuk -	- 13th Jan.
Lieut. Steer - -	- Jugdulluk pass -	- 12th "
Lieut. Vanrenen -	- near Soorkab -	- 12th "
Lieut. Hawtrey -	- Gundamuk -	- 13th "
Lieut. Carlyon -	- Doubtful.	

54th N. I.

Capt. Anstruther -	- Doubtful.	
Capt. Corrie - -	- Ditto.	
Capt. Palmer - -	- Ditto.	
Lieut. Weaver - -	- Gundamuk -	- 13th Jan.
Lieut. Cunningham -	· Ditto -	- 13th "
Lieut. Pottinger -	- Neemla -	- 13th "
Lieut. Morrison -	- Gundamuk -	- 13th "

H. M. 13th Lt. Inf.

Major Kershaw -	- Doubtful.	
Lieut. Hobhouse -	- Gundamuk -	- 13th Jan.

Shah's Service.

Brigadier Anquetil -	- Jugdulluk pass -	- 12th Jan.
Capt. Hay, 35th N. I. -	- Gundamuk -	- 13th "
Capt. Hopkins, 27th N. I.	- near Jellalabad -	- 13th "

Capt. Marshall, 61st N. I.   - Jugdulluk pass   -   - 12th Jan.
Lieut. Le Geyt, Bombay Cav.   Neemla   -   -   - 13th   "
Lieut. Green, Artillery   - Gundamuk   -   - 13th   "
Lieut. Bird, Madras Estab.   Futtehabad   -   - 13th   "
Lieut. Macartney   -   - Gundamuk   -   - 13th   "

LIST OF OFFICERS SAVED OF THE CABUL FORCE.

In imprisonment in Affghanistan.

Political.

Major Pottinger, C. B.   - Wounded at Charekar on   - 6th Nov.
Capt. Lawrence.
Capt. Mackenzie, Madras Estab.   Ditto in action at Cabul on   23d   "

Staff.

Major-Gen. Elphinstone, C. B.   Ditto on retreat at Jugdulluk 12th Jan.
                                          (Died at Tezeen on April
                                          23d.)
Brigadier Shelton.
Capt. Boyd, At. Cy. Gl.
Lieut. Eyre, Arty. D. C. O.   Wounded in action at Cabul 22d Nov.

Horse Artillery.

Lieut. Waller   Ditto   Ditto   - 4th   "

H. M. 44th.

Capt. Souter -   -   - Ditto on retreat at Gundamuk 13th Jan.

H. M. 13th.

Lieut. Mein -   -   - Ditto in action under Gen.
                                   Sale at Khoord-Cabul pass   Oct.

37th N. I.

Major Griffiths   -   - Ditto on retreat in Khoord-
                                  Cabul pass   -   - 8th Jan.
Dr. Magrath.

Shah's Service.

Capt. Troup -   -   - Ditto on retreat in Khoord-
                                  Cabul pass   -   - 8th   "
Capt. Johnson.
Capt. Anderson.

Paymaster.

Capt. Bygrave   -   - The toes of one foot nipped
                           off by frost on retreat.
Mr. Ryley, conductor of Ordnance.

54th N. I.

Lieut. Melville   -   - Ditto on retreat near Huft
                              Kotul   -   -   - 10th Jan

Shah's Service.

Dr. Brydon   -   -   - Escaped to Jellalabad.

NOTE BY THE EDITOR.

I HAVE received information from very high authority, which makes it incumbent on me, in candour, to append this note to a second edition; and I am sorry it was not in time to appear also in the first. I flatter myself that the general tone of this work will prove sufficiently that any supposed misstatement therein will have been made most unintentionally, and on authority which must have appeared to the Author very sufficient. In his absence I cannot do less than append the following observations, which are furnished me to qualify the passages of the text alluded to : —

P. 5. — With reference to the alleged neglect to send a force against the Nijrow chiefs, I am assured that *the Envoy pressed this measure upon the General, but he refused the troops.*

P. 16. — I am assured that Lord Auckland never knew, until after the insurrection, that the pay of the Giljyes had been stopped, and that the measure originated with the Envoy.

P. 28. — Lastly, I am authorised to say that it is not correctly stated that Lord Auckland

did not receive General Elphinstone's resignation as soon as the General wished:
that the General joined the force in April;
and in September, Lord Auckland received
his medical certificate, and wrote to him
by the first mail to beg of him to give up
the command to the next in order, until a
successor could be found.

While readily giving insertion to any counter-
statements so conveyed to me as to guarantee
their accuracy, I must be allowed, on my brother's
part, to express an *opinion* that, being on terms
of intimate friendship with General Elphinstone,
he must have had no less authority than the
General's information for making at least that
statement last referred to: but I am sure he
would regret to be the means of propagating anything not strictly true, from whatever source
derived.

E. EYRE.

THE END.

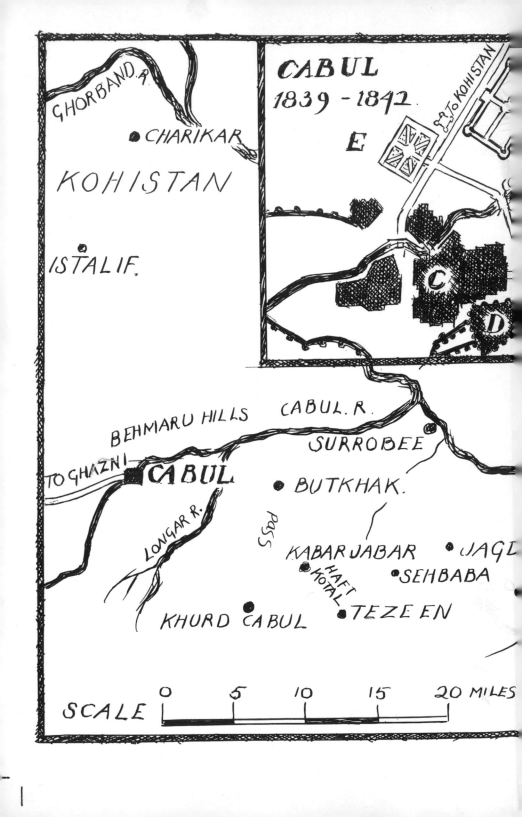